D0926407

THE
NICKY - SUNNY LETTERS

CORRESPONDENCE OF THE TSAR AND TSARITSA

1914 – 1917

ACADEMIC INTERNATIONAL

1970

RUSSIAN SERIES / VOLUME 2

THE NICKY—SUNNY LETTERS. CORRESPONDENCE OF
THE TSAR AND TSARITSA, 1914—1917

Reprint of THE LETTERS OF THE TSAR TO THE TSARITSA,
1914—1917 (London, 1929) and THE LETTERS OF THE
TSARITSA TO THE TSAR, 1914—1916 (London, 1923)

Library of Congress Catalog Card Number: 78—111538

SBN 87569—015—7

DK
258
.A4
A6
1970

Printed in the United States of America

ACADEMIC INTERNATIONAL / ORBIS ACADEMICUS

HATTIESBURG, MISSISSIPPI 39401

THE LETTERS OF THE TSAR TO THE TSARITSA, 1914-1917

TRANSLATED BY A. L. HYNES FROM THE OFFICIAL
EDITION OF THE ROMANOV CORRESPONDENCE AND
NOW PUBLISHED FOR THE FIRST TIME IN ENGLAND
EDITED, WITH NOTES AND AN INDEX, BY C. E. VULLIAMY
WITH AN INTRODUCTION BY C. T. HAGBERG WRIGHT, LL.D.

ACADEMIC INTERNATIONAL

1970

INTRODUCTION

Of the documents bearing on the last years of Imperial Russia none approach in historical value the letters of the late Tsar to his wife written during the war. The correspondence was carried on in English, but the present publication is a translation from the Russian text, the only text available. The letters not only disclose the most intimate traits in the characters of the principal persons responsible for the fate of the country during these disastrous years; but their perusal will also enable anyone to appreciate how the conduct of those who should have been the mainstay of Government was affected by events in the military or political arenas.

The character of the Tsar emerges morally enhanced from the severe ordeal of having his private life laid bare to the world. No impartial historian will in the future pay any attention to the accusations of duplicity and cunning which flooded the Press after the Revolution. The moral value of the man is, however, entirely nullified when his intellectual narrowness as a ruler manifests itself. " The atmosphere round the court was hushed and still," is the short but expressive sentence with which General Voeikov, commander of the Imperial Palaces and one of the Tsar's best friends, summed up the last years of the reign. The private correspondence of Nicholas II now printed corroborates this view. The man with his simple joys and sorrows is almost entirely overshadowed by the robot sitting on the throne and mechanically obeying the voice of tradition. By a curious dispensation of fate he drew his inspiration from a loving but irresponsible wife, who in her turn was under the influence of a vicious adventurer, the instrument of self-seeking cliques.

v

Circumstances placed Nicholas II on the throne at a period when the country was passing through troublous and difficult times. He watched one crisis after another with the alternate placidity and timidity of a child. At the mercy of every change of opinion and every intrigue, he was quite unable to cope with the ever-growing difficulties of ruling many millions of people. Incapable of understanding the real meaning of events, he stood helpless and alone. In the end he met death not only with courage but also with the serenity of a man who foresaw his fate.

The night of the 21st of October, 1894, was fatal in the history of Russia. On that night the last autocrat of Russia died, and the throne of the Romanovs passed into the hands of a weak young man of twenty-six—Nicholas II.

The iron hand of Alexander III had strengthened the power of autocracy so badly shaken during the last years of the reign of his predecessor. The revolutionary spirit had been quelled, but nothing had been done to solve the many political and social problems. The economic condition of the country was bad, while the instability of the political situation emboldened the revolutionary spirits to spread their doctrines. Underground influences continued uninterruptedly to threaten both country and throne with ruin. When the reins of government passed into the nerveless hands of Nicholas II the trouble began, and Russia was immediately faced with indications of approaching civil war.

The story of the reign of Nicholas II is the story of the desertion of the throne by one class after another until it ultimately stood alone without any support and crumbled like a giant with feet of clay. The process of disintegration was certainly hastened by the war, but it was by no means solely due to it; the throne might even conceivably have been saved by an effort of will on the part of the sovereign, but that will was non-existent.

The first indication of the coming storm was given as early as 1895. In that year the Zemstvo presented addresses full of respect, suggesting it would be of advantage if representatives of the people were allowed to participate in the government. The Tsar met these " senseless aspirations "

coldly. The great disaster of May 1896 on the Khodynka
Field outside Moscow, where the people's Coronation fête
was held and where thousands lost their lives, happened
shortly after the reception of the deputation. The reply of
the Tsar seemed to indicate that the policy of the previous
reign would be adhered to. Nicholas did not hesitate to
identify himself with the policy of his father, not because he
had a blind faith in the divine right of kings, but simply
because his father's reign seemed to him to have been a
happy one, since the nation had remained mute and inarti-
culate. The Tsar did not realise that this silence was only
maintained at the cost of a crushing weight of despotism.

A period of political strain accompanied by a series of
murders was the natural consequence. One after another
ministers and governors of provinces fell a prey to the
revolutionaries: Bogolepov and Sipiagin (1903), Plehve
(1904) and the Grand Duke Serge (1904). These melancholy
years were defined by Sir Henry Campbell-Bannerman as
" autocracy limited by assassination."

The crisis was reached during the Russo-Japanese War
(1904–5). Disasters followed in quick succession both in the
field and at sea. Disorganisation became general, and
Nicholas, who threw in his lot with the bureaucracy, soon
found the entire country united in bitter opposition against
him and autocracy. As soon as peace (16th of August, 1905)
was signed revolutionary outbreaks began. A general strike
was proclaimed, and persisted in with such unexpected
unanimity on the part of the people that the Tsar suddenly
found himself isolated, without a single individual on whom
he could rely. Troubles crowded in on him. Persistent
demands from groups of influential members of society urged
him to action. Driven to action he finally gave way, and
issued the manifesto of the 17th of October, 1905, creating
legislative assemblies, the Imperial Duma and the Imperial
Council. At the same time he entrusted the government to
the able hands of Count Witte.

The publication of the manifesto was, however, only the
first step; the most difficult—putting the manifesto into
operation—remained. Some thought a new era of constitu-

tional monarchy had begun, while others considered that a concession had been wrung from the monarch in a moment of weakness, and that it was inadvisable to press matters too far. Nicholas, however, instead of leaving his ministers to settle the question, unfortunately identified himself with those who, feeling too much had been conceded, wished to limit the powers of the Duma. There were hopes of a compromise in 1909 and 1910 when Goremykin was succeeded by a patriotic, able minister—Stolypin.

The revolution of 1905 had given some idea of the terrible desolation which would follow internecine strife in Russia. The craving for land in the soul of the illiterate Russian peasant had become more and more of an obsession, and in many places led to acts of unheard-of cruelty, worse than any "jacquerie" described in history. These wanton murders greatly helped to reconcile the timid bourgeoisie to the Government. A policy of drastic repression was approved, and ministers were given a free hand to deal with the rebels, and by dint of these powers, the reckless destruction which marred the years 1905 and 1906 was soon effectively brought to an end.

Stolypin now turned his mind to the great work of carrying out the promises of the manifesto, but he met with obstacles on all sides. In every council meeting and at every interview with his master he lost ground, until Nicholas himself began to distrust him. Stolypin's ministry was already drawing to a close when he was assassinated in the theatre at Kiev in 1911. It has been established that the pernicious methods of the police were largely responsible for his death. Unconstitutional methods got the upper hand. Offices were filled by "chinovniks" (officials) devoid of political initiative or capacity. No one attempted to originate anything; inertia was supreme.

After 1905 a sudden change in the Tsar's mentality occurred, laying him open to that charge of duplicity and of breaking his word of which so much has been said. The explanation, however, lies in circumstances removed from politics. The Empress gave birth to a son on 30th of August, 1904, and life immediately assumed a new aspect to

husband and wife.   Two or three years of happiness followed.
It was, however, soon broken by the disquieting symptoms
of disease evident in the child.   In 1908 the doctors
announced to the distracted parents that their son was
suffering from an incurable illness—hæmophilia—and the
case was hopeless. [Since no relief could be obtained from
human aid, the Tsar and his wife, already devout, took refuge
in every form of mysticism.] In consequence they were
quickly surrounded by adventurers, who laid claim to gifts
of healing and promised complete recovery if their advice
were followed.   But the wonder-workers were merely the
tools of self-seeking and intriguing " cliques " keen to
exploit the situation.   Indeed only a short time elapsed
before the inner core of Government itself became affected
by these baneful influences and the chief functionaries were
drawn into the vicious circle.   The Tsar, on his side, took the
bold step of declaring that he was Tsar by divine right.
" We are placed," wrote the Tsaritsa, " on the throne by
God, and must keep it untouched and hand it on unshaken
to our son."

    But neither faith-healers—especially the last of them
(Rasputin)—nor functionaries can really be held responsible
for the downfall of the empire.   They were merely the
visible symptoms of the moral decay of that force which
for three centuries had been the only creative force in the
history of Russia.

    Every nerve was now strained to preserve autocracy, and
every method was tried.   The death-struggle had begun.
An audacious move was taken when, in an attempt to corrupt
and degrade the very representatives of the people, " agents-
provocateurs " were introduced into the Duma.   These men
deliberately impeded the work of the country and thwarted
those who were learning how to govern. [When events
finally placed Russia's very existence in the hands of
the Duma, its representatives were found incapable of
shouldering the responsibility.]

    The World War broke out suddenly at the very moment
when the internal struggle had already reached an acute
stage.   As if by magic the country was instantly swept by a

wave of patriotism and all bitterness and discord vanished. In face of a foreign enemy credits were granted and dissension ceased. Unfortunately both the Tsar and the Government misunderstood the situation completely. They failed to seize the opportunity—the last—offered them of putting the affairs of State into better order. Acting on the advice of his wife, the Tsar tried to turn the tide in such a way as would benefit autocracy. If the victory had been won he might have succeeded, but events proved too strong for him. The uncertainty whether or no the army in the field would hold together, and the foolish behaviour of the bureaucracy at home, combined to bring about a serious crisis. To remedy the situation the Tsar took the fatal step of taking over the command of the army (20th of August, 1915). In doing so he identified himself with its fate. He left the control of home affairs almost entirely to the discretion and whims of the Tsaritsa, who sought her inspiration from a narrow-minded, illiterate and self-seeking adventurer. Every nomination to office seemed like a challenge to the public. The Duma, the representative assembly of the people, sounded the alarm; it drew attention to the coming catastrophe, which none of those at the head imagined possible, and it warned the Government that discontent was growing rapidly. But no one listened.

The collection of the letters now published enables us to follow every stage in the history of the catastrophe. Fresh light is thrown on almost every intrigue. We can see how distrust of the Grand Duke Nicholas grew day by day until, against the wish of almost the entire Council of Ministers, the Tsar decided to place himself at the head of his armies. The letter of the 25th August, 1915, is in this respect of supreme value and is one of the greatest confessions known in history. No document could demonstrate more vividly the weakness and fatalism of the Tsar. His decision to take command of the army was fatal, not so much from the military point of view as from that of internal politics. It meant the total estrangement of the throne from the country. All the ministers who had opposed this step resigned one after the other, and were replaced by the nominees of the Tsaritsa.

The Government, at the mercy of the caprices of the Tsaritsa, floundered. Her character was a curious combination of autocratic principles with those acquired from her peculiar Russian surroundings, while she brought to the task of government naïveté, passion and mysticism, but no knowledge of human nature. During the last months of the reign the country was under the control of Protopopov, a man of unbalanced mind. In such circumstances the slightest incident was sufficient to kindle the fire of revolution which began by the looting of several bakers' shops in the last days of February 1917.

On the other hand, the letters afford an opportunity of judging the individual man. When all has been said about the weakness and instability of the Tsar's character, it is quite impossible to avoid a feeling of sympathy with a man overburdened from the outset with the weight of care thrust upon him. Fate had been strangely cruel in placing him on a throne against his inclinations. His outlook on life and his limited intelligence unfitted him for a crown. He was a kind-hearted, anxious and loving father and husband, wrapped up in his family circle with few friends outside; his enjoyments and pleasures were simple. [He was not endowed with a great capacity for learning and was not highly cultured.] He had, however, a keen sense of responsibility and in his actions a complete absence of personal motives. In fact, the intimate life of the Imperial couple presents all the features of a happy bourgeois family life, and amidst his children the Tsar delighted to put aside his obligations. The intimacy and simplicity of his surroundings helped him to rest from the strain due to his exalted position. Unfortunately he forgot that the joys and sorrows of a sovereign are bound up in his people.

He listened to no words of warning. With a strange fatalism he wrote to Stolypin : " You believe, as I do, that the heart of the Tsar is in the hands of God. I am prepared at any moment to render Him an account of all my actions."

Seventeen months after the last letters of the present collection were written, far away in a distant town on the borders of Siberia, a horrible deed was done which humanity will always condemn.

The Tsar and the Tsaritsa always corresponded in English, but the English they used was not always correct, as far as we can judge from the Tsaritsa's letters. The translator of the present collection has performed a difficult task. He has not, of course, been able to reproduce the exact phraseology used by the Tsar, but his version is probably more readable in many respects than the original which is not available, and he seems to me to have preserved that tragic want of comprehension apparent in every letter of the Tsar. The notes give ample explanations of obscure passages and unfamiliar names.

C. HAGBERG WRIGHT.

EDITOR'S PREFACE

THESE letters and telegrams, now presented for the first time to English readers, have been translated from the official Russian publication of "The Correspondence of Nicholas and Alexandra Romanov." The Russian work is edited by Professor M. N. Pokrovsky. Many of the Tsaritsa's letters, which form the bulk of this correspondence, have already been published in this country, after having passed through the hands of German editors and German printers, with an excellent introduction by Sir Bernard Pares. The authenticity of the correspondence has never been questioned.

The present work consists of a close translation of the published Russian text. In view of the fact that the original documents (inaccessible to the student) are written in English, it is clear that the text must contain minor variations of the original wording. But the substance, not the style, of these letters is of the first importance, and that substance is here literally reproduced.

Although the Russian edition is, on the whole, carefully prepared, it is evident that it contains errors. These, where obvious, have been corrected; and in one or two doubtful cases alternative readings are given. The index to the Russian work is admirable, and has been of much use to the present editor.

The paragraphing of the text conforms, generally, to that of the original. It was the Tsar's custom to write in paragraphs, and these are sometimes at variance with literary practice. Abbreviations are frequent. In cases where these are doubtful they have been extended or omitted, except in the case of personal names, where they are retained. A certain number of words and phrases were written in Russian in the original letters, but are not always clearly indicated in the published text. Where there is no ready equivalent or where there is some doubt in the matter, these words have been transliterated, and explained in the notes. Square brackets are used to enclose alternative readings or necessary extensions by the present editor. Round brackets are printed as used in the original letters. Stops have been placed in accordance with English usage, and do not always agree with those in the Russian text. Words underlined in the letters are here printed in italics. A few unimportant telegrams have been omitted, but no letters. Passages of an extremely intimate character, or those touching on delicate subjects, have been omitted, and such omissions are indicated by dots in the usual manner.

No attempt has been made to improve the style of the letters or to twist them into literary forms which would have been uncongenial to the writer. The Tsar's simple and resourceless personality expressed itself in a simple and resourceless manner. Only in one or two passages has a slight modification been necessary.

The notes have been made as ample as possible. The great historical value of these letters, as well as their intense human interest, can only be appreciated through adequate knowledge of the characters and events to which they refer. It is hoped that the notes will supply at least a part of that knowledge. Capitals have been used for all first references to personal names, in order that these may be quickly located when using the index. In the case of persons of historical importance, or those who figure largely in the correspondence, the biographical notes are longer than in the case of those who are of less interest. Where the text itself affords adequate information, a note is clearly unnecessary. In a few instances the editor has not been able to trace allusions or references. Abbreviations of personal names are included in the index. There are no biographical notes on the Tsar himself or on the Tsaritsa, neither are the members of the Imperial Family described. It will be remembered that the Tsar had four daughters—Olga,

Tatiana, Marie and Anastasia—and one son, the Tsarevitch Alexis or Alexey, usually referred to as " Baby " or " the Little One."

The dating of the correspondence is in accordance with the old Russian calendar : it is therefore thirteen days behind the modern reckoning.

A considerable number of works, papers and periodicals have been consulted by the editor in the preparation of the present volume. Those which are actually quoted in the notes are contained in the appended bibliography, and they are subsequently referred to only by the author's name. Sincere thanks are due to Dr. C. Hagberg Wright, and to the staff of that most valuable literary institution, the London Library.

BIBLIOGRAPHY OF WORKS QUOTED

" With the Russian Army, 1914–1917."   Major-General Sir Alfred
     Knox, K.C.B., C.M.G.
" Memories and Impressions of War and Revolution in Russia,
     1914–1917."   General Basil Gourko.
" The Emperor Nicholas II as I Knew Him."   Sir John Hanbury-
     Williams, K.C.B.
" Russia's Ruin."   E. H. Wilcox.
" Critical Decisions at Headquarters."   General von Falkenhayn.
" My War Memories."   General von Ludendorff.
" Fateful Years."   Serge Sazonov.
" Le Tragique Destin de Nicholas II."   Pierre Gilliard.
" La Russie des Tsars."   Maurice Paléologue.
" The Russian Turmoil."   General A. I. Denikin.
" L'Assassinat de la Famille Imperiale Russe."   N. Sokolov.

THE LETTERS OF THE TSAR
TO THE TSARITSA, 1914–1917

Radiotelegram.

Kronstadt. 20 *June,* 1914.

The English squadron passed by the yacht exactly at noon. It was a beautiful picture; the weather is lovely, hot. We shall be home to dinner. All embrace you.

NICKY.

Telegram.

Novoborissov. 21 *September,* 1914.

Sincere thanks for dear letter. Hope you slept and feel well. Rainy, cold weather. In thought and prayer I am with you and the children. How is the little one? Tender kisses for all.

NICKY.

Telegram.

Stavka. 21 *September,* 1914.

Praise be to God, who granted us yesterday the victory at Souvalky and Mariampol. I have arrived safely. A thanksgiving Te Deum has only just been sung in the local military church. Have received your telegram; am feeling splendid. I hope all are well. Embrace you.closely.

NICKY.

Telegram.

Stavka. 22 *September,* 1914.

Hearty thanks for sweet letter. General Rouszky was presented to me to-day. He told me much of interest about his famous battles in Galicia. I have appointed him Adjutant-General. Here it is quiet and calm. Embrace all closely.

NICKY.

ROUSZKY: General N. V. Rouszky, the Commander of the 3rd Army. He had been a professor in the Military Academy, and had

B

held various Staff appointments in the Guards. In the Manchurian campaign of 1904-5 he was Chief of Staff to General Kaulbars, who commanded the 2nd Army. Shortly before the war of 1914 he was assisting the Minister of War, Soukhomlinov, in the reorganisation of the forces. He succeeded Jilinsky as Commander of the North-west Front in September, 1914. General Polivanov (who became Minister of War in 1915) considered him as the best general in the service, and he was described by Sir Alfred Knox as " a clear thinker." At the time of the Tsar's abdication he played an important part in the course of events. Killed by the Bolsheviks in October 1918.

Stavka. 22 September, 1914.

MY BELOVED DARLING WIFY,

Sincerest thanks for dear letter which you gave to my messenger—I read it before going to sleep.

How terrible it was parting from you and the dear children, though I knew that it was not for long. The first night I slept badly, because the engines jerked the train roughly at each station. I arrived here the next day at 5.30; it was cold and raining hard. Nicolasha met me at the station at Baranovitchi, and then we were led to a charming wood in the neighbourhood, not far (5 minutes' walk) from his own train. The pine forest reminds me strongly of the wood in Spala; the ground is sandy and not at all damp.

On my arrival at the Stavka I went to a large wooden church belonging to the Railway Brigade to a short thanksgiving Te Deum, at which Shavelsky officiated. Here I saw Petiusha, Kyrill, and the whole of Nicolasha's Staff. Some of these gentlemen dined with me, and in the evening Yanoushkevitch made a long and interesting report to me in their train, where, as I expected, the heat was terrible ! I thought of you—how lucky that you are not here !

I insisted on their changing the sort of life they lead here, at least before me.

To-day at 10 o'clock I was present at the usual morning report, which N. receives in a little house beside his train, from his two chief assistants, Yanoushkevitch and Danilov.

They both report very clearly and concisely. They read

through the reports of the preceding day which have come in from the Army Commanders and ask for orders and instructions from N. for the next operations. We bent over enormous maps covered with blue and red lines, numbers, dates and such like. On my return home I shall give you a short summary of all this.—Just before lunch General Rouszky arrived, a pale, thin man, with two new Orders of St. George on his breast. I have appointed him Adjutant-General for our last victory on the Prussian frontier—the first since his appointment. After lunch we had our photographs taken in a group with the whole of N.'s Staff. In the morning, after the report, I went for a walk round the whole of our Staff quarters and passed through the ring of sentries, then came on the outposts of the Cossack Life-Guards, set out far into the forest. They spend the nights in mud huts, quite warmly and comfortably. Their duty is to keep a look-out for aeroplanes. Excellent, smiling fellows, with tufts of hair sticking out from under their caps. The whole regiment is quartered very near the church, in the little wooden houses of the Railway Brigade.

Gen. Ivanov has gone to Warsaw and will return to Kholm on Wednesday, so that I shall stay here for another 24 hours, not changing my programme in other respects.

I am leaving here to-morrow night, and shall arrive in Rovno on Wednesday morning; shall stay there till 1 o'clock, and then start for Kholm, where I shall arrive about 6 o'clock in the evening. On Thursday morning I shall be in Bielostok, and, if it proves possible, shall look in without previous warning at Osovetz. I am not sure about Grodno—that is, I do not know whether I shall stop there—I am afraid all the troops have set out for the frontier.

I had a delightful walk with Drenteln in the wood, and on my return found the thick package with your letter and six books.

Warmest thanks, my dear, for your precious lines. How interesting is that part of Victoria's letter which you have so kindly copied for me !

I had heard from Benckendorf some time ago about the friction between the English and the French at the beginning of the war. Both of the foreign attachés here have gone to Warsaw for a few days, so that I shall not see them this time.

It is difficult to believe that a great war is raging not far from this place; everything seems so peaceful and quiet. The life here reminds me more of those old days when we stayed here during manœuvres, with the single exception— *that there are no troops whatsoever in the neighbourhood.*

Beloved mine, I kiss you again and again, because just at present I am quite free and have time to think of my Wify and my family. It is strange, but it is so.

I hope that you are not suffering from that abominable pain in your jaw and are not over-tiring yourself. God grant that my Little One may be quite well on my return !

.   .   .   .

Always your old hubby
NICKY.

Give my regards to Ania.

The word Stavka, which appears at the head of most of these letters and telegrams, requires explanation. It has no connection with our own word Staff. In archaic Russian it meant the military camp of a chief, and in modern times it was applied to General Headquarters. Although Stavka and G.H.Q. are generally regarded as one and the same thing, the Stavka had a peculiar significance in the history of the last years of the Tsarist regime, and possessed extraordinary powers. At the beginning of the war the Stavka was situated at Baranovitchi, a small Polish town on the line between Minsk and Brest-Litovsk, and well placed behind the centre of the Russian front. Baranovitchi was the headquarters of a Railway Brigade, and in 1914 the Stavka was housed partly in the Grand Duke's train, drawn up in a special siding, and partly in the wooden huts of the Brigade and in the Commander's house.

NICOLASHA : the Grand Duke Nicolai Nicolaievitch (here, and often subsequently, referred to as " Nicolasha ") was Commander-in-Chief of the Russian forces in 1914. He was certainly the most popular figure in the dynasty, a man of commanding presence, and regarded with esteem and affection by the troops. It is said that Rouszky had a poor opinion of his capacity as a military leader; but that opinion was not shared by Ludendorff or by Hindenburg.

He was disliked and distrusted by the Tsaritsa, partly on account of his popularity, which, in the Army, so completely overshadowed that of the Tsar, and partly because of his bluff opposition to Rasputin and the court camarilla. He was the Tsar's cousin.

SHAVELSKY: G. I. Shavelsky was the Chaplain-General of the Forces. He is often referred to as O. Shavelsky—O. being an abbreviation of Otetz or Father. PETIUSHA: the Grand Duke Peter Nicolaievitch, brother of the Grand Duke Nicholas. KYRILL: the Grand Duke Kyrill Vladimirovitch, head of the Naval Staff, attached to the Stavka in that capacity. A man of advanced liberal opinions, who, at the outbreak of the Revolution, went over to the Provisional Government. YANOUSHKEVITCH: General N. N. Yanoushkevitch was Chief of Staff at G.H.Q. He was ill-fitted for this post, for he had seen no active service and had never commanded any unit larger than a company. He had joined the War Ministry at an early age, and was Chief of the General Staff at the outbreak of the war. He was assisted by a man of a very different type, General G. N. DANILOV, the Quartermaster-General, a stern disciplinarian and a very capable soldier.

" Our last victory on the Prussian frontier." The fighting at Souvalky and Mariampol hardly amounted to a victory. It represented, at best, a partial and local recovery after the crushing defeat of Tannenberg a fortnight previously.

IVANOV: General N. Y. Ivanov was Commander-in-Chief of the South-west Front—an old but energetic man of patriarchal appearance. DRENTELN: one of the Tsar's A.D.C.'s, a Colonel in the famous Preobrajensky Regiment. VICTORIA: Princess Victoria of Battenberg, wife of Prince Louis, the sister of the Tsaritsa, and before her marriage Princess Victoria of Hesse. BENCKENDORF: Count A. C. Benckendorf, Marshal of the Court and Ambassador to Great Britain from 1902 to 1916. He died in the winter of 1916.

ANIA: Anna Vyroubova. She is frequently referred to in these letters as " A," " Ania " or " her." She is credited with having possessed great political significance, but it is most improbable that this was actually the case. It is unnecessary to repeat here the many fantastic and scandalous stories of which she was the subject. The daughter of Tanaiev, the Keeper of the Privy Purse, she entered the court circle at an early age, and became the Tsaritsa's favourite maid-of-honour from 1903 onwards. After her unhappy marriage with Lieutenant Vyroubov, and its consequent dissolution, she lived on the most intimate terms with the Imperial Family. Sazonov (p. 296) describes her as " an ambitious but by no means intelligent woman, who combined with a slavish obedience to Rasputin an ecstatic devotion to the Empress and to the Tsar." Paléologue (Vol. II, p. 239) says : " Physically she is heavy, commonplace, the head round, the lips fleshy, the eyes clear and expressionless. . . .

To explain her situation and her rôle at the Imperial Palace, it is perhaps sufficient to adduce her personal attachment to the Empress, the attachment of an inferior and servile creature to a sovereign who is always ill, crushed by her position of authority, besieged by terrors." Gilliard, the tutor to the Tsarevitch, spoke of her as " an unintelligent woman, limited, simple, garrulous, sentimental and mystic. Her reasoning was puerile, and she was destitute of ideas " (Sokolov Inquiry, p. 111). He says elsewhere that she had " the mentality of a child " and that " her unhappy experiences had exalted her sensibility without ,ripening her reflexion." There is little doubt that she was sentimentally attached to the Tsar. She lived in a small house at Tsarskoe Selo, close to the Palace, and was a constant intermediary between the Empress and Rasputin. Her book, " Memories of the Russian Court," published in 1923, consists mainly of foolish tittle-tattle. She was brought before a Commission of Inquiry and acquitted on the 25th August, 1917. This acquittal sufficiently disproves the allegation that she had political power.

Stavka. 23 September, 1914.

MY BELOVED WIFY,

My warmest thanks for your sweet letter, and for the one which you, the girls, Ania and N. P. have written conjointly. The words you write are always so true, and when I read them their meaning goes right to my heart, and my eyes are often moist. It is hard to part, even for a few days, but letters like yours are such joy that it is worth while parting for the sake of them. To-day it is raining in buckets, but of course I went for a walk with Dr., which was very good for me. Last night poor old Fredericks had a slight repetition of what happened to him not long ago in town—a little blood-spitting.

He is better now, but both Feodorov and Malama insist on his keeping quiet and motionless for 24 hours. It will be very difficult to make him obey them. They advise that he should remain here, and not go with me to Rovno— he can catch up my train at Bielostok in two days' time— on Tuesday. The presence of the old man here in these circumstances complicates the situation considerably, as he is a constant encumbrance to me and generally embarrasses everybody.

I feel quite well again and, I assure you, for the last few days even rested, thanks especially to good news. Alas! as I feared, Nicholasha will not let me go to Osovetz, which is simply intolerable, as now I shall not be able to see the troops which have been lately in action. In Vilna I intend to visit two hospitals—the military and the Red Cross one—but I have not come here solely for that !

Among the honours, which I have confirmed, General Ivanov has presented Keller for the Order of St. George. I am so glad !

And so I shall at last see Olga to-morrow and spend the whole morning in Rovno. I must finish, because the courier is waiting to be sent off.

Good-bye, my sweet, beloved Sunny. May God bless and keep you and the dear children; as for me, I kiss you and them tenderly.

Always your hubby,

NICKY.

N. P. refers to Nicolai Pavlovitch Sablin, a captain in the Gvardeisky Equipage (described in a subsequent note) and a close personal friend of the Imperial Family. He was senior officer on the Imperial yacht " Standart " from 1912 to 1915, and was A.D.C. to the Tsar. FREDERICKS : Count Fredericks, an old and devoted servant, was Minister of the Imperial Court. FEODOROV : Professor S. P. Feodorov, the chief Court physician. MALAMA : Dr. B. Z. Malama, honorary physician to the Tsar. KELLER : General Count F. A. Keller of the Cavalry Guards, formerly the commander of the Life-Guard Dragoons. He commanded in succession, during the war, the 10th Cavalry Division and the 3rd Cavalry Corps. A dashing leader and a great friend of the Tsar's. He was killed by Ukrainians in Kiev in December 1918. OLGA : the Grand Duchess Olga Alexandrovna, the Tsar's younger sister, occupied with hospital work. She married Prince Peter of Oldenburg (" Petia "), but divorced him and married Colonel Koulikovsky. The divorce is referred to later in the present correspondence.

Telegram.

Brest. 24 *September*, 1914.

Am very grateful for news. Was so glad to see Olga in Rovno. Inspected her hospital and the local one. Not many wounded left. The weather is cold, bad. Embrace all closely.

NICKY.

Telegram.

Grodno Railway.   25 September, 1914.

Have stopped in Bielostok all the same and visited Osovetz; found the garrison looking very well. Many projectiles have fallen into the fortress, one can see everywhere the funnels which they have made. I shall inspect hospitals in Vilna. To-morrow, God willing, we shall see each other. Hope all are well. Tender embraces.

NICKY.

Telegram.

Stavka.   22 October, 1914.

Have arrived safely. In the morning inspected two hospitals in Minsk; found them in splendid order. It is not cold, foggy. . . .

Telegram.

Stavka.   23 October, 1914.

Tender thanks for news. The weather is milder than at home. There is no snow. Petia is here. He has become much quieter since having been under heavy fire in Galicia. He and Kostia's boys have meals with me. Hearty greetings.

NICKY.

PETIA : Prince Peter of Oldenburg, referred to in the preceding note. KOSTIA : the Grand Duke Constantine Constantinovitch.

Telegram.

Stavka,   23 October, 1914.

The joyful news has been received that the Austrian army is in full retreat from Sanok. Am going to a moleben [Te Deum] now. Embrace you closely.

NICKY.

Telegram.

Stavka. 24 October, 1914.

Sincerest thanks to you and the children for letters. I am very glad that you have been to Louga. Yesterday your squadron of the Alexandriisky Hussars joined our troops after an absence of four weeks in the extreme rear of the enemy with very few losses. I embrace you all tenderly.

NICOLAI.

Telegram.

Stavka. 25 October, 1914.

Mank thanks for letter and magazine. Yesterday I watched with pleasure the regiment of Hussars and their distribution. To-day am inspecting two hospitals of wounded and the Cavalry Guards. Unfortunately had no time to write. I am going for 24 hours to Kholm and Sedletz. Am returning on the 27th in the morning. I hope you are well. Embrace all tenderly.

NICKY.

Telegram.

Brest. 26 October, 1914.

Spent the morning in Kholm; went to Mass and inspected a large Red Cross hospital. We passed Vlodava. The weather is calm, warm. I embrace you and the children closely.

NICKY.

Stavka. 27 October, 1914.

MY BELOVED, DARLING SUNNY,

At last I am able to write a few lines to thank you for your sweet letters, the sight of which on my table makes my old heart jump for joy !

The first days of my stay here I had to see old General Panteleiev with regard to the sad story of Samsonov; then old Trotzky, who is going to Kiev to establish order there; after that, Professor Scherbatov concerning our horses. I found old Petiusha here, who has only just returned from Lvov and from a battle into which he was taken by Radko-Dmitriev.

They spent three hours under the fire of the Austrian heavy artillery. From other telegrams it is clear that Petia conducted himself with the utmost coolness and he requests an award for himself; I therefore gave him the Georgievskoe orougiye [Arms of St. George], which made him nearly mad [with joy]. He had not expected it. At present he has a cold and is confined to an empty barrack near the train. On the whole, it seems to us that he has become very much less expansive than usual, most likely because he has been under fire. I had the pleasure of spending the whole of Saturday with Misha, who has become quite his old self and is again charming. We went to vsenoshchnaia [vespers] together and parted after dinner. Both the evenings I spent with the Cavalry Guards and with my Hussars. The horses of the Cavalry Guards are almost all in condition, but those of the Hussars have a most lamentable appearance. It is curious that, judging from what they say, the German horses which they have captured stand the hard work much worse than ours.

Now about my programme. Wednesday I shall spend in Rovno; Thursday in Lyublin and Ivangorod; Friday again in Ivangorod and on the adjoining battlefield (Kozenitzy), and Saturday in Grodno. If you could come there to meet me it would be splendid. I have spoken to Voeikov, and all preparations will be made.—I was intending to spend the whole of Saturday in Grodno (hospitals and fortress) and arrive at Pskov on Sunday morning to attend Mass in church, then to the hospital and be home for dinner. But if you only go there, of course Pskov falls out.

Well, my own Wify, I must finish this letter. I hope that you are feeling stronger and are well again. I kiss you and the children tenderly. God bless you !

Always your old
NICKY.

PANTELEIEV : General A. I. Panteleiev, Adjutant-General and a member of the Council of State. SAMSONOV : General Samsonov commanded the 2nd Army, which was annihilated at the Battle of Tannenberg on 18th August, 1914. His military career had been a brilliant one, and he had attained the rank of Major-General at the age of forty-three. He was fifty-five in 1914. After having witnessed the defeat of his army, and finding himself an exhausted straggler on the battlefield, he committed suicide. TROTZKY: General V. I. Trotzky, formerly commanded the Life-Guard Pavlovsky Regiment, and during the war was Governor of the Military District of Kiev. RADKO-DMITRIEV: General Radko-Dmitriev, one of the most daring and courageous leaders on the Russian side, was a Bulgarian. He was born in 1859 at Grodetz. After passing through the military school in Sophia, he studied in the Academy at Petrograd. He was involved in the plotting which led to the abdication of Prince Alexander, and was exiled by Stambulov. He then served for ten years in the Russian army, and returned to Bulgaria on the accession of King Ferdinand. He was Chief of the Bulgarian General Staff in 1902, led an army in the Balkan War, and was the victor of Kirk-Kilisse and Lule-Burgas. He then returned to the Russian service. During the war he commanded in succession the 8th Army Corps, the 3rd Army, and the 12th Army. MISHA: the Grand Duke Michael Alexandrovitch, the Tsar's brother. VOEIKOV: General Voeikov was Commandant of the Imperial Palaces. He married the daughter of Count Fredericks. Gourko (p. 153) represents the Count as saying, " Here [at the Stavka] everyone intrigues, and most of all my son-in-law." He is frequently mentioned in these letters as " Voeik." or " V."

" Sunny " was the Tsar's favourite name for his wife, and appears thus written in a published facsimile of one of his letters. In her girlhood she was known at the English Court as " Sunshine."

Telegram.

Stavka. 28 October, 1914.

Thank you heartily for your letter and news. Of course I can see M. I am in full agreement about the question of change of Governor in the South. Wrote to you yesterday about my plans. I shall arrive in Grodno on the 1st of November in the morning. Shall spend the whole day there. Will you not meet me in that place? To-morrow I shall spend in Rovno, then two days in the fortress. Am longing for you passionately. Kiss you tenderly.

NICKY.

M. refers to Maklakov, the Minister of the Interior. Lavrinsky, the Governor of the Crimea, was to be replaced by Kniazevitch, apparently on the recommendation of Rasputin.

Telegram.
                    Army in the Field.   29 October, 1914.

Am very glad to be here again and to see Olga.   Have
been to her hospital; now I am going to see the military
hospitals.   The weather is splendidly warm.   Am staying here till to-night.   Thanks for letter.   Embrace you
closely.

                                   NICKY.

Telegram.
                    Ivangorod Fortress.   30 October, 1914.

Many thanks for letter of 28th.   In the morning I inspected in Lyublin three hospitals in good order.   Found
here much of interest, of which I will tell you at our meeting.   Saw many troops and sailors whom I knew.   I am
so glad to find them here.   The weather is quite warm.
To-morrow I shall drive round the battlefields.   I said that
we would stop in D[vinsk].   Embrace all closely.

                                   NICOLAI.

                    In the train.   18 November, 1914.

MY BELOVED SUNNY AND DARLING WIFY,

We have finished breakfast and I have read your
sweet, tender letter with moist eyes.   This time I succeeded
in keeping myself in hand at the moment of parting, but it
was a hard struggle.

The weather is dismal; it is pouring with rain; there is
very little snow left.   When we moved off, I visited the
gentlemen [of the suite] and looked in at each coupé.   This
morning I found among the papers of the Minister of War
the paper relating to Rennenkampf and signed it.   He will
have to leave his Army.   I do not know who Nic. has in
view for his place.

What joy and consolation it would be if we could make
the whole of this journey together !   My love, I miss you
terribly—more than I can express in words.   Every day a
courier will leave the town with papers.   I shall try to

write very often, as, to my amazement, I have come to the conclusion that I can write while the train is in motion.

My hanging trapeze has proved very practical and useful. I swung on it many times and climbed up it before meals. It is really an excellent thing for the train, it stirs up the blood and the whole organism.

I like the pretty frame which you have given me. It *lies* in front of me on the table for safety, because a sudden jerk might break the lovely stone.

All the miniatures are good, with the exception of Marie. I am sure that everyone will appreciate their merit. What a joy and consolation it is to know that you are well and are working so much for the wounded! As our Friend says, it is by God's grace that in such a time you can work so hard and endure so much. Believe me, my beloved, do not fear, have more *confidence* in yourself when you are left alone, and all will go smoothly and prosperously.

May God bless you, my beloved Wify! I kiss you and the children lovingly. Sleep well and try to think that you are not lonely.

Your hubby
NICKY.

RENNENKAMPF: General P. Rennenkampf, commanding the 1st Army, whose failure to advance after the victory of Gumbinnen was partly responsible for the disaster of Tannenberg. He had greatly distinguished himself in the Japanese War, after which he became a Corps Commander, and was later appointed to the Governorship of the Vilna Military District. In 1915 he deserted his army, was accused of treachery and dismissed from the service. Killed by the Bolsheviks in 1918. OUR FRIEND: Gregory Rasputin. We are not yet in a position to judge correctly the true character or to measure the full power of this mysterious man. There can be no doubt, however, that his influence in Imperial and political circles was immense, though his motives in gaining and in using that influence are still obscure. We shall have occasion, later, to note his interference in matters military and political, and to observe the Tsar's attitude towards his strange adviser. Such a figure at the Russian Court was by no means a novelty, and he was but the successor of John of Kronstadt and the magician Phillippe.

Telegram.

Stavka. 19 November, 1914.

Have arrived in good time; thanks for letter and telegram. The weather is as it was yesterday, without frost. Kyrill and Dmitry are at present here. Embrace you and the children.

NICKY.

DMITRY : the Grand Duke Dmitry Pavlovitch, son of the Grand Duke Paul. He was the Tsar's cousin, an elegant and perhaps decadent young man, who wrote verses, and who assisted at the murder of Rasputin in December 1916.

Stavka. 19 November, 1914.

MY PRECIOUS WIFY,

Sincerest thanks for your sweet letter (the second), received to-day after dinner. I arrived exactly at 12.30. N. met me at the big station behind the wood. He looks well and calm, though he has lived through terrible moments, more correctly days, when the Germans were penetrating deeper and deeper.

The only great and serious difficulty for our troops is that we have again an insufficiency of munitions. In consequence of this, our troops have to observe economy and discretion during action, which means that the brunt of the fighting falls upon the infantry; owing to that, the losses at once become colossal. Some of the Corps of the Line have become divisions; the brigades have shrunk into regiments, and so forth.

Reinforcements are coming in well, but half of them have no rifles, as the troops are losing masses. There is nobody to collect them on the battlefields.

Apparently the Germans are drawing the Austrians up to the north; several Austrian corps are fighting on our soil, as if they have come up from Thorn.

And all of these troops are commanded by Prussian generals. It is said that the Austrian prisoners abuse their allies for that. Petiusha is here again and is feeling well. I also saw Kyrill, Dmitry and Yoanchik, who has asked me to appoint our Olga president of the committee for the building of the large cathedral, if he should be killed.

Four foreign generals dined with me. I had a talk with them in the evening. They have travelled not a little round the places where there is heavy fighting at present—Soukhachev, Seradz, Lodz, etc. To-day we had no detailed reports from the front.

My beloved Sunny, I love you with an undying love; as you see, I could call it " un puits d'amour "—and this after twenty years. God bless you, my darling ! May He guard you and the children. I kiss you all tenderly.

YOUR NICKY.

In this letter the Tsar speaks of the shortage of munitions— after little over three months of war. It is now commonly known that the shortage was largely due to the incompetence, if not to the criminal neglect, of the Minister of War, Soukhomlinov, of whom we shall speak in a later note. The Russian army, at the beginning of the war, was deplorably equipped for service. General Alexeiev said that the shortage of rifles reached an acute phase in September 1914. According to E. H. Wilcox, the correspondent of the *Daily Telegraph* at Petrograd, reinforcements sent to Galicia were " absolutely unarmed." Soldiers were not only trained with sticks instead of rifles, but were actually sent into the trenches with them. At one time 40,000 troops were waiting at Tarnopol without weapons. Robert Wilton, *The Times* correspondent, says : " Proportionately speaking, the Russian Army was not so well prepared for war in 1914 as it had been in 1904. Eleven artillery brigades on mobilisation were found to be without guns." And Gourko states that in 1914 his Division " possessed neither light nor heavy motor transport."

YOANCHIK : Prince Ioan Constantinovitch.

Telegram.

Dorogobuzh. 20 November, 1914.

Thanks for telegram. In Smolensk I thought of our stay in 1912. Visited four hospitals there. All are in excellent order. It is warm, still. In thought I am with you. . . .

Telegram.

> Toula.   21 *November*, 1914.

Warmest thanks for both sweet letters.   I advise you, if you are well, to go to K[ovno] and V[ilna].   This morning after church I visited a munition factory—very interesting—ten thousand workers.   Now I am going to hospitals, there are about 40.   I have no time to write here.   I kiss and embrace all ardently.

> NICKY.

Telegram.

> Kharkov.   23 *November*, 1914.

Sincerest thanks for dear letters.   I hope that yesterday's papers have arrived.   Have seen numbers of hospitals, but had no time to see the son of Count Keller.   The reception was so touching.   I am leaving at four o'clock for Ekaterinodar. . . .

Telegram.

> Stanichnaia.   24 *November*, 1914.

Have spent three happy hours at Ekaterinodar.   Thanks for telegram.   I remember about Olga.   Embrace you all closely.

> NICKY.

> *In the train.*   25 *November*, 1914.

MY BELOVED, DARLING SUNNY,

It seems to me as though it is ages since we parted ! —Two days ago I received your letter from Kharkov, with our group taken in Dvinsk.   To-day is my first free day.

We are passing through picturesque country which is new to me, with beautiful high mountains on one side and steppes on the other.   Since yesterday it has been much warmer, and to-day the weather is lovely.   I sat for a long time at the open door of the carriage and breathed in the warm fresh air with delight.   At each station the platforms are crowded with people, especially children; there are thousands of them, and they are charming with their tiny papakha [fur caps] on their heads. Naturally, the receptions in every town were touchingly cordial. But yesterday I experienced other and still better impressions in Ekaterinodar, the capital of the Kouban province—it was as pleasant as on board ship, thanks to crowds of old friends and the familiar faces of the Cossacks, which I remember from childhood, in the Convoy. Of course I drove in my car with the Ataman [Hetman], General Babysch, and inspected several excellent hospitals, containing wounded from the Caucasian Army. Some of the poor fellows have frostbitten legs. The train is jolting terribly, so you must excuse my writing.

After the hospitals I looked in for a minute at the Kouban Girls' Institute and at a large orphanage dating from the last war, all of them Cossack girls, real military discipline. They look well and unconstrained; here and there a pretty face. N. P. and I were very pleased with what we saw.

I have just finished lunch. It is quite hot in the train.

We are running along by the Caspian Sea; it rests the eye to look at the blue distance; it reminded me of our Black Sea and wafted me into melancholy. Not far off are mountains, beautifully lit up by the sun. It is a pity— why are we not together? On the whole, travelling about here means being infinitely further removed from the war than being in Kovno or Grodno. N. P. and I were very glad that you went there and saw our friends. I shall send this letter by courier from Derbent. Of course it was Peter the Great who took this little old place in 1724—I cannot remember where the keys are kept. I know that they must be in one of the palace churches, because I have seen them, but I am not sure precisely in which.

Tell Olga that I thought of her a great deal yesterday in the Kouban province. This country of the Cossacks is magnificent and rich; a large number of orchards. They are beginning to be wealthy, and above all they have an inconceivably high number of small infants. All future subjects. This all fills me with joy and faith in God's mercy; I must look forward in peace and confidence to what lies in store for Russia.

c

This second telegram from our Friend was handed to me at a small station where I got out for a walk. I find it highly comforting.

By the way, I have forgotten to explain to you why my programme was slightly changed. When I was at the Stavka, the old Count Vorontzov asked me by telegram whether I would care to visit both of the Cossack provinces and both chief towns; as we had a little spare time on our journey, Voeikov quickly arranged this matter, and has thus given me an opportunity for seeing some more useful and important places [bases?]—Ekaterinodar, and on our journey back to the north, Vladikavkaz—of the Tersky Army. During my passing visits to Toula, Orel, Koursk and Kharkov I was too busy and bewildered to be able to write to you or even to telegraph—you must have noticed it, whereas to-day we are all enjoying a real rest; the gentlemen are as much tired as I am. But I repeat again : *all* our impressions are *delightful*. What the country is achieving and will go on achieving till the end of the war is wonderful and immense. Part of this achievement I saw with my own eyes, and even Feodorov, from a purely medical point of view, was astounded.

But I must finish now, my love. I kiss you and the dear children warmly and tenderly. I am longing for you so much, so much in need of you ! God bless and keep you !

Always your hubby
NICKY.

The Tsar was never so happy, during the war, as he was on these tours of inspection. He had no knowledge of the terrors of war, and his army was usually presented to him on the parade ground. Such tours, moreover, provided an escape from the " beastly papers " and the dull routine of the Stavka.

Ataman or Hetman, the title of a Cossack commander.

" Palace churches "—the churches which stood within the Imperial precincts.

VORONTZOV : General Count Vorontzov-Dashkov, Lord Lieutenant of the Caucasus and a member of the Council of State.

The letter was written in the train between Petrovsk and Baku.

Telegram.

Tiflis. 26 November, 1914.

Have arrived safely; the reception was wonderful. The old Count is not very well. I shall visit some hospitals to-day. I am sorry that you are not here. Close embrace for you and Ella.

NICKY.

ELLA : the Grand Duchess Elizabeth, widow of the Tsar's uncle, the Grand Duke Sergey (assassinated in 1905), and the elder sister of the Tsaritsa. She was a beautiful and remarkable woman, who, after the death of her husband, became the Mother Superior of a convent in Moscow. Her tragic life was tragically ended on the 17th July, 1918—on the day following the murder of the Imperial Family—at Alapaievsk in the Oural Province, where she was killed by the Bolsheviks.

Telegram.

Tiflis. 27 November, 1914.

Thank you heartily for dear letter with the enclosed letters from Marie and Alexey. The Count and Countess are very touched with your greetings. There was a grand reception in the morning—saw two young officers of the Nijni-Novgorod Regiment, both wounded. Thank you for your congratulations. I have seen above a thousand wounded in two days. Please distribute medals to seriously wounded men in my name. Am tired, but very pleased and satisfied with what I have seen and heard. Embrace you and the children closely.

NICKY.

Telegram.

Tiflis. 28 November, 1914.

Hearty thanks for letter about your delightful journey to Vilna and Kovno. I have been visiting educational institutions all day long. The Countess took me round your sklad here in the house. Saw not less than 200 ladies and women at work—I was much embarrassed. I went to tea with the nobility; masses of pretty faces—felt shy. Everything has made an excellent impression on me. All of them are very desirous of seeing you and the children some time. Fond kisses for all the six of you.

NICKY.

Sklad : a depot for Red Cross supplies.   The Tsaritsa was devoted to hospital work, in which she took an active and practical part.

Telegram.

Tiflis.   29 November, 1914.

Sincere thanks for dear letter, also to Olga and Alexey for their letters.   Ideally warm weather.   After a grand reception of deputations this morning I visited the Girls' Diocesan School and after that the Military College.   I have received crowds of people.   After lunch walked here in a charming garden; am now going into the town to tea.   I am leaving for Kars in the evening. . . .

Telegram.

Kars.   30 November, 1914.

Have arrived this morning.   Real winter, but luckily not cold, 4 degrees.   Went to Mass in a very ancient church, which is now the garrison church.   Saw heaps of troops, very few wounded.   Drove in a car round the fortress; very interesting, but a thick fog was hiding the distance. I kiss all many times tenderly.

NICKY.

Telegram.

Sarykamysh Railway.   1 December, 1914.

Thank you and Tatiana sincerely for letter; I have only just arrived, and see on the station, to my joy, my Company of the Kabardinsky Regiment.   Embrace you closely.

NICKY.

Telegram.

Kars.   1 December, 1914.

Have spent an ever-memorable day.   I drove from Sary-kamysh in a car to Medginghert, right on the frontier.

There were collected all the lower ranks of all the parts of the Caucasian Army who had most distinguished themselves, about 1200 men. I distributed crosses and medals of St. George among them; they had come straight from the advanced positions, and had an excellent sunburnt appearance. The weather has been warm there for the last few days. The young Gandourin has recovered and will return to his regiment in three days' time. I was exceedingly glad to see the famous Kabardintzy. The road up to the frontier is excellent. I have passed over two beautiful mountains covered with woods. I am now returning. Tender embraces for all.

NICKY.

Telegram.

Kiurdamir. 2 *December*, 1914.

I thank you heartily for two letters, Tatiana also. Towards the morning we descended from the mountains and it became warmer again. I hope you are not tiring yourself in the hospitals. . . .

Telegram.

Derbent. 3 *December*, 1914.

I thank you and Olga heartily for dear letters. I am free to-day. I am now going for a walk along the Caspian Sea. To-morrow morning I am going to Vladikavkaz. The weather is warm, damp. I embrace all closely.

NICKY.

Telegram.

Novocherkask. No date.

Many thanks for last letter. I am glad to be on the Don. Am very pleased with the reception. Have been to see many hospitals. Am leaving at 7 o'clock in the evening. I am very happy to meet you to-morrow. Tenderly embrace you and the children.

NICKY.

Telegram.

                                        Novoborissov.   13 *December,* 1914.

Saw to-day an echelon of recovered wounded, who are returning to the army. It is clear; 4 degrees of frost, without snow. Thanks for letters. Embrace all tenderly.

                                                                NICKY.

Telegram.

                                        Stavka.   14 *December,* 1914.

Thanks for telegram. There is no news to-day, as it is quiet along almost the whole front. I have had a long walk. I have felt tired ever since leaving Moscow. Goodnight. Sleep well. Warm kisses.

                                                                NICKY.

Telegram.

                                        Stavka.   15 *December,* 1914.

Thanks for telegram. Am very sorry for poor Botkin. Here nothing is known. The regiment of Infantry Guards has been recalled, and I want to inspect them. I hope you will not mind if I return on Friday night. . . .

BOTKIN : Dr. E. S. Botkin, physician to the Tsar. He was one of the most devoted attendants of the Imperial Family, and was murdered with them at Ekaterinburg. The allusion is to the death of his son, who was killed in the war.

Telegram.

                                        Stavka.   16 *December,* 1914.

Warmest thanks for charming scented letter; and Marie also. Everything is quiet here. Reports are good. Yesterday I inspected the new 53rd Don Cossack Regiment, which is commanded by Zvegintzev. A. Orlov is not wounded. I am sorry for Boutakov. I kiss you tenderly.

                                                                NICKY.

ORLOV : A. A. Orlov, an officer in the Life-Guard Hussars. BOUTAKOV : probably A. I. Butakov, a senior lieutenant in the Gvardeisky Equipage, who " died on duty."

Telegram.

Stavka. 16 *December,* 1914.

Warmest thanks for dear letter. Am leaving to-day at 9.30; to-morrow morning I hope to see the infantry division and after dinner our Rifles. Cold, keen wind.

NICKY.

Telegram.

Garvolin. 17 *December,* 1914.

In the morning I saw the First Division and a company of Her Majesty's Gvard. Equipage. Wonderfully healthy, cheerful appearance. The weather is warm here. Shall send news in the evening.

NICKY.

The Gvardeisky Equipage was a unit for which the Tsar and Tsaritsa had a special affection. In 1867 all the Russian naval commands were condensed into "rotas" (companies), and these were grouped in "Equipages," each about 2000 strong. The Gvardeisky Equipage—sometimes translated as Marine of the Guard, or Garde Équipage—was a part of the Imperial Guard, and its members served on the Royal yachts and, during the winter, as a part of the Petrograd garrison. In addition to service on the Royal yachts, the Equipage acted as Marines on the ships of the Baltic Fleet. They represented the Navy in the general establishment of the Guards. During the war a battalion of the Equipage was on active service. The Gvardeisky Equipage were on duty at the palace of Tsarskoe Selo on the eve of the Revolution, and their desertion to the Duma, under the leadership of their commander, the Grand Duke Kyrill, appeared to the Tsaritsa as a bitter revelation of disloyalty and ingratitude.

Telegram.

Sedletz. 17 *December,* 1914.

Thanks for telegram. I was delighted with the Rifles and Grabbe's Cossacks. The weather is spring-like. Am in a happy mood. Good-night.

NICKY.

GRABBE: Count A. N. Grabbe commanded the Cossacks of the Imperial Guard, and was an intimate friend of the Tsar's. According to Gourko (p. 153): "It was said of him that, by his natural tact, greatly surpassing his inborn mental qualities, he kept himself wonderfully clear of the influences of the different parties. . . . The Tsar greatly appreciated his abstinence from everything which did not concern him." His name occurs frequently in these letters.

Telegram.

Stolbtzy. Al. Rly. 18 *December*, 1914.

Many thanks for two letters; also to Tatiana and Olga. I saw to-day the Moskovsky, Pavlovsky and Atamansky Regiments. The weather was warm. We are returning home. So glad to be with you all to-morrow night. Tender embraces.

NICKY.

Telegram.

Novosokolnikovo Rly. 19 *December*, 1914.

N. P. has received your telegrams, but has not received A.'s letters. The weather is warm. Am glad to return. Embrace you closely.

NICKY.

Telegram.

Stavka. 23 *January*, 1915.

Sincere thanks for two telegrams. Here everything is well. The weather is the same as with you. Give her my greetings. I kiss you and the children warmly.

NICKY.

Stavka. 24 *January*, 1915.

MY BELOVED SUNNY,

Both your sweet letters have deeply touched me—I thank you with all my heart for them.

It was hard to leave you and the children this time, because of the poor Little One's foot. I am so afraid that it may last a long time. Please do not overtire yourself now that you have to be upstairs with him so often—except, perhaps, when you are at the hospital.

Our journey has proved agreeable and quiet. How fortunate it is that the gentlemen have got accustomed to each other and no incidents occur! In the evening we

played with Mamma's new dominoes and listened to Voeikov
or Feodorov, who read Ania's amusing book to us.

I have found Nicolasha's Staff here in very good spirits.
I am very glad to see old Ivanov, who has come for a few
days on duty. Luckily he grumbled less than usual. He
asks you to send him your new photograph; please do so—
it will please the dear old man. Kyrill and Petia are here;
the latter will remain at N.'s disposal. I was so pleased to
see the jolly, stout old Veselkin; he had dinner and tea
with us and told us, mixed up with serious and interesting
things, such stories that everyone shook with laughter. It is
now the seventh time that he has travelled by the Danube to
Serbia with his Supply Expedition. The risk increases more
and more, as the Austrians are doing all in their power to
blow up our steamers. God grant that they may be spared!

As on all my previous visits here, the first day turned out
to be a frightfully busy one : only after lunch did I manage
to get in a good walk, but for the rest of the time I received
people until the evening.

Well, good-bye, my beloved Wify-teeny. May God bless
you and the children! I kiss you and them affectionately.
Give my warm greetings to A.
Always your hubby
NICKY.

" The Little One " : the Tsarevitch, Alexis. He is referred to as
" Baby," " the Little One," or " Alexey." At this time he was
ten years old.

The words " except, perhaps, when you are at the hospital "
must be taken as meaning " try to spare yourself as much as you
can, except, perhaps, when you are on duty at your hospital." The
Tsaritsa was untiring in her work as a nurse, and even assisted at
operations.

VESELKIN : Rear-Admiral M. M. Veselkin, attached to the Stavka.
He administered the flotilla commands in the Danube-Dobroudja
area. Commanded the warship " Borodino."

Telegram.
Stavka. 24 *January,* 1915.

Hearty thanks for dear letter. Both thank you for your
greetings. It is cold, clear, windy. I saw to-day Engalychev,

the Governor-General. His first steps are successful. I
have written. Blessings and tender kisses to all.

NICKY.

ENGALYCHEV : Prince P. N. Engalychev, Adjutant-General. He
was the Governor of Warsaw, and had formerly commanded the
Life-Guard Hussars. At one time the head of the Nicolaievsky
Academy.

Telegram.

Stavka. 25 *January*, 1915.

Tender thanks for letter and telegram. To-day after
divine service I distributed orders and crosses to the officers
and other ranks of my composite Cossack Regiment. I had
no time whatever to-day for writing. It is warmer, but
windy. I embrace all closely.

NICKY.

26 *January*, 1915.

MY DEAR, BELOVED WIFY,
       I thank you tenderly for your letters. I am so sorry
that I did not write yesterday, but I had endless receptions.
In Baranovitchi, after church, Crosses of St. George were
distributed among my black, handsome Cossacks—many of
whom have speared or cut down several of the enemy. I
visited Nicholasha and inspected his new railway carriage;
a very comfortable and practical one, but the heat in it is
such that one cannot endure it above half an hour. We
discussed thoroughly several important questions and, to
my joy, came to an entire agreement on all those we touched
upon. I must say, that when he is alone and in a good
humour he is sound—I mean to say, he judges correctly.
Everybody has noticed a great change in him since the
beginning of the war. Life in this isolated place, which he
calls his " hermitage," and the sense of the crushing responsibility which rests on his shoulders, must have made a
deep impression upon his soul; and that, if you will, is a
great achievement too.

I arrived here this morning, and was met by dear Olga and some others. She looks and feels absolutely well and sound again. We drove in my car to her hospital. After having visited the wounded, I went to her room, where we sat for a little while, and then returned to the train.

We had lunch and then sat together. As the weather was magnificent she suggested a drive. We drove out of the town, went up a steep hill and returned by another road through a pretty wood. Mordv[inov], Drent. and N.P. came with us, and we all derived much pleasure from our walk. K. enjoyed it very much. At present we are both busy writing to you in my coupé, sitting so cosily side by side. My train leaves at 7 o'clock. Only think! I have just received a telegram from Doumbadze to the effect that the infamous " Breslau " has fired about 40 rounds on Yalta and considerably damaged the " Russia " Hotel. Swine!

Well, good-bye; God bless you and the dear children. Thank them for their letters.

Your dearly fondly loving and always, my treasure,

Your old

NICKY.

MORDVINOV : A. A. Mordvinov, formerly A.D.C. to the Grand Duke Michael. He was one of the Tsar's favourite A.D.C.'s during the war, and was very much liked by the Tsaritsa and her daughters. DOUMBADZE : General J. A. Doumbadze, a member of the Imperial suite and the mayor of Yalta, a fashionable watering-place in the Crimea. It will be remembered that the German cruiser " Breslau," together with the " Goeben," passed through the Mediterranean.

Telegram.

Kiev. 27 January, 1915.

Hearty thanks for letters. Have inspected a charming hospital belonging to both of the sisters, and then the hospital of the nobility for 85 officers. Agreeable, frosty weather. Had a very cordial reception. Tender kisses for all of you, and A.

NICKY.

Telegram.

Sevastopol.   29 January, 1915.

Have only just arrived.   2 degrees of heat.   A great deal of snow.   The fleet returned yesterday.   I am now preparing to visit it.   Tender kisses.

NICKY.

Telegram.

Sevastopol.   29 January, 1915.

Thanks for telegram.   I am so happy to be here and to have an opportunity for thanking all those who work and serve so zealously.   Before lunch I spent a little time on board the " Eustaphia " and the " Kagoula " and in the naval hospital.   At noon I inspected the young sailors and visited the barracks of the naval training college for boys. The impression made by everything is delightful.   Clear, mild, calm weather. . . .

Telegram.

Sevastopol.   30 January, 1915.

Have visited all the fortifications and batteries on the north side.   Saw a few wounded who have recovered. Pleasant, warm weather. . . .

Telegram.

Sevastopol.   30 January, 1915.

Warm thanks for letter.   Drove round the southern batteries in a car.   I had inspected some of them in 1913. In the town I saw wounded officers and men from the front, sent here for treatment.   A magnificent day.   I am leaving now.   Good-night.   Tender embrace.

NICKY.

Telegram.

Ekaterinoslav.   31 January, 1915.

Sincere thanks for sweet letter and two telegrams.   I am very pleased with my cordial reception.   Have inspected two splendid hospitals. The weather is still sunny. In the course of the day I shall inspect the Briansky arms factory. I embrace all closely.

NICOLAI.

Telegram.

Lopasnia. 1 *February*, 1915.

Hearty thanks for two letters and news. The weather is mild; it is thawing. All send their greetings, and N. P. and M. their thanks. Am looking forward to seeing you to-morrow. I embrace you and the children.

NICKY.

The reader should be reminded that, at this time, the " winter battle " of the Masurian Marshes was raging without intermission. On the day on which this telegram was sent, Lyck was taken by the Germans; two days later, Litzmann occupied Augustovo, and in a fortnight's time the Russians had lost 110,000 men in prisoners alone. The 10th Army was, in fact, wiped out.

28 *February*, 1915.

MY BELOVED DARLING,

Although it is naturally very sad for me to leave you and the dear children, I am going this time with *such* calm in my soul that I am myself surprised. Whether it is because I had a talk with our Friend last night, or because of the newspapers which Buchanan gave me, telling of the death of Witte, or perhaps because of the feeling that something good will happen in the war—I cannot say, but in my heart reigns a truly paschal peace. How I wish that I could leave it with you too !—I was so happy to spend those two days at home—perhaps you noticed it, but I am foolish, and never speak of what I feel.

What a nuisance it is to be always so busy and not to have an opportunity for sitting quietly together and having a talk ! After dinner I cannot stay indoors, as I long to get out in the fresh air—and so all the free hours pass, and the old couple seldom get a chance of being together, especially now that A. is unwell and cannot come to us.

Do not overtire yourself, my love; remember your health; let the girls work for you sometimes.

God bless you and them; I am sending you my tenderest love and kisses. Always with boundless love,

Your hubby
NICKY.

I shall always let you know where I am going.

BUCHANAN : Sir George Buchanan, the British Ambassador to Russia. WITTE : Count S. Y. Witte, the great Liberal statesman and President of the first Duma. He was careless and caustic in speech, and referred openly to the war as " folly." It is not surprising that he was disliked, and probably feared, by the Tsar and Tsaritsa. After Stolypin, perhaps the most able statesman of the reign of Nicholas II.

The reference to " the old couple " alludes to the Tsar's recent visit to Tsarskoe Selo, when many demands were made on his time.

Telegram.

Stavka. 1 *March*, 1915.

Thank you sincerely for letter and telegram. I am terribly sorry about poor Strouve. The weather here is very mild; there is practically no snow. The news from everywhere is good. George is here and very busy. I kiss you and the children fondly.

NICKY.

STROUVE : Captain S. G. Strouve, on the Staff of the Life-Guard Cavalry, killed in action on the 27th February, 1915. He had been A.D.C. to the Tsar. GEORGE : the Grand Duke George Mikhailovitch.

Telegram.

Stavka. 2 *March*, 1915.

Warmest thanks for dear letter and news. It is warm, but dull. I am very busy and have to speak a great deal. Find time for the usual long walks after lunch. I shall write. Embrace everyone closely.

NICKY.

Stavka.   2 March, 1915.

MY TENDERLY BELOVED,

I thank you from my heart for your two sweet letters. Every time that I see the envelope with your firm writing, my heart leaps several times, and I shut myself up and read, or more correctly absorb the letter.

Of course the girls can bathe in my swimming-bath; I am glad that the Little One enjoys it so much; I asked the rogue to write to me about all this!

I am here for the seventh time—only think of it! At the front everything is quite satisfactory. N. is in a good humour and as usual demands rifles and ammunition. The question of supplying our railways and factories with coal has assumed an alarming character, and I have asked Roukhlov to take it all into his hands. Only imagine, if the manufacture of military supplies were to cease! And this because of a lack of coal, or rather owing to an insufficient output of it in our mines in the South! I am convinced that energetic measures will pull us out of these difficulties.

George looks quite well and very sunburnt; he has told me many interesting things, which he will presently pass on to you. Petiusha is here, quite recovered now. I have learnt from him that Roman had typhoid fever, but is getting better. To-day a charming old man, Pau, a French general, came from Galicia—he is delighted with his journey and with having been under Austrian fire. Sazonov arrived as well this morning, so that they all lunched with me. To-morrow Paléologue is due to arrive, who is supposed to bring the official reply of France concerning Constantinople, and also her wishes with regard to the Turkish booty.

3 *March.*

In the course of the day we had a lengthy conversation —N., Sazonov, Yanoushkevitch and I—which ended to our mutual satisfaction. So many questions have accumulated that it is impossible to solve them in one day. My plans are not yet quite clear. N. would not hear of my going to

Lomja to start with. He says that German aeroplanes are flying there above our troops, searching for our reserves; that all the roads are blocked with transport and wagons; and that, for these reasons, he does not advise General Pau to travel in that direction. I shall see what I shall do. I have sent Djounkovsky to find out what is happening there, and, as he is a practical man, he will be able to judge whether this journey is possible.

To-day the news from everywhere is quite good. Little Osovetz is holding out satisfactorily against the bombardment; all that is damaged in the day-time is repaired at night; the spirit of the garrison is magnificent and they are in sufficient strength. I have sent them my thanks. This time the Germans are further away from their objective than they were the first time in September.

Yesterday N. brought me Ivanov's report from Broussilov and Khan-Nakhichevansky about the splendid behaviour of Misha's division in the February fighting, when they were attacked in the Carpathians by two Austrian divisions. The Caucasians not only repelled the enemy, but actually attacked him, and were the first to enter Stanislavov, while Misha was the whole time in the line of fire. Everybody is asking me to give him the Cross of St. George, which I shall do. N. is sending one of his adjutants this evening with my letter and order to Misha; I am very glad for his sake, as I think that this time he has really earned this military distinction, and it will show him that he is, after all, treated exactly as all the others, and that by doing his duty well he also gets a reward.

The little Admiral is behaving very well and often makes us laugh during our evening games of dominoes by his witty remarks about Tatishchev and Svechin, who bore him with their interminable talks. It is true that the latter likes to tell dull anecdotes, interspersed with French sentences, when we are having lunch or tea, and he is beginning to try the patience of us all. The Admiral has become great friends with Feodorov, and they discuss nothing but points of strategy.

Well, I have talked enough nonsense, and you must

forgive me, my darling Wify. God bless you and the children ! I kiss you all tenderly.

Always your old devoted hubby

NICKY.

The military situation had greatly improved, and the Austrian centre had been broken by a counter-offensive near Smolnik in the Carpathians.

ROUKHLOV : S. V. Roukhlov, Secretary of State, Member of the Council of State, and Minister of Ways and Communications from 1909 to October 1915. PAU : General Pau had commanded the army in Alsace at the beginning of the war, and had taken Mulhause. He came to Petrograd via Salonika, and brought with him a number of decorations for the Russian army. He visited Russia twice during the war. SAZONOV : S. D. Sazonov, Minister of Foreign Affairs from 1910 to July 1915. A capable and honest statesman, perhaps lacking in subtlety, but not in sincerity or intelligence. His book, " Fateful Years," has recently been published in England. His enmity to Rasputin and the sinister and " occult " influences of the Court led to his dismissal—and thus deprived Russia of the services of one of her few reliable Ministers. PALÉOLOGUE : Maurice Paléologue, the French Ambassador, whose delightful book, " La Russie des Tsars," is the best contemporary work on the social and political life of Russia during the war. DJOUNKOVSKY : General V. F. Djounkovsky, Governor of Moscow. He was an A.D.C. to the Tsar, and Assistant-Minister of Internal Affairs. He was accused by the Tsaritsa of having fostered the " seditious popularity " of the Grand Duke Nicholas (Paléologue, Vol. II, p. 70), and he had the courage to speak to the Tsar concerning certain scandals in which Rasputin was involved. As a result of this, he was dismissed from his office in September 1915, and was given the command of the 8th Siberian Rifle Brigade. BROUSSILOV : General A. A. Broussilov, then commanding the 8th Army, was the most vigorous, and the most fortunate, of the Russian generals. In 1916 he succeeded Ivanov as Commander-in-Chief of the South-west Front, and conducted a brilliant offensive in the Carpathians. He was sixty-one at the outbreak of war, and his career up to that time had not been in any way distinguished. He became Commander-in-Chief under the Provisional Government in 1917, but resigned. KHAN-NAKHICHEVANSKY : a cavalry general, commanding the 2nd Caucasian Division.

" The little Admiral "—Admiral C. D. Nilov, formerly the commander of the Imperial yacht " Standart," and then Flag-Captain to the Tsar, who was particularly fond of him. TATISHCHEV : General Count I. L. Tatishchev, one of the Tsar's most loyal friends. He accompanied his sovereign to the Ourals in 1917, and was

D

murdered by the Bolsheviks. SVECHIN : Colonel V. V. Svechin of the Preobrajensky Regiment of Life-Guards. A.D.C. to the Tsar.

It is not clear why the Tsar should have been so anxious to visit Lomja, a small town in northern Poland, about eighty miles north-west of Warsaw, and at that time close to the front line.

Telegram.

Stavka. 3 *March*, 1915.

Warmest thanks for charming letters from you and the children. I was busy all the evening with conversations, reading and writing. Foul, wet, windy weather. Good news from everywhere. I kiss you all fondly.

NICKY.

Telegram.

Stavka. 4 *March*, 1915.

I have finished my notepaper. Could you not send me my paper—in the blue box on the shelf opposite the first window? I have very stupidly forgotten it. All is well. The weather is nasty, a snowstorm. I kiss you tenderly.

NICKY.

Telegram.

Stavka. 4 *March*, 1915.

Warm thanks for letter and two telegrams. I am in despair at your being worn out. I am very grieved about your poor wounded officer; I quite understand you. . . .

Stavka. 5 *March*, 1915.

MY BELOVED LITTLE BIRD, SUNNY,

My warmest thanks for your long, precious letter. How well do I understand your sorrow for the sad death of the poor fellow, without a single relative near ! Truly, it is better to be killed outright, like Strouve, as death in battle comes in the presence of the whole division or regiment and is entered in history.

To-day the weather is good, but it is frosty with a lot of snow. The sun is shining beautifully through the trees which are in front of my window. We have only just come back from our after-dinner walk. The roads among the fields are very slippery, and my gentlemen sometimes fall down. Some days ago Sazonov fell, while crossing from the train to his carriage, and bruised his nose and leg. Yesterday Drenteln slipped in the same place and tore the tendon of his ankle; he had to lie down, and Feodorov is attending him. To-day, during our walk, Grabbe fell, but luckily without hurting himself. Towards the end he fell through the ice into a ditch, but also without taking harm.

From all this you can see that we spend our time quietly and without notable events. This morning I spent an hour or an hour and a half with N. and two Staff officers.

I see George often—he has improved remarkably; everybody who has seen him since his return from the Caucasus notices it. After having made inquiries as to how the *plastouni* (my special weakness) have conducted themselves, I have appointed myself Chief of the 6th Koubansky *plastouni* battalion, and him—George—Chief of the 4th Koubansky *plastouni* battalion, because he was with them in their trenches—that is extraordinary, is it not? Tell Olga about it.

All these splendid men are leaving Batoum in a few days for Sevastopol, to get ready for the final expedition.

Now I must finish, my love. God bless you and the dear children! I kiss you tenderly and lovingly and remain, my darling,

Unchangeably your old hubby
NICKY.

The " sad death " of one of the patients in the Tsaritsa's military hospital at Tsarskoe Selo.

Plastouni. The plastouni battalions were Kouban Cossack units, consisting of picked marksmen. They were originally attached to the various infantry units of the Black Sea forces, but in 1870 they were formed into independent battalions—six battalions in peace time and sixteen in war.

The " final expedition " was to have been to Constantinople—the fulfilment of the long cherished hopes of Russian imperialism.

Telegram.

Stavka. 6 *March,* 1915.

Hearty thanks for dear letter with the note about your 21st Regiment.   Thank her and give her my greetings. The weather is lovely and frosty.   I hope your heart is better.   You must take care of yourself.   I embrace and kiss you tenderly.

NICKY.

Telegram.

Stavka. 7 *March,* 1915.

Warmest thanks for dear No. 283.   About the New Testaments—yes.   I shall tell you about the plastouni.   The gentlemen thank you all.   It is warm to-day, thawing. . . .

" About the New Testaments."   The Tsaritsa wished to send 10,000 New Testaments to the prisoners of war in Germany, and was anxious to know whether these might be sent in her name, and with an inscription to that effect.   She asked him to telegraph his reply.

Stavka. 7 *March,* 1915.

MY BELOVED SUNNY,
                I thank you countless times for your sweet letter No. 282, and am angry with myself for not writing to you every day, as I intended.   The courier leaves at 6.30, and after 5 o'clock I am always in a hurry with the papers, and when I am busy with the usual morning report there is hardly time enough left to write letters before lunch.   We are all amazed here at the time going so quickly.   The prolongation of my stay here has proved useful, as we had to discuss a number of serious and pressing questions; if I had not been here it would have taken much more time and an exchange of telegrams.

It seems to me you think that N. is holding me back on purpose, with the idea of not letting me move about and see the troops.   In reality that is not quite correct.

About a fortnight ago, when he wrote to me advising me to come here, he said that I could easily visit three army corps, because they were grouped together in the rear.

Since then much has changed, and they have all been sent to the front line; that is true—I receive proof of it every morning during the Reports. Even General Pau was not allowed to go to Lomja (my little place). He only went through Warsaw to Bzoura and Ravka, where at the present moment all is quiet. Yesterday I drove out 24 versts in a car and walked in a charming wood and in the camp of the 4th Army Corps—the place is called the Scobelevsky Camp. On the huts occupied by the officers their surnames are inscribed; they are surrounded by little gardens, with benches, gymnastic apparatus, and all sorts of amusements for the children. I thought with sadness of those who will never again return here.

It was terribly cold driving in an open car, but we were warmly clothed. To-day it is thawing. Chemodourov bought these cards for me at the post office. Give A. my greetings and tell her that I liked the verses which she copied for me.

I hope that you are feeling better now, my love, my sweet Wify. God bless you and the children ! I am always with you in prayer and thought.

Ever your loving
NICKY.

CHEMODOUROV : T. I. Chemodourov, the Tsar's valet. He accompanied the Imperial Family to the Ourals in 1917, fell ill at Ekaterinburg, was transferred to the prison infirmary and forgotten, and thus escaped with his life.

Telegram.

Stavka. 8 March, 1915.

Warmest thanks for letter, for the delightfully scented lilies, and two telegrams. I am very glad about Irina. The news is good from everywhere. I am leaving on Tuesday, shall be home on Wednesday morning. I kiss you fondly. Give her my kind regards.

NICKY.

IRINA : the daughter of the Grand Duke Alexander Mikhail-ovitch and wife of Prince Yussoupov. She had given birth to a daughter.

Telegram.

Stavka.   9 March, 1915.

Przemysl is taken.   Praise be to God !

NICKY.

The capture of Przemysl was an event of supreme military importance.   It was the chief fortified town of Galicia, and its fall had a
stimulating effect, not only on the moral of the Russian armies, but
also on that of the Allies.   No fewer than 126,000 prisoners were
taken, and 700 heavy guns.

Stavka.   9 March, 1915.

MY BELOVED SUNNY,

How am I to thank you for your two charming letters
and for the lilies ?   I press them to my face and kiss often
the places which I think were touched by your dear lips.
They stand on my table day and night ; when the gentlemen
pass my doors I give them the flowers to smell.   God grant
that I may return by the 11th—probably at 10 o'clock in
the morning.   What joy to be again in one's own nest—
snugly and closely (in every sense) together !   Just at this
very minute, 11.30, Nicolasha came running into my
carriage, out of breath and with tears in his eyes, and told
me of the fall of Przemysl.   Thanks be to God !   For two
days we have been waiting for this news with hope and
anxiety.   The fall of this fortress has an enormous moral
and military significance.   After several months of despondency, this news strikes as an unexpected ray of sunshine,
and exactly on the first day of spring !

I began this letter in a calm mood, but now everything
has been turned upside down in my head, so you must excuse
the second part of this letter.   Oh, my dear, I am so profoundly happy at this good news, and so grateful to God for
His mercy !   I have ordered a thanksgiving Te Deum to be
sung at 2 o'clock in the local church, where I was present
last year at the thanksgiving molebni [services] !   Yesterday
I drove in a motor car to the same charming wood near the
Scobolevsky Camp, and had a good walk on the other side
of the big road—it was warm and thawing hard.

As Drenteln has hurt his ankle, Grabbe is taking his

place at our games of dominoes; he is so amusing with the little Admiral that they make me and N. P. roll with laughter. I am thinking of sending Grabbe to the army in Przemysl with heaps of orders and thanks for the officers and men.

3 o'clock.

I have just returned from church, which was packed with officers and my splendid Cossacks. What beaming faces! Shavelsky spoke a few moving words; everyone was in a sort of paschal mood!

Well, good-bye, my treasure, my Sunny! May God bless you and the dear children! I am tremendously happy to return home again.

.   .   .   .   .   .

Always your old hubby,
NICKY.

Telegram.

Stavka. 10 *March,* 1915.

I forgot to thank you for your dear letter; was very excited over the happy news. A colossal number of prisoners was taken there. Lovely sunny weather. Am leaving at 3 o'clock. I kiss you warmly.

NICKY.

Telegram.

Louga. 4 *April,* 1915.

Hearty thanks for dear letter. I have changed the beginning of my programme; am first going to the Stavka and then to the two other places which I wrote down in your pocket-book. Am feeling splendid. I kiss all tenderly.

NICKY.

Telegram.

Stavka. 5 *April,* 1915.

Hearty thanks for sweet letter with violets, and for the telegram. All is well. I shall stay here several days. I shall explain my plans in my letter. Kiss you tenderly.

NICKY.

Stavka.   5 *April*, 1915.

MY BELOVED SUNNY,

I thank you from the depth of my old loving heart for your two charming letters, the telegram and the flowers. I was so touched by them ! I was feeling so sad and down-hearted, leaving you not quite well, and remained in that state until I fell asleep.

On my way here, Voeikov informed me that it would be better to turn off from Vilna, as German aeroplanes were dropping bombs on the railway lines and the trains going through Bielostok, and that General Alexeiev was not in Sedletz ! That is why we arrived here this morning at 9 o'clock. I had a long conversation with N.; then the usual Report, and [afterwards went] to church. He suggested [advised] that I should go as soon as possible to Przemysl and Lvov, as later it would be necessary to take certain measures in Galicia. Bobrinsky told me the same thing several days ago. I shall be accompanied by N., as it will be my first visit to the conquered area. Naturally, this visit will be of very short duration, [as] both local railway lines are blocked up with trains. After that I shall see Ivanov and Alexeiev and continue my journey to the South. I cannot yet ascertain the date, but of course I shall inform you in good time.

It is quite interesting to spend a few days in this manner, and in some ways passes the bounds of the ordinary. Petiu-sha and Petia are here, and are both well. Old Fredericks has just had his talk with N. At dinner I shall be able to judge by the expression of their faces how this conversation has passed off. I had a good walk with my people; the wind blew hard, but the sun gave considerable warmth. The snow which had fallen during the night had thawed, the birds sang merrily in the wood, and my Life-Guard Cossacks were practising with their machine-guns, making a terrible noise. I went up to them on my way home and watched them.

Well, my love, I must finish. The courier is leaving now —at 6.30.

Tenderly and most affectionately do I kiss you, my darling Wify, and the children, and remain

Unchangeably your devoted hubby,
NICKY.

God bless you !

ALEXEIEV : General M. V. Alexeiev, at that time Commander-in-Chief of the North-west Front, became, later, Chief of Staff to the Tsar, and the virtual director of the Russian campaign. He was fifty-seven in 1914. The first ten years of his military career were spent in an infantry regiment at Mogilev. In 1877–78 he saw active service on the Danube. He became a professor at the Military Academy, and served on the Quartermaster-General's branch at Army Headquarters. In the Manchurian War of 1904–5 he was Quartermaster-General of the 3rd Army. From 1908 to 1912 he was Chief of Staff of the Kiev Military District, and he then commanded the 13th Corps. At the beginning of the war he was Ivanov's Chief of Staff. He was a spruce, energetic little man, with an affable yet firm personality. John Pollock, who saw him at the Stavka, describes him as " a Russian of the Russians, with the wide face and large brow of the good peasant stock from which he has sprung." He was undoubtedly a valuable Chief of Staff, and if he lacked brilliance he possessed the great qualities of honesty and resolution. In the matter of work he spared neither himself nor his subordinates. He died in the winter of 1917.

BOBRINSKY : Count G. A. Bobrinsky, Adjutant-General, was appointed Governor-General of Galicia on the first occupation of that province.

Telegram.

Stavka. 6 April, 1915.

Warm thanks for dear letter and telegram; thank Marie also. There is no special news. I saw Engalychev. The weather is much better and warmer. Fond kisses.

NICKY.

Stavka. 6 April, 1915.

MY PRECIOUS SUNNY,

Countless loving thanks for your sweet letter, which has arrived this morning. Yes, it is curious—setting off at

2 o'clock by the Warsaw line, one arrives here at 9 o'clock in the morning; whereas, leaving at 10 o'clock in the morning one gets here only at about 12 by the Vindavo-Rybinsk railway; it is a bad line and the trains move slowly on it.

Yesterday, after lengthy discussions, it was decided that we should start from the Stavka on Wednesday evening and arrive at the old frontier station of Brody on Thursday morning. Thence, N., I and some of our suite will drive in cars to Lvov, and the rest with Fredericks will go by train.   In this way we shall follow the route which was taken in August by our Third Army, and shall see the battlefields, spend the night in Lvov and in the morning proceed via Sambor, where Broussilov is, to Przemysl.—Here we shall spend the night and return by the same route.   Between those two places I shall perhaps manage to get in touch with the Third Caucasian Corps, who are concentrating in the reserve.

Think what a delight it would be if I should really succeed in doing so !   All these changes will add only one extra day to the whole of my journey, so I hope that my Wify will not be very cross with me.

I was glad to see dear Olga.   To-day the weather is really delightfully warm.   We had a fairly long walk in the fields and got into an evil-smelling swamp.   Some amusing scenes occurred here, especially when Grabbe, having tucked up his skirts, tried with all his might to pull himself out of the deep mud.   You can imagine in what a charming condition we returned !   Well, my love, my little bird, I must finish; it is time to dispatch the courier.   We are all going to the cinematograph.

Ever, beloved mine,

Your hubby
NICKY.

Brody, a small town formerly on the frontier between Austria-Hungary and Poland, but now in Poland, forty miles from the Ukrainian border.   Lvov is more usually known in this country as Lemberg.

Telegram.

Stavka. 7 *April,* 1915.

Thank you tenderly for dear letter, Olga and Alexey as well. The weather is divine. I was very busy in the morning. Drove in a car to our wood; wonderful air. I hope that you are better. Tender embraces.

NICKY.

Stavka. 7 *April,* 1915.
MY BELOVED SUNNY,

I thank you heartily for your dear letter and am returning you the Countess's letter. I do not think that any difficulties will arise about that question; a little goodwill on our side and the thing will be done, and we shall have one annoyance the less in our lives. Of course I shall discuss it with the old man.

To-day I had a very busy morning—after the reports I received Grunwald, who has come from Vilna, where he inspected all the hospitals, and later on I saw Engalychev, as well as our Vielopolsky, looking like a king who has lost his kingdom.

They all had lunch. N. received the Belgian Mission and entertained them in his train.

Darling mine, I do not agree with you that N. ought to remain here during my visit to Galicia. On the contrary, precisely because I am going in war-time to a conquered province, the Commander-in-Chief ought to accompany me. It is he who accompanies me; not I who am in his suite.

As I wrote to you yesterday, I hope to see the 2nd Caucasian Corps near Sambor, and get in touch with the 8th Army of Broussilov. Unless one counts last year's visit to the Caucasus, I have so far not had the opportunity of being near troops, and especially those troops which have been victorious since the very beginning of the war!

To-day we drove in a car along our well-known, charming road, and went further into the delightful wood. It was quite hot, and we found some flowers—here is one of them! —To-morrow is the anniversary of our betrothal; how many joyful recollections ! God bless you, my treasure, and the children ! Thank Olga and Alexey for their letters. I kiss you all affectionately, and remain

Ever your old hubby

NICKY.

Give A. my greetings.

The Countess : Countess Hohenfelsen, morganatic wife of the Grand Duke Paul, and later given the title of Princess Paley. In her letter she asked for the title of Princess, and referred to various family matters. GRUNWALD : General A. A. von Grunwald, Chief Equerry. VIELOPOLSKY : Count Vielopolsky was Master of the Imperial Preserves in Poland.

Telegram.

Stavka. 8 April, 1915.

Warm thanks for letter, telegram and flowers. In prayers and thought I am more than ever with you. A delightful warm day. I hope you are feeling better. I kiss you and the children fondly.

NICKY.

Stavka. 8 April, 1915.

MY PRECIOUS DARLING,

My warm and loving thanks for your dear letter, full of tender words, and for both telegrams. I too have you in my thoughts on this our 21st anniversary ! I wish you health [or well-being] and all that a deeply loving heart can desire, and thank you on my knees for all your love, affection, friendship and patience, which you have shown me during these long years of our married life !

To-day's weather reminds me of that day in Coburg—*how sad it is* that we are not together ! Nobody knew that it was the day of our betrothal—it is strange, how soon people forget—besides, it means nothing to them.

Krivoshein has arrived, who, in my presence, gave N. his opinions on various suggestions about measures which could be adopted in regard to the reward of officers and men who are leaving the army at the end of the war ; those who have distinguished themselves, those who have been crippled, and all wounded in general. Excellent suggestions, which I shall impart to you at home. Of course I have forgotten all the names they mentioned to me.

To-day I had no time to write to you before the courier's departure, as I was in a hurry with my usual papers. I am sending this letter to-morrow from the border station of Brody. I am afraid I shall not have time to write from Galicia, but I shall write later, from the South.

Before the evening I drove along the old road to the town of Slonin in the province of Grodno. It was extraordinarily warm and pleasant; and the smell of the pine forest—one feels enervated and softened !

I am sending you Ella's telegram to be deciphered—I cannot understand what she wants.

Brody, 9 April.

Here I am, on what was once Austrian soil. Wonderful hot weather. I heard the reports in N.'s train, which is standing alongside of mine, and after lunch I am going to Lvov by car. God bless you, my precious Sunny ! I kiss you and the children tenderly.

Always your hubby

NICKY.

" That day in Coburg "—in 1894. It was the anniversary of the Tsar's betrothal. Three years later, a prisoner at Tobolsk, he noted the same anniversary in his diary.

KRIVOSHEIN : A. V. Krivoshein, the Minister of Agriculture.

Telegram.

Brody. 9 April, 1915.

Have arrived at 10 o'clock; the weather is lovely. Am leaving for Lvov at 1 o'clock. I have sent a letter from here. Embrace you closely.

NICKY.

Telegram.

Lvov. 9 April, 1915.

Thanks for news. Am deeply impressed; an interesting route; a great number of soldiers' graves. I had a touching reception here. Saw Ksenia [Xenia] and Olga in her hospital. Summer-like weather. Tender kisses.

NICKY.

KSENIA : Ksenia or Xenia, the Tsar's elder sister, married the Grand Duke Alexander Mikhailovitch.

Telegram.

Telegraph Office 152.   10 *April,* 1915.

Have arrived safely in Khyrov via Sambor. Saw the wonderful Caucasian Corps. The district is delightful. The weather is summer-like. Have received very deep and joyful impressions. I embrace you tenderly.

NICKY.

Telegram.

Telegraph Office 152.   11 *April,* 1915.

Last night I received the ikon, letter and photograph. I am very grateful. Am going to look over the fortifications [or defences]. After lunch back to Lvov, and thence in the evening to Brody. The weather is splendid. Everything is bursting into bud. . . .

Telegram.

Brody.   12 *April,* 1915.

Arrived here already last night; have found two letters. Many thanks. I am leaving now for the South; am carrying away the happiest impressions. . . .

NICKY.

Imperial Train. Proskourov. 12 *April,* 1915.

MY PRECIOUS DARLING,

First of all, my warmest thanks for your two letters and the ikon of St. Simeon the Holy, and for Baby's photograph, which I have, alas ! dropped out of the box and broken the glass. That happened in Przemysl. Well— how difficult it is to describe rapidly all that I have seen, or, more correctly, lived through, in the last three days !

On the 9th of April I arrived in Brody, after having

crossed the old frontier. N. was already there with his Staff. When the reports were over I finished my last letter and papers, had lunch and went out in a motor with N. It was hot and windy. The dust we raised covered us like a white shroud. You cannot imagine what we looked like ! We stopped twice and got out of the car to look at our positions and those of the Austrians at the time of the first great battles in August of last year; there are a great number of crosses on the common [the word in the Russian text is " fraternal "] graves and on the single ones. It is amazing what long marches the army then made every day, in addition to fighting ! About half-past five we cleaned up a little—Bobrinsky met us on the hill and we drove straight to Lvov. It is a very handsome town, slightly resembling Warsaw, a great number of gardens and monuments, full of troops and Russians ! The first thing I did was to go to an enormous riding school, which has been converted into our church, and can hold 10,000 people; here, in the guard of honour, I saw both my sisters. Then I went to Olga's hospital; there are not many wounded there now; saw Tam. Andr. and other acquaintances from Rovno, doctors, sisters, and so forth—and just before the sun set drove up to the Governor-General's palace. A squadron of my Life-Guard Cossacks was drawn up in front. Bobrinsky led me to his rooms, ugly and uncomfortable, rather like a big railway station, in the same style, without doors, if you do not count the doors into the bedroom. You may be interested to know that I slept in old Franz Joseph's bed.

10 April, I left Lvov by rail, in Austrian carriages, and arrived at Sambor at 1 o'clock in the afternoon; there I was met by Broussilov and, to my great astonishment, by a guard of honour of my splendid Rifles of the 16th Odessa Regiment. The company was commanded by my friend the Sergeant-Major, as all the officers were wounded and the captain killed. While they were passing, the band played the march which we liked so much at Livadia, and I could not hold back my tears. I went to Broussilov's house; he presented the whole of his Staff to me, and then we had lunch. Later, I returned to my train, and arrived

at Khyrov, situated picturesquely in the mountains, at 4 o'clock.   Here, on a large field, were drawn up all the troops of the 3rd Caucasian Corps.   What magnificent regiments they are !   Among them were my Shirvantzi and Alexeiev's Saliantzi.   I recognised only one officer and one ensign.   They had arrived there only a day or two before from Osovetz, and were very pleased at getting into a warmer climate and being able to see the mountains.   I went down three long lines on a ploughed field, and nearly fell several times, because the ground was very uneven, and I had to think of Dmitry.   As we had very little time left, I passed along [the remainder of] the troops in a car, thanking them for their faithful service.   I and N. were frightfully shaken up.   I returned to the train quite hoarse, but I am very pleased and happy at having seen them.   An hour later we arrived in Przemysl.

It is a small town, with narrow streets and dull grey houses, filled with troops and Orenberg Cossacks.   N. and I stayed, with several gentlemen [of the suite], in a fairly clean house, the owner of which had fled before the fall of the fortress. The little place is surrounded by mountains and looks very picturesque.   We dined in the garrison mess, where everything has remained untouched.   Slept badly.

11 April.   I got up early and went with the whole of our company to look over the defences.   They are most interesting, colossal works—terribly fortified.   Not an inch [vershok] of ground remained undefended.   Charming views open out from the forts ; they are completely covered with grass and fresh flowers.   I am sending you a flower which I dug up with Grabbe's dagger.   At 12 o'clock I returned to the town, lunched at the mess, and drove by another route to Lvov, via Radymno and Yavorov, again past the fields of the September battles.   The weather was beautiful the whole time.

Ksenia and Olga came to me before dinner.   I left Lvov at 9.30 by rail and arrived in Brody at 12.30 at night. Here I changed over to our train.

To-day I got up late, heard the usual reports and left N. at 2 o'clock.   Forgive me for this short and dry account,

but I have no time for more. God bless you, my beloved
Sunny, and the children. I kiss you all fondly.

Ever your old hubby

NICKY.

Telegram.

Proskourov. 13 *April*, 1915.

Thanks for telegram. Am glad that your health is
better. I am now going to Kamenetz-Podolsk to inspect
the Trans-Amur Borderers. The weather is excellent.
To-morrow Odessa. Tender embraces.

NICKY.

Telegram.

Gmerinka. 13 *April*, 1915.

Thanks for telegram. I saw the splendid Trans-Amur
Borderers and your Crimeans. They are in beautiful con-
dition. They asked me to give their greetings to their Chief.
I was very glad to come across them here by chance. . . .

Telegram.

Rasdelnaia. 14 *April*, 1915.

Warmest thanks for letter. To-day I saw our fine fellows
[our beauties] in Odessa at a grand inspection. Visited two
hospitals. Lovely summer-like weather. Kyrill is going
to two other places. Tender kisses.

NICKY.

Telegram.

Nicolaiev. 15 *April*, 1915.

Sincere thanks for the news. Saw our new ships and went
over magnificent docks. After lunch I shall continue the
visiting of other shipbuilding and ammunition factories. It
is extremely interesting. Cold, windy weather. At 6 I am
leaving for dear Sevastopol. . . .

Telegram.

Sevastopol. 17 *April*, 1915.

Best thanks for dear letter and telegram. This morning
I heard of a sad disaster connected with an explosion. The

E

weather to-day is beautiful, but not hot. Drove round the ships and went on board some of them. Visited the hospital ship. Now I am going to inspect my plastouni on the platform in front of the train. To-morrow all the others are to be inspected. . . .

Sevastopol. 17 *April,* 1915.

MY BELOVED SUNNY,

I thank you with all my heart for your dear letters, which have brought me such joy and consolation in what is, when all is said, my solitude. Although this time, no matter where I went, I was surrounded by members of the family—in Galicia, at Odessa and here. This will probably be my last letter. My trip to Kamenetz-Podolsk has given me immense pleasure. The town is very pretty, and I have simply lost my head over the Trans-Amur men and your delightful Crimeans. The first, who have only recently arrived from Kharbin, look magnificent. They are well equipped and smart, like Guard regiments. The Tartars have rested, and all smiled broadly as I was passing along them. I was not surprised that they had *few* officers.

The following day Odessa was full of enthusiasm. Perfect order was observed in the streets. Our splendid fellows of the Gvard. Equip. were more impressive than ever before—the whole lot of them are magnificent men. I had to address a few warm words to them, and to reward about twenty men with decorations. By the side of them stood the new Caucasian Regiment, which I had not seen in Kars—the 9th Caucasian Rifle Regiment—; at that time they were fighting the Turks, and lost approximately 600 men and 14 officers. But now their numbers are made up again. In addition to them, the 53rd and 54th Don Regiments were at the inspection. The 53rd was at the Stavka last year. The next day it suddenly became intensely cold in Nicolaievo. It would take too long to describe all that I saw there—it was wonderfully interesting, and fine to see what our nation is capable of—how it approaches matters in a serious spirit :

three dreadnoughts, four cruisers, nine destroyers, and a vast number of large submarines, engines, turbines and shells [shrapnels] without number.

I was so pleased yesterday to find the fleet here. After dinner I played about on the quay with my 6th Battalion of *plastouni*, and to-morrow I am arranging to inspect them all in their camp.

I like this place. God bless you, my precious Wify, and the children. I kiss you lovingly.

Ever your hubby
NICKY.

Telegram.

Sevastopol. 18 *April*, 1915.

Warmest thanks for dear letter and telegram. I have just returned from an inspection of all the 11 battalions of the plastouni. An interesting, beautiful sight, and unique of its kind. I have appointed Alexey Chief of the 3rd Batt. Be kind enough to telegraph to them in his name. . . .

Telegram.

Sevastopol. 18 *April*, 1915.

Thirteen thousand ikons have arrived. I intend to drive by car beyond the Baidars. Tender embraces.

NICKY.

Telegram.

Likhachevo South. 19 *April*, 1915.

Sincerest thanks for letter No. 301. I thank also all the children. Divine weather. Yesterday I went half-way to Yalta; saw the big landslide. It is much cooler there. The old man is well, sends his thanks. We stopped in Borki. I embrace you tenderly. How is her leg?

NICKY.

It may be noted that, on this day, von Mackensen broke through the Russian front on the middle Dounayetz. In the course of the next few days the second and third Russian lines were taken, and the Russian armies were withdrawn northwards over the Carpathians. This withdrawal, according to Falkenhayn (p. 90), degenerated into a rout on a front more than 100 miles wide. But here again, as at the time of the Masurian battles, the Tsar makes no comment on the disastrous course of events. It is inconceivable that he was not informed.

Sajnoe. 19 *April,* 1915.

MY LOVE,

These photographs were taken in Sevastopol, when I was playing about with my plastouni. You will return them to me, will you not? when I come back. The heat in the train is terrible—22 degrees.

I love you immensely and kiss you.

Your

NICKY.

Telegram.

Orel. 20 *April,* 1915.

Warm thanks for dear letter. I have spent a very interesting and full day at the Briansky factory. In the morning it was terribly hot; now, after a thunderstorm and rain, the temperature has fallen to 6 degrees. To-morrow morning I shall see Ella. I kiss you affectionately.

NICKY.

Telegram.

Tver. 21 *April,* 1915.

Sincerest thanks for last letter. Saw Ella for ten minutes. I am now going into the town until evening. Cold, chilly weather. So glad to be home to-morrow. Fond kisses.

NICKY.

Telegram.

Stavka. 5 *May,* 1915.

Have just arrived safely. Lovely weather. The woods are now quite green and smell delightful. Now I am off to church. Thanks for telegram. I embrace you tenderly.

NICKY.

Telegram.

Stavka. 6 *May*, 1915.

I am very touched by your lovely presents and good wishes. Am sorry that we are not together. I thank Ella. I kiss you and the dear children fondly.

NICKY.

The Tsar's birthday.

Telegram.

Stavka. 6 *May*, 1915.

Again I thank you tenderly and warmly for your good wishes. Be kind enough to thank our Friend for his moving words. After great heat and a night's downpour it has become much cooler now. . . .

Telegram.

Stavka. 7 *May*, 1915.

Best thanks for sweet letter. Tell her that I was touched by her note. The news is unsatisfactory. I wish you a happy journey, and hope that it will not prove fatiguing. I kiss you fondly.

NICKY.

Here we have an acknowledgment of the fact that the news was not good. Mackensen was bombarding Przemysl, and Lutkov had fallen the day before.

Telegram.

Stavka. 8 *May*, 1915.

Thanks for letter and telegram. I hope that you were not very tired. To-day there was a ray of light in the news. I think it will be better for me to stay here several days more, till matters clear up. I am sure you will understand. It is warm but dull. I kiss and embrace you tenderly, also O[lga] and T[atiana].

NICKY.

Telegram.

Stavka. 9 *May*, 1915.

I am glad to hear that you have returned. Hearty thanks for news. The situation has improved slightly. The weather has at last become lovely. Please thank the three younger ones for their letters. I embrace you tenderly.

NICOLAI.

Telegram.

Stavka. 10 *May,* 1915.

Many thanks for letter and news. Thank God the news is better. The weather is also wonderful, not very hot. I am sad because we are not together. I embrace you closely. The old man asks me to send his greetings.

Stavka. 11 *May,* 1915.

MY OWN DEAR LOVE,

It is exactly a week to-day since I went away. I am so sorry that I have not written to you since then ! But, one way and another, it happens that I am just as busy here as at home. The morning reports, as you can imagine, have been lengthy. Then church, nearly every day, endless conversations and so forth. This took up nearly all my time, if one does not count half of the early evening, which is filled up with useful occupations. After tea there is a hasty survey of the papers, often vsenoshchnaia [vespers] and dinner—with the result that I have a headache in the evening and am completely exhausted. But that has all passed, and everything has become better and more normal, as it used to be.

When I arrived, a mood of depression and despondency reigned here. In a half-hour's talk, N. has clearly explained the whole state of affairs. Ivanov's Chief of Staff, poor General Dragomirov, went off his head, and he began to tell people right and left that it was necessary to retreat to Kiev. Such talk, coming from above, naturally affected the spirit [moral] of the generals in command and, combined with desperate German attacks and our terrible losses, led them to the conclusion that there was nothing left for them to do except to retreat. Since January, N. had given them all strict orders to fortify their positions in the rear. This was not done. Therefore, Radko-Dmitriev was compelled to leave his army, while Lesh was appointed his successor. Dragomirov was replaced by Gen. Savitch, an excellent man, who has arrived from Vladivostok with his Siberian Corps. Ivanov had given orders to evacuate even Przemysl. I felt all this before N. told me of it. But now, after the appointment of Savitch, thanks to God and also to his (Savitch's) strong and cool will and clear head, the mood of the generals has changed. Danilov, who came back yesterday, is absolutely reassured by what he has seen and heard. The moral condition of our troops is admirable, as it always has been; the only thing which causes anxiety, as in the past, is the shortage of munitions.

Fancy, the same thing has happened to the Germans—according to what the prisoners tell our officers—namely, that they were obliged to hold up their attacks owing to their supplies of ammunition being exhausted and their terrible losses. N. is very pleased with Gen. Alexeiev, my cross-eyed friend, and thinks him a man in the right place.

Now you can judge for yourself whether I could go away from here in such difficult circumstances. It would have been understood as meaning that I avoided staying with the army at critical moments. Poor N., while telling me this, wept in my private room, and even asked me whether I thought of replacing him by a more capable man. He was not at all excited [overwrought]; I felt that he was saying exactly what he thought. He kept on thanking me for staying here, because my presence here supported *him personally.*

That is how it is. I have explained it all to you, my treasure. Now my conscience is clear. I hope to return about the morning of the 14th—that is, if everything goes smoothly.

The sudden death of Admiral Essen is a heavy loss to the country! Admiral Kanin will be appointed to Essen's post—a man whom the latter valued very highly. For the last few days the weather has been magnificent, the woods smell so delightfully and the birds sing so loudly. It is a veritable rustic idyll—if only it were not for the war! I drive about in a car, look at new places, get out and walk.

I am sending you this telegram of N.'s, which was received only this morning. I am delighted with your regiment; of course Bat. will receive his cross.

I must finish. God bless you, my darling Sunny, and the dear children ! Give A. my greetings. I kiss you tenderly and remain

Ever your loving old hubby

NICKY.

LESH, appointed to the 3rd Army in succession to Radko-Dmitriev. SAVITCH : General Savitch, appointed to be Chief of Staff to General Ivanov, was a capable and reliable soldier. ESSEN : Admiral N. O. Essen. He had taken part in the Japanese war, and commanded first the cruiser " Novik " and then the battleship " Sevastopol." He was Chief of the Operations Department of the Naval General Staff, and later commanded a part of the Baltic Fleet, hoisting his flag on the cruiser " Rurik." His death took place at Helsingfors. KANIN : Admiral V. A. Kanin, a member of the Council of State.

Telegram.

Stavka. 12 *May*, 1915.

Warmest thanks for news and dear letter. Divine weather; the lilac has come out in bloom. I am leaving to-morrow at 2 o'clock. I kiss you tenderly.

NICKY.

Telegram.

Stavka. 13 *May*, 1915.

Sincerest thanks for dear letter. I have been for my last walk. It is very warm. Am leaving after lunch. Am happy to be returning. Kiss you fondly.

NICKY.

Telegram.

Stavka. 11 *June*, 1915.

Have arrived safely. During the journey had heavy warm rain. Thanks for news. There is nothing specially bad to report. I hope you will soon feel quite strong again. . . .

According to Sir Bernard Pares (Introduction to " Letters of the Tsaritsa "), the Russian losses by this time were 3,800,000. He

had the figures from the Russian War Office, and considers them
an under-statement.   Mackensen was pressing forward, and two
days before the dispatch of this telegram the enemy had re-occupied
Lemberg.   In order to make good these terrible losses it was decided
to call up the Reservists : see the following note.

Telegram.

Stavka.   12 June, 1915.

Hearty thanks for charming letter; I also thank Olga for
her letter.   After a rainy night we are having dull, warm
weather.   I have a great deal of work to do, but shall try
to write. . . .

Stavka.   12 June, 1915.

BELOVED WIFY MINE,
          I thank you most warmly for both your sweet letters
—they have refreshed me.   This time I left with such a
heavy heart ! I thought of all the various and difficult
questions—of the change of Ministers, of the Duma, of the
2nd Category, and so on.   When I arrived, I found N.
grave, but quite calm.   He told me that he understood the
seriousness of the moment, and that he had received a
letter to that effect from Goremykin.   I asked him whom
he would recommend in Soukhomlinov's place.   He answered
—Polivanov.
          Having looked over the list of Generals' names, I have
come to the conclusion that, at the present juncture, he
might prove a suitable man.   He has been sent for, and
arrived this afternoon.   I spoke absolutely frankly with
him, and told him why I had been dissatisfied with him
before—A. Goutchkov, etc.   He replied that he knew it,
and that already, for three years, he had been carrying the
burden of my displeasure.   He has lost his son during the
war, and has greatly and efficiently helped Alek.
          I hope, therefore, that his appointment will turn out to
be successful.
          To-day I saw Krivoshein as well, and had a long con-
versation with him.   He was less nervous, and consequently
more judicious.   I sent for Goremykin and several of the
older Ministers; to-morrow we shall discuss some of these

questions and shall pass over nothing in silence. Yes, my own darling, I am beginning to feel my old heart. The first time it was in August of last year, after the Samsonov catastrophe, and again now—it feels so heavy in the left side when I breathe. But what can one do!

Alas! I must finish; they are all gathering for dinner at the big tent. God bless you, my treasure, my consolation and happiness! [Literally, "treasure, consolation and happiness mine!"] I kiss you all warmly.

Always your hubby

NICKY.

The weather is divine.

"The Second Category." The Second Category of the Opol-chenie or Reserve, consisting of untrained men between the ages of twenty-one and forty-three. The Opolchenie had only twice been called up—in 1812 and in 1854. It was eventually decided to call up this category, and the decision was a grave one, indicating a state of desperate emergency.

GOREMYKIN: I. L. Goremykin, then over eighty years of age, an obstinate and senile reactionary, President of the Council of Ministers, and absolutely incapable of performing his duties. SOUKHOMLINOV: General Soukhomlinov, the Minister of War. He was dismissed from office on the day on which this letter was written. It is not easy to decide whether he was deliberately treacherous or merely incompetent, but it is known that the inadequate equipment of the army was mainly due to his neglect. The Tsar was fond of him, and parted from him with reluctance. He was a pleasure-loving old man, wholly indifferent to his responsibilities. He was charged with having given information to the traitor Miassoyedov, knowing him to be the enemy's agent, and with betraying secrets of State to other foreign spies. He was further indicted with criminally neg-lecting to supply the army with munitions, and with placing con-tracts for his own benefit. His sentence was penal servitude for life. After serving a term of imprisonment, he was brought before a special tribunal in 1917. Of this trial General Denikin says (p. 30): "When the man who was responsible for the military catastrophe faced his judges . . . his personality produced a pitiful impression. The trial raised a more serious, painful question: How could this irresponsible man, with no real knowledge of military matters, and perhaps even consciously a criminal, have remained in power for six years?" POLIVANOV: General A. A. Polivanov, who succeeded Soukhomlinov, was an extremely capable organiser. Sazonov says of him (p. 287): "The new Minister of War was a very intelligent man and an indefatigable worker. He had very much resented having to serve under such a chief as Soukhomlinov." GOUTCHKOV : A. I. Goutchkov, the leader of the Octobrist (moderate Liberal) party, and Vice-President of the Duma, was strongly opposed to the Rasputin clique, and therefore hated by the Tsaritsa and her advisers. He possessed a vigorous, uncompromising personality. During the South African War he saw active service with the Boers. In 1912 he fought a duel with Miassoyedov (hanged at Warsaw in March 1915 as a spy) in consequence of a newspaper article. He founded, and became the head of, the General Association of Industries, and was Minister of War in the Provisional Government of 1917. One of the most able and most honest of Russian statesmen. ALEK : Prince A. Oldenburg, the father of Prince Peter.

Telegram.

Stavka. 13 *June*, 1915.

I thank you sincerely for your dear letter; Tatiana and Alexey as well. I have written to Marie for her birthday. The weather is splendid. The news is not so bad. This is a very busy day. I kiss you all fondly.

NICKY.

Telegram.

Stavka. 14 *June*, 1915.

Warm thanks for dear letter, and best wishes for Marie's birthday. I have only just returned from church. After lunch we are having the conference of Ministers. Lovely days and cool nights. . . .

Stavka. 15 *June*, 1915.

MY BELOVED, DARLING SUNNY,

My tenderest thanks for your two sweet letters. Yesterday I had not a minute to spare to write to you, as I was busy all day long. It was Marie's birthday, and it gave me happiness to be able to go to church in the morning.

I spoke to Shavelsky about arranging, for some day or other, krestny khod [the procession of the Cross] all over Russia. He thought it a very good idea, and suggested for it the 8th of July, the day of the Mother of God of Kazan, which is celebrated everywhere. He sends you his deepest respects. In our conversation he alluded to

Sabler, and said that it would be necessary to replace him. It is remarkable how everyone understands this, and wishes to see a clean, pious and well-meaning man in his place. Old Gorem., and Krivoshein and Shcherbatov have all told me the same thing, and believe that Samarin would be the best man for this post.   I remember now that, about six years ago, Stolypin wished to have him in his Ministry, and spoke to him with my permission, but he declined.   I have given Gorem. leave to send for him and to offer him this appointment.   I am sure that you will not like this, because of his being a Muscovite, but these changes must be brought about, and it is necessary to select a man whose name is known to the whole nation and who is unanimously respected.   One can work with such men in the Government, and they will all hold together [or use their force together—*i.e.*, in harmony]—that is quite obvious.

Fortunately yesterday's conference was held in the large tent, and lasted from 2 till 5 o'clock.   I was rather tired, but N. and all of them were greatly pleased.   Old Gor. expressed the opinion that this conference here was more productive of results than three months of their ordinary work.

In my next letter I shall tell you some of the details of it ; to-day I have no time.   My papers are neglected, and I must look through them.

Somehow I miss you particularly in these days, my Ray of Sunshine !   God bless you !   I kiss you and the dear children tenderly.

Unchangeably your old hubby

NICKY.

SABLER : V. K. Sabler, Procurator of the Holy Synod.   SHCHER-BATOV : Prince N. B. Shcherbatov, Minister of the Interior.   SAMA-RIN : A. D. Samarin, Marshal of the Nobility at Moscow.   He succeeded Sabler, and, according to E. H. Wilcox, he was " one of the best Procurators," but he was dismissed not long after his appointment.   STOLYPIN : P. A. Stolypin, the great Liberal states-man, at one time Governor of Saratov, and then Minister of Internal Affairs and President of the Council of Ministers.   He was assassi-nated at Kiev on 14th September, 1911.

Telegram.

Stavka. 16 *June,* 1915.

I thank you most warmly for your letter, also Marie and Alexey. It is very hot, but not sultry. Nothing new, but they are still pressing in some places. I kiss you all fondly.

NICKY.

Stavka. 16 *June,* 1915.

MY BELOVED SUNNY,

I thank you with all my heart for your sweet, long letter, in which you give me an account of your conversation with Paul. You gave perfectly correct answers on the questions of peace. That is precisely the chief point of my rescript to old Goremykin, which will be published.

With regard to Danilov, I think that the idea of his being a spy is not worth an empty eggshell. I am quite aware, too, that he is not liked, that he is even hated in the army, beginning with Ivanov and ending with the last officer. He has a terrible character, and is very harsh with his subordinates.

N. knows this, and from time to time puts him in his place; but he considers it impossible to dismiss him after 11 months of hard work—so well does this man know his duties.

Even Krivoshein spoke to me on this subject—he thinks, for instance, that N. ought to make alterations among his Staff, and choose other men in place of Yanoushkevitch and Danilov. I advised him to tell N. of it, which he did— from his own point of view, naturally. He told me later that N. had obviously not liked his frankness.

The conference, which was held some days ago, dealt with three problems : the regime for the German and Austrian nationals who are still domiciled in Russia; the prisoners of war; the text of the above-mentioned rescript; and finally the soldiers of the Second Category. When I told them of my wish, that the men of 1917 should be called up, all the Ministers heaved a sigh of relief. N. agreed at once.

Yanoushkevitch only asked that he might be allowed to work out the preparatory measures in case of necessity.

Of course, should the war continue for another year, we shall be obliged to call up some of the younger ages of the Second Category, but now it is not required.   Yussoupov, whom I sent for, was present at the conference on the first question; we cooled his ardour slightly, and gave him some clear instructions.   He caused some amusing moments when he was reading his reports of the Moscow riots—he became excited, shook his fists and banged them on the table.

I hope soon to go to Beloveje by car for a whole day, and to do it quite unexpectedly.   The old man and Voeikov thank you very much.   Well, I must break off this letter. God bless you, my darling Wify.   Fondly I kiss you and the dear children.

Your
NICKY.

YUSSOUPOV : General Prince F. F. Yussoupov, Chief of the Moscow Military District.   Father of Prince Felix Yussoupov, who took an active part in the murder of Rasputin.   He was obliged to relinquish his post, about this time, in consequence of anti-German pogroms in his district.   The Moscow riots were the outcome of a popular demand for the removal of Soukhomlinov, Maklakov (Minister of the Interior) and Shcheglovitov (Minister of Justice).

Beloveje : one of the Royal Preserves in Poland, where deer and big game were kept on a large scale.

Telegram.

Stavka.   17 *June*, 1915.

I am very grateful for letter and two telegrams.   Thanks to Tatiana and Olga.   It is very hot and windy.   There are 22 degrees of heat in our carriages.   Please do not worry, and see Goremykin, who will calm you.   Fond kisses for all.

NICKY.

Telegram.

Stavka.   19 *June*, 1915.

My warmest thanks to you for your sweet letter, to Anastasia also.   S. is coming here to-night.   Fine hot weather. I hope that you are feeling strong and reassured. Tender embraces.

NICKY.

S.—Samarin, who was coming for an interview in connection with his appointment to the Synod.

19 *June*, 1915.

MY DARLING SUNNY,

I beg your pardon for sending you an empty cascara bottle, but I require some more. I am putting my candle-end into it—give it to Alexey for his collection.

How grateful I am to you for your dear sweet letters, for all your devotion and love for me ! They give me strength. I embrace you closely, beloved mine ! It is too hot to write on such a subject. I am glad that you have seen the old man. Has he reassured you?

I am sending you a minute photograph which Djounk. took here last time. I have decided to leave here on Tuesday, and with God's help we shall see each other at last.

The Guards and other units are at present being trans-ferred to the side of Kholm and Lyublin, as the Germans are pressing us in that direction. That is why I am sitting here till the concentration [of troops] is accomplished. I am quite well again; I merely had a shooting pain in the left side at the bottom of the spine, which hurt me in my efforts to take a deep breath; it was especially painful at night, but now it has quite gone. Owing to the heat, we are going for long drives in the car, but walk very little. We have chosen new roads, and are driving about the neighbouring country with the aid of a map. Mistakes often occur, as the maps are obsolete, having been made 18 years ago; new roads have been made, new villages built, some forests have disappeared, all of which alters the map. Sometimes the horses with the carts which we meet begin to bolt—then we send the chauffeurs to the rescue. On Monday I hope to go to Beloveje.

It is well that you have seen Shcherbatov; try now to see

Polivanov, and be frank with him. Well, it is time to dispatch the courier. God bless you, my Wify, my treasure ! I kiss you and the children fondly.

Ever your hubby

NICKY.

Give her my greetings.

Telegram.

Stavka.   20 June, 1915.

I thank you heartily for your sweet letter; also Marie and Alexey. The heat is terrific. I saw Samarin, who has accepted, but asked to postpone his appointment for a fortnight. . . .

Telegram.

Stavka.   21 June, 1915.

Countless thanks for sweet letter and telegram. I had no time to write. To-morrow I am going for the whole day to Beloveje. I think I ought to stay here for a little longer, for military considerations. I kiss you tenderly. Sleep well.

NICKY.

Telegram.

Beloveje.   22 June, 1915.

I have arrived here all right. I remember; am thinking of you all. The forest is beautiful. I embrace you closely.

NICKY.

Telegram.

Stavka.   23 June, 1915.

My warmest thanks for dear letter. I derived great pleasure from my trip yesterday. I am writing about it. Returned at 11 in the evening. The weather is wonderful. I have remembered the date of her birthday and sent a telegram. . . .

Stavka.   23 June, 1915.

MY DEAR WIFY,

I thank you for your dear letter. Yesterday I really enjoyed myself in Beloveje. It was quite strange to be there alone, without you and the children. I felt so lonely and sad, but was none the less glad to see the house and our charming rooms, to forget the present and to live through past days. But the night before my departure I spent anxiously. No sooner had I finished playing dominoes than N. appeared and showed me a telegram he had just received from Alexeiev, which said that the Germans had broken through our lines and were penetrating far into the rear. N. left immediately in his train, and promised to telegraph to me in the morning from Sedletz. Naturally, I could not start for Beloveje at 10 o'clock as I had intended. All [those] around me became greatly discouraged, except Voeikov, as they did not know the cause of N.'s sudden departure. At last, at 11.40, a telegram came, to the effect that the proriv [breach] was repaired by a strong counter-attack of three of our regiments, and that the enemy was repulsed with heavy losses. So at 12 o'clock I ran off with a light heart, accompanied by the old man and all my gentlemen.

The road to Beloveje stretches for 183 versts, but it is a very good and even one. Three towns lie on the route—Slonim, Roujany and Proujany. I arrived at our house at 3.20, and the others at intervals of five minutes, because of the frightful dust. A cold lunch was served for us in the dining-room, and then I showed the gentlemen all over our and the children's rooms. Then we drove to the zverinetz [preserve] to see some wild bison and other animals. We were lucky enough to meet a large herd of buffaloes, who looked at us quite calmly.

We drove in the forest on excellent grass paths and got on to a main road at the end of the poushcha [wood]. The weather was magnificent, but this year there is such a drought that even the marshes have disappeared, and a thick dust pervades even the forest; all who took part in the drive were made unrecognisable by the black dust, especially the little Admiral. The Keeper of Beloveje is new—he is called Lvov, a fat man, related to the Admiral. The old priest is dead, as well as Neverli, whom I did not know. His successor is Bark, a relation of the Minister,

F

who has served here for 20 years in the capacity of Forester—
an energetic man, who knows the forest and the game to
perfection.   On our way back, the tyres of all the cars began
to burst—on my car three times—owing to the heat of the
day and a mass of scattered nails.   These stoppages came in
very opportunely, as they gave us a chance of getting out
and stretching our legs.   In the evening and during the
night it was beautifully fresh, and the air in the forest
wonderfully aromatic.

We arrived here at 10.45, just at the time when N.'s
train was slowly moving to its place.   After a talk with
him I had supper with my gentlemen, and immediately after
went to bed.   He told me that, on the whole, the situation
had not changed for the worse since yesterday, and that it
would improve if the Germans ceased to press us at the
same point for several days.   In that case we should have
to collect new (fresh) troops and try to stop them.   But
again there crops up this damnable question of the shortage
of artillery ammunition and rifles—this puts a check on
any energetic movement forward, as, after three days of
hard fighting, the supply of munitions might be exhausted.
Without new rifles it is impossible to make good the losses,
and the army is at present only just a trifle stronger than
in peace-time.   It should be—and at the beginning of the
war it was—three times as strong.   That is the position
we are in at this moment.

If there was no fighting for the duration of a month our
position would be far better.   Of course, I am giving this
information only to you; please do not speak of it, darling.

This letter has become rather lengthy, and I have no time
for more.   God bless you, my beloved Sunny!   Tenderly,
tenderly I kiss you and the children.   Be well and strong
again!

Ever your hubby

NICKY.

With regard to the continued shortage of rifles, it may be noted
that the troops were now using, in addition to those of Russian
manufacture, Japanese, Austrian and Mexican rifles.   The order
for American rifles had been held up by Soukhomlinov (Knox,

p. 222). There was an increasing scarcity of cartridges, and innumerable orders were issued to the army commanders laying stress on the need for economy. (See Gourko, p. 103.)

Telegram.

Stavka. 24 *June,* 1915.

I am infinitely grateful for dear letters—yours and Marie's —which came at 9, instead of in the morning. The weather is beautiful. I bathed in the little river in my favourite wood. I kiss you tenderly. Sleep well.

NICKY.

Telegram.

Stavka. 25 *June,* 1915.

Thanks for sweet letter; Tatiana also. The weather is sultry to-day. I hope to return on Sunday after dinner. The news is better. I kiss you fondly.

NICKY.

Telegram.

Stavka. 26 *June,* 1915.

Thank you heartily for your dear letter, and Alexey's. At lunch we had a refreshing thunderstorm. The krestnyie khodi [processions of the Cross] are fixed for the 8th of July. Am inexpressibly happy to be going home to-morrow. . . .

Stavka. 26 *June,* 1915.

MY PRECIOUS SUNNY,

My warmest thanks for your three dear letters. I could not write before, as I was busy with my beastly papers, which I get at the most inconvenient hours. This was caused by great numbers of military trains going from Vilna to Bielostok.

Yesterday I was glad to see the 6th Squadron of my Hussars, which was passing through the station. The train was stopped for 15 minutes; all the men got out—and brought out the colours. I saw them settle down again and start off, gaily shouting " hurrah ! " What a joyful, refreshing feeling !

The Dragoons also went through here, but your Uhlans went past by another line. I agree with you, my darling, that my chief work is the inspection of troops. I have often spoken of this to Voeikov—from the practical point of view it is very difficult to organise from here.

From Beloveje it is, of course, easier. But not being here [so in the text : presumably he means " there."], I do not know what troops are where, and those which are behind the front line are constantly shifted backward and forward and are difficult to find. Travelling round in the train is now out of the question. It is like a blind alley, as the French say !

I am very grateful to you for forwarding me Victoria's letter—she always writes so clearly and positively.

During lunch to-day a thunderstorm passed over us; the downpour was heavy and lasted for an hour. It has freshened the air wonderfully, having lowered the temperature from 23 to 15 degrees.

This is my last letter to you, my dear little Birdy—I am truly happy to be returning home to my family.

I kiss you tenderly, tenderly, and the children too. I hope to arrive on Saturday at 5 o'clock in the evening. May God bless you, my beloved, darling Sunny !

Always your old hubby

NICKY.

Telegram.

Stavka.   27 June, 1915.

I thank you warmly for your dear letter with the papers; Olga and Alexey as well. I am leaving now with good impressions. The news, thanks be to God ! is definitely better. I hope that you are feeling better. I kiss you tenderly.

NICKY.

Telegram.

Vitebsk.   23 August, 1915.

Thank you heartily for your dear letter, the children too. I slept well; am feeling strong and resolute. I hope that you are calm, and not very tired. I shall telegraph to-night, when all is over. I bless you and love you infinitely.

NICKY.

This telegram, sent after two months' residence at Tsarskoe Selo, was dispatched when the Tsar was on his way to supersede the Grand Duke Nicholas and to take over the Supreme Command. He was undoubtedly led to this fateful decision by the insistence of the Tsaritsa and of Rasputin. The military and internal situations were now critical. Falkenhayn, in his report to the Commander-in-Chief this month, said: " That the enemy has already been decisively defeated cannot be doubted by anybody who visualises the fact that the Russians have lost in three months about three-quarters of a million men in prisoners alone, endless material, Galicia, the kingdom of Poland and the Duchy of Courland." The Tsar's step was opposed by his Ministers. Sazonov (p. 290) says that " The Tsar's sudden decision to remove the Grand Duke Nicholas from the Supreme Command and to take his place at the head of the Army caused a great outburst of public anxiety." Even Goremykin was in opposition. A letter of respectful protest was sent to the Tsar, signed by the Procurator of the Synod (the newly-appointed Samarin) and by the majority of the Ministers. " We venture once more to tell you," they said, " that to the best of our judgment your decision threatens with serious consequences Russia, your dynasty and your person." As to the effect of this change on the army, Sir Alfred Knox (p. 332) says : " Misgiving . . . was almost universal. . . . It was felt that the new appointment would produce a crop of intrigues." Ludendorff was grimly satisfied at the removal of the " strong personality " of the Grand Duke, whom he regarded, and rightly, as a formidable opponent. Sir J. Hanbury-Williams (p. 46) says that there had been rumours of this change as far back as July. It would seem that the Tsar was fated, on the rare occasions on which he made a critical decision, to assert himself in a manner disastrous to his own prestige and to the interests of his country. By thus absenting himself from the capital, he virtually abandoned the control of appointments to the Tsaritsa, who, in her turn, was directly influenced, if not actually governed in her choice, by Rasputin.

Telegram.

Stavka. 23 August, 1915.

Thanks for news. The meeting has passed off wonderfully well and simply. He is leaving the day after to-morrow,

but the change over has taken place to-day already. Now
all is done. I kiss you and the children tenderly.

NICKY.

The Stavka had been moved, a short time previously, to Mogilev,
about 180 miles to the north-east of Baranovitchi, in consequence
of the steady forward movement of the enemy. It now became
known as the Tsarskaia Stavka or Tsar's Headquarters. Mogilev
was a town of some importance on the banks of the Dnieper, and
the capital of the province of the same name.

Telegram.

Stavka. 24 August, 1915.

Hearty thanks for news. Yesterday I signed the papers
of the military appointments. I have begun my work with
Alexeiev, who thanks you for the ikon. The town is well
situated by the river. I had a drive in the car and a walk.
The weather is beautiful. I am content and calm. I kiss
you, the children, " all," tenderly.

NICKY.

Stavka. 25 August, 1915.

MY OWN BELOVED, DARLING SUNNY,

Thank God it is all over, and here I am with this
new heavy responsibility on my shoulders ! But God's will
be fulfilled—I feel so calm—a sort of feeling after the Holy
Communion !

The whole morning of that memorable day, Aug. 23,
while coming here, I prayed much and read your first
letter over and over again. The nearer the moment of our
meeting, the greater the peace that reigned in my heart.

N. came in with a kind, brave smile, and asked simply
when I would order him to go. I answered in the same
manner that he could remain for two days; then we discussed the questions connected with military operations,
some of the generals and so forth, and *that was all.*

The following day at lunch and dinner he was very
talkative and in a very good mood, such as we have not
seen him in for many months. Pet. too; but the expression

on his adjutant's face was of the gloomiest—it was quite amusing.

I must do justice to my gentlemen, beginning with old Fr.—they behaved well, and I did not hear one discordant note, not one word at which one could cavil.

Naturally, while N. is here I have requested him to be present both mornings at the report. Alexeiev makes them so well. He was touched by the little ikon and the blessing which you sent through me. N. repeated to me that he was going from here quite calmly, knowing that I had *such help* in Alexeiev. We spoke a good deal about the Caucasus. He is fond of it, and is interested in the people and in the beautiful country, but he begs not to be left there for long after the end of the war. He has immediately put on a beautiful old Circassian sword [shashka]—a present which Shervashidze gave him several years ago—and will wear it all the time. He intends to stay in Pershin for twelve days, and then go straight to Tiflis and meet the old Count V. at Rostov-on-Don. The whole collection of black women will join him at Kiev at his place, and they will all go together !

A new clean page begins, and only God Almighty knows what will be written on it !

I have signed my first prikaz [order] and have added a few words with a rather shaky hand !

We have only just finished our evening meal, after which I had a long conversation with Laguiche, and later with Gen. Williams.

Both Georgie and the King of the Belgians have replied to my telegrams, in which I informed them of our changes here—and so promptly !

I am so glad that you have spoken to old Gor. and have consoled him. Please tell him, next time, from me, that as soon as the Council of State and the Duma finish their work they must be adjourned, no matter whether I shall be back by that time or shall still be here !

Why not see Kroupensky?—he is a trustworthy man, and might perhaps tell you something worth while.

Think, my Wify, will you not come to the assistance of your hubby now that he is absent? What a pity that you have not been fulfilling this duty for a long time [long ago] or at least during the war !

I know of no more pleasant feeling than to be proud of you, as I have been all these past months, when you urged me on with untiring importunity, exhorting me to be firm and to stick to my own opinions.

We had only just finished playing dominoes when I received through Alexeiev a telegram from Ivanov, who reports that to-day our 11th Army (Shcherbatchev's) in Galicia attacked two German divisions (the 3rd Guard and the 48th Infantry) with the result that they have captured over 150 officers and 7000 men, 30 guns and many poulemeti [machine guns].

And this happened immediately after our troops learnt that I have taken upon myself the Supreme Command. This is truly God's blessing, and such a swift one !

Now I must finish; it is already late, and I must go to bed.

God bless you, my beloved treasure, my Ray of Sunshine !

Tenderly and again tenderly do I kiss you and the dear children.

Always your old hubby
NICKY.

Give her my warm greetings.

The second paragraph of this notable letter shows that the Tsar felt keenly the strain of his approaching meeting with the Grand Duke.

Alexeiev was now Chief of Staff, and the future conduct of the Russian campaign was actually in his hands.

" The whole collection of black women "—possibly a reference to the two Montenegrin Princesses, Anastasia and Melitza, married respectively to the Grand Duke Nicholas and the Grand Duke Peter. SHERVASHIDZE : Prince G. D. Shervashidze, Chief Steward of the Household of the Dowager Empress. Count V. : Vorontzov-Dashkov, already referred to. LAGUICHE : General Laguiche, the French attaché at the Štavka. WILLIAMS : General Sir John Hanbury-Williams, the British attaché. GEORGIE : King George V. KROUPENSKY : P. N. Kroupensky, Lord Chamberlain, Councillor of State.

The Russian counter-offensive on the Sereth at Tarnopol and Trembovla was successful for a few days. 8000 prisoners were taken

Telegram.

Stavka. 26 August, 1915.

My warmest thanks for letter No. 332. Last night I received a telegram from Ivanov about the glorious success of our army in Galicia, where two German divisions have lost over 150 officers and 7000 men prisoners, and 30 guns, taken by us. This happened immediately after the declaration of my appointment. Praise be to God for such a consolation ! Fond kisses.

NICKY.

Telegram.

Stavka. 27 August, 1915.

Hearty thanks for letter and greetings. In view of the dampness of the wood, where the train was standing, I have taken up residence in the Governor's house. The Staff is also here, next to me, which is still more convenient. Everyone is pleased with this move. Cool, rainy weather. I hope that all are well. Fond kisses.

NICKY.

Mogilev. 27 August, 1915.

MY OWN DARLING, PRECIOUS SUNNY,

My heartfelt thanks for your 2 sweet letters. How long it takes for them to reach me ! The trains move very irregularly, owing to the tremendous work on the lines. From a military point of view, this is one of our greatest difficulties.

The troops, the war materials, the supplies go in one direction, and the evacuation—and especially these unhappy begentzi [refugees]—in the opposite !

It is quite impossible to restrain these poor people from abandoning their homes in face of the attacking enemy, as nobody wishes to be left in the hands of the Germans or Austrians. Those who cannot find room in the trains walk or travel by road, and, as the cold weather is coming, this pilgrimage is beginning to be terribly distressing ; the children suffer very acutely, and many of them, unfortunately, die on the way.

All local authorities and the members of various committees work hard and do all in their power—I know that; but they confess frankly that they cannot do everything. It is frightful to think how many *unforeseen* sufferings the war has brought with it, not counting the usual calamities which always follow in its wake !

And yet it must finish some time ! ! !

I cannot tell you how pleased I am with Gen. Alexeiev. What a conscientious, clever and modest man he is—and what a worker !

His reports are of quite a different sort from the ones I received before.   He works alone, but has two little Generals —Poustovoitenko and Borissov—who have been with him for many years, and who help him in details and in questions of secondary importance.

But I am afraid that I am boring you with this dry subject.   Thanks for sending me N.'s letter—I believe that he is sincere and wrote what he thinks.   In any case it is very interesting, as it shows that sometimes he has an opinion of his own, independent of what those around him think.

I am very glad of Vol. Troub.'s exploits; this man has undoubtedly earned the Cross of St. George, which I hope he will soon receive.

I see Mitia Dehn every day now.   He looks quite well, walks fairly decently, but has nothing to do, and is desperately bored after ten years of active life on the Black Sea. He wants to get some work near us.   And the old man suggested : could he not be put in charge of our garage instead of that fat Orlov?   What do you think of it?   I think it is a very good idea.

The little wood in which our train stood was very snug, but owing to the rains it became damp there, even in the carriages; therefore I decided that it would be better and simpler to move into the town, in order to be nearer my Staff and to live in a house.   The building is old, but quite convenient, with a little garden and a delightful view over the Dnieper and the distant country—positively Kiev in miniature.

N. was in the habit of inviting foreigners to lunch, and I

mean to continue this custom. There are only 20 of us at the table in a spacious dining-room.

The last two mornings, since my coming to the town, I received, before the reports, the dvorianstvo [nobility] and the higher ranks of the administration. Now the official part of my residence here is finished [the official ceremonies in connection with my coming into residence here are over]. I drove twice in the car to the other side of the river—a charming, attractive piece of wooded country with excellent roads. Dmitry's bad temper has entirely vanished—I am thinking of the mood he was in that day at Tsarskoe. He is now doing orderly officer, taking turns with N. P. and Dm. Sherem. He asked me to send you his greetings—he has become his old self again.

I have been fasting for the last three days and shall try to go to church before Sunday. Good-bye, my precious Wify, my Ray of Sunshine. I kiss you and the dear children fondly. God bless you !

Always your old hubby
NICKY.

I have just received your sweet letter No. 334. Thousands of thanks ! I am glad that you are calm.

The terrible sufferings of the refugees are described by John Pollock in the *Fortnightly Review* of September 1916.

POUSTOVOITENKO : General M. S. Poustovoitenko, the Quarter-master-General. BORISSOV : General V. E. Borissov, adviser on military operations. VOL. TROUB. : Vladimir Troubetzkoy. MITIA DEHN : a naval officer, the husband of Madame Lily Dehn, one of the Tsaritsa's favourite ladies-in-waiting. He served on the Imperial yacht " Standart." The words " in charge of our garage " are literally transcribed, but the meaning is obscure. Prince Vladimir Orlov was head of the Tsar's Military Chancery. DM. SHEREM. : Count Dmitry Sheremetiev, one of the A.D.C.'s on duty.

Telegram.

Stavka. 28 August, 1915.

God bless you, my own darling ; I am very glad that you will again receive the Sacrament. I am now going to church ; to-morrow again. This morning I saw our magnificent

Cossacks from Pavlovsk; they are going there. I told the commander to present himself to you. Quiet, sunny weather. I embrace all tenderly.

NICKY.

Telegram.

Stavka. 29 August, 1915.

In prayers and thoughts I am with you, darling, and all of you. I am glad that you had this consolation. I kiss you affectionately.

NICKY.

" This consolation "—public confession.

Telegram.

Stavka. 30 August, 1915.

Heartfelt thanks for two dear letters, which I received yesterday evening. I saw the old man; we spoke of many things, but I postponed the final decision till my return. To-day, to my great joy, Keller suddenly appeared, looking well. He is returning to the front. I gave him your greetings. Delightful weather. . . .

Telegram.

Stavka. 31 August, 1915.

I have received all your letters; hearty thanks. I have been very busy for the past few days, so could not write. I thank the girls for their letters. The weather is lovely. It would be better for us if it rained more. I kiss all of you fondly.

NICKY.

Mogilev. 31 August, 1915.

MY PRECIOUS, DARLING WIFY,

How grateful I am to you for your dear letters ! In my loneliness they are my *only* consolation, and I look forward to them with impatience, but I never know when they will arrive.

During the time of fasting I went to church daily—either in the morning or in the evening—and was, moreover, occupied with Alexeiev, so that I had little time left for writing letters, and I have, naturally, neglected my usual papers.

Here I go out once only after dinner, although there is a very small garden here, adjoining the Governor's house, bathed in sunshine and prettily laid out.

What do the children say to my living in the Governor's house? He is an excellent, clever and energetic man. His surname is ugly—Pilz; that is why there are so many mushrooms round here! We eat them every day, and the foreigners are beginning to like them, especially the Japanese General.

Sandro spent two days here. He appeared with the Report, and then we had a long and interesting talk. He is very pleased with the change; he told me the same thing that Nicolai M. wrote to you, and was amazed at my enduring this false position for so long.

He has now gone to Smolensk. Yesterday Kyrill arrived here. I was very glad to see the charming Keller, who came quite unexpectedly, and departed the same evening for his Cavalry Corps. Unfortunately I could not speak to him for long, as old Goremykin arrived the same morning : it was a Sunday. I received the old man after lunch—but, at any rate, I talked to Keller across the table, and everybody listened to the interesting things he spoke of.

He asked me to convey to you his deepest respects and gratitude. I am glad that Alexeiev has a high opinion of him too.—I can see that you think Mogilev too far removed from home. If you remember, I thought so too. before my coming here; but now I think it is the most suitable place. It is situated in the centre behind the whole of our front, to one side of the main movement of the troops, and so on. From Tsarskoe Selo it is no further than Vilna, and when the railways begin to work normally again it will not seem far at all.

Now a few words about the military situation.—It looks threatening in the direction of Dvinsk and Vilna, grave in the centre towards Baranovitchi, and good in the South (Gen. Ivanov), where our successes continue. The gravity lies in the terribly weak condition of our regiments, which consist of less than a quarter of their normal strength; it is impossible to reinforce them in less than a month's time, as the recruits will not be ready, and, moreover, there are very few rifles. And the battles continue, and with them the losses.

In spite of this, great efforts are being made to bring up all available reserves from other parts to Dvinsk, to push back the enemy at that place. But again, we cannot rely upon our worn-out railway lines, as in former times. This concentration will only be accomplished towards the 10th or the 12th of September, if, God forbid! the enemy does not appear on the scene there before.

For this reason I cannot decide to come home before the dates indicated. I beg you, my love, do not communicate these details to anyone; I have written them only for you.

Just at this moment, Katov has brought me your dear letter No. 339, together with another letter for N. P. Be quite calm and sure of me, my darling Sunny. My will is now strong and my brain sounder than before my departure. Yesterday we had a good and conclusive talk with Gor.; you will probably see him on Thursday, when the Duma will be adjourned. He will be able to repeat our conversation —but I have quite forgotten to mention Khvostov. It is better to leave these questions over till my return.

Your charming flowers, which you gave me in the train, are still standing on my table before me—they have only faded a little. That is touching, is it not?

I shall finish this letter to-morrow. Good-night, my love, my little bird!

1 September.

It is a divine day. All the morning, from 10.30 to 12.30, I sat in the Staff Quarters by an open window, as usual, and worked with my Gen. Alexeiev and, to start with, Gen. Poustovoitenko.

Yesterday we made a delightful excursion, crossed the Dnieper on a ferry with our cars, and returned by a different route.

The country and the views are really magnificent, and have a calming effect upon the soul. May God bless you, my beloved, and the children! Warmly and tenderly I kiss you and them. Ania too.

Always your old hubby

NICKY.

Pilz is the German word for mushroom.

SANDRO : the Grand Duke Alexander Mikhailovitch, husband of the Tsar's elder sister, Ksenia. NICOLAI M. : the Grand Duke Nicolai Mikhailovitch, a keen student of history and a writer on historical matters. KATOV : a valet. KHVOSTOV : A. A. Khvostov, the Minister of Justice, successor to the reactionary Shcheglovitov.

Telegram.

Stavka. 1 September, 1915.

My sincerest thanks to you and to Marie for your dear letters. Kyrill and Dmitry thank you very much. To-day I went for a long drive in the car. Wonderful country and weather! I kiss you fondly.

NICKY.

Telegram.

Stavka. 2 September, 1915.

Hearty thanks for dear letter; also Alexey and Anastasia. The news, on the whole, is better. Summer-like weather. In thought I am always near you. I kiss all tenderly.

NICKY.

The Russians were stiffening their resistance on the Niemen; they had occupied Czernovitz, and were again advancing towards Przemysl.

Telegram.

Stavka. 3 September, 1915.

Warmest thanks for dear letter, and for Olga's. I hope that you do not tire yourself with all that you do. I feel well and determined. Boris has arrived, sent by the officer commanding the Guards, with the report of their losses. . . .

Telegram.

Stavka.   4 September, 1915.

I thank you for your dear letter; Tatiana as well. I have made arrangements about a motor car for Ella. She will receive it in a week's time. It is cooler after the rain. Greetings to you from the cousins who are here. I kiss all tenderly.

NICKY.

Mogilev.   4 September, 1915.

MY OWN DARLING,

I kiss you countless times for your dear letters; the last two smelt delightfully of your scent, which has come through—even through the envelope, in the form of a greasy patch!

When you see Paul, tell him that I intend to send him later on to the armies. George is now transferring from one army to another. He telegraphed that, on the 1st of September, his train was bombed at Lida by Zepp. and aeroplanes, and that about 20 people were killed!

Boris arrived yesterday with interesting papers for me from Gen. Olokhov—he has replaced Besobrazov. It is pleasant to hear from all sides such praise of Boris, and of how he is loved, not only by his regiment, but by others as well. I have had the idea of appointing him Field Hetman in place of the excellent Gen. Pokotilo, who has gone back about a fortnight ago to the Don. I am sure that you will ask me : why not Misha?—but I want to try keeping him with me; and later on we will see. Perhaps he can get the command of the Cavalry Corps of Khan-Nakhichevansky.

A few days ago I received a request from Yussoupov, asking me to release him from Moscow, and I have agreed to it, all the more readily as the very good and energetic Gen. Mrosovsky has only just been appointed Commandant of the troops of the Moscow military district.

He commanded a grenadier corps there, and in the war, knows the town and will prove his worth, I hope, when the moment comes.

You ask me about the reception of the 3 German sisters. I think, of course, yes—especially as Mamma is receiving them. Here such things seem very much simpler and clearer. My darling, I miss you so terribly at times, and I feel so lonely ! ! !

The Germans are pouring into the gap between our troops at Dvinsk, and through others at Vilna; this causes great anxiety to Alexeiev, as there are no details and no information. Their cavalry patrols, with the infantry following behind, have come up to the railway line at Polotzk ! This movement upsets our plans of bringing up reserves to the two towns mentioned. It is enough to make one desperate when one is unable to move and concentrate troops as quickly as one would desire.

He (Alex.) told me to-day that he considers it imperative to move the Stavka, and he thinks Kalouga a suitable place for it. This vexes me very much, as I shall again feel myself far away from the army. He has sent someone, as well as Voeikov, to select a suitable locality. Perhaps he is right, but I do not like the idea at all. If God will again vouchsafe us His blessing, we shall be able to stop this advance of the enemy—then, of course, the Stavka will remain at Mogilev, which is both convenient and expedient —everything is near at hand here.

My friend, Gen. Williams, has shown me a telegram telling me of the safe arrival of two new submarines in the Baltic Sea. We have now five English submarines in our fleet. That, if you remember, is the result of my telegram to Georgie—the one I sent him before my departure. Have you seen in the newspapers the speeches by Kitchener and Lloyd George on the war, and on the part played in it by Russia? It is very true. If only God would grant that they and the French began now—it is long overdue !

I have just received your dear letter, with two newspaper cuttings and Marie's letter. I thank you with all my heart for all that you write to me, and for the box of sweets, which are delicious. To-morrow I shall receive Shcherbatov, who is coming here, and also Polivanov. Dimka

G

Golytzin has asked permission to go later to Tiflis—he will make a good assistant to Nicol., as he knows the local society and people well—and I have allowed him to follow N. It is better for him to be surrounded by good men !

Well, I must finish; it is already late. Good-night, sleep well, my precious Wify.

5 September.

Good-morning, my beloved Sunny. It is dull and cold and looks like rain. I have now to receive two deputations, and afterwards I am going to the usual Report. It is Ella's namesday to-day. God bless you, my precious Wify, you and the children ! I kiss you all tenderly.

Ever your old hubby
NICKY.

Please give this little note to A.

PAUL : the Grand Duke Paul, the Tsar's uncle, morganatically married to Countess Hohenfelsen, later Princess Paley. He had served in the Guards under Besobrazov. Killed by the Bolsheviks in 1919. BORIS : the Grand Duke Boris Vladimirovitch, the Tsar's first cousin. OLOKHOV : General V. A. Olokhov, who commanded in succession the 1st Infantry Guard Division, the 23rd and the 2nd Guard Corps. BESOBRAZOV : General Besobrazov, the commander of the Guard Corps, had been guilty of insubordination.—" Field Ataman " is a free translation of Pokhodny Ataman—thus written in the text.—DIMKA GOLYTZIN : General Prince D. B. Golytzin, a cavalry leader, Chief Master of the Imperial Hunt.

Telegram.

Stavka.   5 September, 1915.

Thanks for letters, yours and Marie's. It is very sad about Ortipo. I have just received your telegram. Be quite assured of my firmness with Shch. I have written to-day. It is cold, rainy. Tender kisses.

NICKY.

Ortipo : a pet bulldog, apparently referred to in Marie's letter. Shch. : Prince Shcherbatov, Minister of the Interior, suspected of Liberal tendencies of the Court circle.

Telegram.

Stavka. *6 September,* 1915.

Thank you with all my heart for your letter and the flowers, which have arrived quite fresh. It is cold, rainy, stormy. Vilna was evacuated last night. I hope that in a few days the news from that place will be better. I kiss all fondly.

NICKY.

Telegram.

Stavka. *7 September,* 1915.

Thanks for your letter and Olga's. Also for the information. This man's behaviour is beginning to drive me mad. . . .

" This man "—Sazonov. The Tsaritsa had lodged a bitter and foolish complaint against him in her letter of the previous day.

Mogilev. *7 September,* 1915.

MY BELOVED SUNNY,

My warmest thanks for your dear letter, in which you spoke of your visits to the begentzi [refugees] in various parts of the town ! What an excellent idea, and how splendid that you should have been and seen everything for yourself ! I can judge of the way your brain works by the abundance of thoughts and names which you mention in your letters. I shall inquire about Ploto and shall try to do what is possible. It is the right thing—to send members of the suite to the factories which are working for the army, and I shall tell this to the old man, who throws himself at your feet !

Yesterday George returned quite unexpectedly. He looks well and sunburnt. He saw the 30th Army Corps, but could not reach the Guards of the Northern Army, as fierce battles were raging. He told me a great number of interesting things. To-day I sent Kyrill to visit Gen. Ivanov and his three magnificent armies, after their recent successes. He is taking with him 4200 crosses and also officers' decorations · he is delighted to have been given such a job.

Yesterday, although it was Sunday, was a very busy day. At 10 o'clock, church; from 11 to 12.30, work on the Staff, a big lunch, then Shcherbatov's report; I told him everything. A half-hour's walk in the garden. From 6 to 7.30, Polivanov's report in the presence of Alexeiev, and after dinner his private report, and then a mass of beastly papers for signature. This time, Shcherbatov has made a much better impression on me than he did at Tsarskoe; he was much less timid, and reasoned soundly. Concerning Moscow, he repeated that there is no cause for alarm about the Syiezd [Assembly], for, if they make stupid resolutions, they will not be passed for printing, and so no harm can result. Right !

I . . . would give a great deal to be able to nestle in our comfortable old bed; my field bedstead is so hard and stiff ! But I must not complain—how many sleep on damp grass and mud !

God bless you, my love, and the children ! Tenderly and passionately I kiss you times without number.

Ever your old hubby

NICKY.

PLOTO : a German officer on parole. He was arrested on Russian territory at the beginning of the war.

The Syiezd or Assembly of Town Councils was a progressive organisation and, as such, distasteful to the Tsar.

Telegram.

Stavka.   8 September, 1915.

Thanks for telegram. It is difficult to dismiss him without having chosen somebody in his place. Could not the old man give you a list to choose from, and you send it on to me ? To-day, Mordvinov, who is accompanying George, told me a great deal of good news about the army. I kiss you tenderly.

NICKY.

" Him " refers to Samarin, the Procurator of the Synod, already in disfavour with the Tsaritsa. It will be remembered that he was one of those who signed the letter of protest to the Tsar. Most of the Ministers who signed this letter were eventually replaced.

Telegram.

Stavka.   9 September, 1915.

I thank you heartily, my love, Tatiana and the Little One.
I hope that you are not tiring yourself out.   Misha has
asked for permission to come here.   I shall be very glad to
see him in the near future.   The news is a trifle better.
God grant that in a few days it may be really comforting.
The weather is cold, clearer. . . .

Mogilev.   9 September, 1915.

MY OWN DEAR, BELOVED SUNNY,

I thank you, I thank you for your dear, long letters,
which now come more regularly—about 9.30 in the evening.
You write just as you speak.   The behaviour of some of the
Ministers continues to amaze me !   After all that I told them
at that famous evening sitting, I thought they understood
both me and the fact that I was seriously explaining precisely what I thought.   What matter ?—so much the worse
for them !   They were afraid to close the Duma—it was
done !   I came away here and replaced N., in spite of their
advice ; the people accepted this move as a natural thing
and understood it, as we did.   The proof—numbers of telegrams which I receive from all sides, with the most touching
expressions.   All this shows me clearly one thing : that the
Ministers, always living in town, know terribly little of what
is happening in the country as a whole.   Here *I can judge*
correctly the real *mood* among the various classes of the
people : everything must be done to bring the war to a
victorious ending, and no doubts are expressed on that
score.   I was told *this* officially by all the deputations which
I received some days ago, and so it is all over Russia.
Petrograd and Moscow constitute the only exceptions—two
minute points on the map of the fatherland !

The charming Shavelsky has returned from his journey
to the 2nd Corps at Dvinsk and the 3rd behind Riga.   He
communicated a great many consoling things to me—naturally sad ones too—but a brave spirit pervades all.   I hear
the same thing from George, Mordvinov and the fat Kakhov-

sky, who accompanied him. They are still waiting here for the first opportunity of going to other troops in the North. Misha inquired by telegraph whether he might come towards the end of the week; I shall be very glad to see him here.

Well, my precious little bird, I must finish. God bless you and the children! I love you so much and pray for you fervently every day. I am sending our Friend's telegram—his son is taken, then. I bless and kiss you ardently.

Always your
Nicky.

KAKHOVSKY : G. V. Kakhovsky, an officer in the 4th Life-Guard Rifles.

" His son is taken . . ." According to Professor M. N. Pokrovsky, the editor of the Russian text, Rasputin's son was a private in the Second Category, and his father implored the Tsaritsa to save him from being called up for active service. It appears that the Tsar paid no attention to this matter, and there is no further reference to the young Rasputin in the correspondence. Pokrovsky quotes messages from Rasputin urging the Tsaritsa to prevent the calling up of the Second Category, which, he said, would bring ruin on all Russia. The Tsaritsa, accordingly, used her influence with her husband in order to have the project cancelled or indefinitely delayed. When the Category was actually mobilised, Rasputin sent a telegram to Madame Vyroubova in which he says : " Have suddenly received a telegram that my son is called up. I say in wrath—is it possible that I am Abraham ? "

By this time the moral of the troops was seriously affected. " The number of men who reported ' sick ' was enormous. Any excuse was good enough to get away from the front. They said there was no good in their fighting, as they were always beaten " (Knox, p. 350).

Telegram.

Stavka. 10 *September,* 1915.

I thank you, the girls and Alexey, heartily for your last dear letters and for the telegram. I am glad that you went to Peterhof. I hope you are none the worse. Here it is also fine and a little warmer. I kiss all fondly.

Nicky.

Telegram.

Stavka. 11 *September*, 1915.

Thanks for dear letters, yours and Tatiana's. It is again fine and warm. Misha has just arrived, he looks well. To-day I inspected some troops. I am writing. I kiss you all tenderly. Thank her for the ikon.

NICKY.

Mogilev. 11 *September*, 1915.

MY PRECIOUS SUNNY,

Bless you for your two sweet letters ! I often re-read them, and then it seems to me that you are lying on your sofa and that I am listening to you, sitting in my armchair by the lamp. When will that happy moment come? If God will grant that matters improve at Dvinsk and the position of our troops is consolidated, I might find an opportunity for flying over to Ts. S. But there is so much to do here—these changes of Ministers, and the strengthening of the old man's position ! I shall call him out here; there is no time to lose ! Old Fred. understands this admirably, and exhorts me to hold on to Gor., which is very nice of him.

I have explained all this to V. also, during our walks. He seems to have understood it properly at last.

This morning V. reported to me the absurd rumours which are being circulated here in the town, that somewhere near Orsha (90 versts from here) a German patrol of cavalry scouts has been seen. Mounted police were at once sent out in all directions—and part of our convoy. Of course, so far they have not discovered so much as a rat. It is all so foolish; I laughed heartily.

After dinner to-day, going out in my car, I stopped to look at a field battery which has come from some distance away to protect this town from aeroplanes. I can understand that ! [*i.e.*, that is the right thing !] It was very pleasant to see the officers, men and horses, who have such a splendid healthy appearance—17 men received decorations. Further on I met a large detachment of soldiers who were marching towards the town. I stopped, got out and let them pass by me. It was the 2nd Battalion of the Vladi-vostok Garrison Artillery; they have come from Brest-Litovsk, exactly a month's march by the main road, and are on their way to the north of Orsha. To all appearances, the men have arrived in very good condition; they have a few sick in their carts, whom they will leave in the hospitals before going from here.

Misha has just arrived. He is sitting in my room, reading the newspaper. He has asked permission to stay a little longer. Yesterday two of his regiments launched a splendid attack and took 23 officers and over 400 prisoners—all Hungarians.

You ask me about the trip to Novgorod—of course, go now without me, as most probably I shall not have time when I return home. There is no thought of my leaving here before the 15th—20th.

Well, my little bird, I must finish. I love you passionately with an everlasting love. A thousand thanks for your sweet No. 350, which I have only just received. God bless you and the children! Tenderly, tenderly I kiss you all. Always, my darling Sunny,

Your old
NICKY.

" The old man's position " refers to a desperate attempt to keep the amiable and futile Goremykin in office, and to induce the other Ministers to work under his Presidency. As he was an extreme Conservative, and incapable of causing trouble, his retention was consistent with the policy of the camarilla.

Telegram.

Stavka. 12 *September*, 1915.

My warmest thanks for dear letter. The old man has telegraphed that he is coming on Monday; have written him an encouraging letter. It is out of the question for me to come before a week's time. Lovely, summer-like weather. In thought I am always with you.

NICKY.

Telegram.

Stavka. 13 *September,* 1915.

Hearty thanks for dear letter and telegram, also to Anastasia and Alexey. Wonderful summer-like weather. Have been to church twice. The news is better, but I cannot yet find out for certain about the losses. I have told Boris to inform me. He is returning now. Goodnight. I kiss you fondly.

NICKY.

Mogilev. 14 *September,* 1915.

MY OWN BELOVED, DARLING SUNNY,

My heartfelt thanks for your dear letters, which are always a source of joy and consolation to me. The old man (Gor.) has just arrived, and I shall receive him at 6 o'clock. I am very sorry for you, that you had to tire yourself so much during these busy days. . . .

So far it is difficult for me to settle the day of my coming home, because it depends on the Stavka being moved to Kalouga; that will take five or six days—so that, God willing, we shall spend about a week together! What happiness!

The story of the German patrols has ended as I thought it would—in a comic fashion. It was our own patrol of 7 Cossacks, which, having gone astray, broke off from one of the cavalry divisions to the north of Dvinsk. They were looking for the German cavalry, and got to the south as far as Mogilev. How silly it was to invent such a story!

The weather continues to be lovely. I go out every day in a car with Misha, and we spend a great part of my leisure together, as in former years. He is so calm and charming —he sends you his very heartiest greetings.

On the whole, things at the front are not bad. The Germans are still pressing at the top [probably, " at the extreme end of the line " or " at the extreme north "] at Dvinsk, and from the direction of Vilna, to the east, as well as from Baranovitchi. Serious fighting is going on in these places all the time.

Well, my dear, I must finish. God bless you and the dear children! Next time I shall write to Anastasia. I kiss you all tenderly.

Always your
NICKY.

Telegram.

Stavka. 14 *September,* 1915.

Hearty thanks for telegram. I have just seen the old man. I have decided to call all the Ministers here. He asked for it to be done. I have written. The weather is warm. I am sorry for old Arseniev's death. Please give Shcheglov orders to take back into the library all the letters and papers which I allowed him to use. I kiss you fondly.

NICKY.

ARSENIEV: General D. S. Arseniev, formerly tutor to the Grand Dukes Sergey and Paul. SHCHEGLOV: V. V. Shcheglov, the Imperial Librarian at Tsarskoe Selo.

Telegram.

Stavka. 15 *September,* 1915.

I thank you sincerely for letters, yours and Olga's, and for the telegram. The news is good. Ideal weather. I am glad that you are feeling better. In thought I am with you. Do not worry about my conference to-morrow. I will show them. . . .

Telegram.

Stavka. 16 *September,* 1915.

Thanks for good wishes. The conference passed off well. I told them my opinion sternly to their faces. I am sorry that I had no time to write. Lovely weather. The news is much better. I love you and kiss you fondly.

NICKY.

Mogilev. 17 *September,* 1915.

MY BELOVED SUNNY,

The courier leaves before the evening, at such an hour that I never have any time to write quietly. Misha

often sits with me, and I lose my free time, and in the
evening I am obliged to rummage through my papers.
Praise be to God, things go well with us, and our wonderful
troops are pushing forward between Dvinsk and another
place at Sventzy. It gives me an opportunity for coming
home for a week—I hope to arrive on Wednesday morning !
That will be a happy day !

Alexeiev hopes that perhaps there will now be no necessity
to move the Stavka, and that is a good thing, especially
from the moral point of view. Yesterday's sitting [con-
ference] has clearly shown me that the Ministers *do not wish*
to work with old Gor., in spite of the stern words which I
addressed to them ; therefore, on my return, some changes
must take place.

It is a pity that I have no time to answer all your questions.
God bless you, my dear precious Wify ; I think incessantly
of our meeting. I kiss you and all the children fondly and
remain

Ever your old

NICKY.

Misha thanks you and sends his greetings.

Telegram.

Stavka. 17 *September*, 1915.

Sincerest thanks for your dear letter, and for Marie's and
Anastasia's letters. Misha has gone home, but will come
again. I have written to-day. I hope that you are well.
Charming weather. The news is still good. I kiss all fondly.

NICKY.

Telegram.

Stavka. 18 *September*, 1915.

I have immediately ordered the old man to find out about
old Felix. I think it is a misunderstanding. The French
General D'Amade and two officers are here, sent by Joffre.
To-morrow they are leaving for town. They will ask to be
received by you ; please see them. Good-night. I kiss
you fondly.

NICKY.

Old Felix : Prince Yussoupov. He had asked to be relieved of his office as Governor of the Moscow District, and it was rumoured that he had been suspended.

Mogilev. 18 *September,* 1915.

PRECIOUS, BELOVED SUNNY,

Your dear letters move me *so* deeply that I am quite in despair at being unable to answer in the same manner.   I give you, perhaps, only a tenth part of what you give to me by your loving lines.

I find that, the longer our separation lasts, the deeper and firmer become the ties which bind us.   A month is much. It is strange how accurately our Friend foresaw the length of time during which I was to be absent : " Thou wilt spend a month there, and then thou wilt return."   Now, when I leave, our Cossacks (the escort) will, of course, remain here; the other half is stationed at Tsarskoe; so Grabbe has asked me to put the barracks at your disposal—the new ones—for your wounded, till the end of the war.   He came and asked me to write to you about it, knowing that this will give you pleasure.

I have just received your last dear letter of the 17th, in which you speak of the good impression which young Khvostov made on you.   I was sure of it, knowing him of old, when he was Governor of Vologda, and later in Nijni. And in order not to lose time, I shall see him immediately on the day of my return, at 6 o'clock.   Perhaps the elder Khvostov will do for S.'s place.

The day after our conference he asked permission to see me, and came in trembling with indignation against the others.   He wanted to know whether I wished to keep him. I naturally said that I wished to do so—but now he will occupy another post.   I did not tell him this, as I did not know it myself then.

19 *September.*

It is true that the old man mentioned Kryjanov., but I rejected him.   Krasheninnikov is an excellent, energetic man, and will be all right in the capacity of Minister of Justice.   These are the chief questions, which I conse-

quently hasten to answer. And now I must finish. God
bless you, my precious, beloved little Birdie ! Passionately
and tenderly I kiss you and the children ! Thank A. for
her letter.

Always your old hubby
NICKY.

KHVOSTOV : A. N. Khvostov, the younger, nephew of the Minister
of Justice, later appointed to the Ministry of the Interior in succession
to Prince Shcherbatov. KRYJANOV. : Senator S. E. Kryjanovsky, a
Secretary of State. KRASHENINNIKOV : I. S. Krasheninnikov, a
Senator, who held office in the Court of Criminal Appeal. He was
at the head of the official inquiry into the summer riots at Moscow.

Telegram.

Stavka. 19 *September*, 1915.

Thanks for dear letter. I remember Khvost. I should
like to see him on Wednesday at 6 o'clock; could you not
tell him? . . .

Telegram.

Stavka. 20 *September*, 1915.

Warmest thanks for dear letter and two telegrams. I
have given your greetings to Grabbe. Amazing, heavenly
weather; for the last three days 16 deg. in the shade. Have
had a delightful trip on the river, rowing with my gentlemen,
in three boats. I kiss you and the children tenderly.

NICKY.

Telegram.

Stavka. 22 *September*, 1915.

I am leaving at 4.30, hope to arrive at 10 in the morning.
To-day I saw Sandro. The news is good. Hearty thanks
for dear letter yesterday evening. I kiss you all fondly.

NICKY.

Telegram.

Pskov. 1 *October*, 1915.

Hearty thanks for dear telegram. We miss you greatly.
I sat with Alexey, played various games, walked about on

the stations. Have just had dinner with Marie and the Generals. To-morrow I shall inspect the troops further on. Good-night. Sleep well. . . .

Alexey: the Tsarevitch was accompanying his father to G.H.Q. It was considered that his presence would have a favourable effect on the moral of the troops, and that he would gain an insight into military matters which would have a definite educative value in his training as the future Tsar. MARIE: the Grand Duchess Marie Pavlovna, who worked in the hospitals at Pskov.

Telegram.

Rejitza. 2 October, 1915.

Thanks for news. I had the great joy to-day of seeing the wonderful 21st Corps. The weather is splendid, sunny. In thought I am with you and the children. We are now on our way to Mogilev. Alexey and I kiss you all fondly.

NICKY.

Telegram.

Stavka. 3 October, 1915.

Hearty thanks for dear letter sent by courier. Of course the Little One was present at yesterday's magnificent review and was very pleased. We arrived during the night, left the train at 10 in the morning, and have settled down quite cosily. Clear but cold. We went for a walk in the wood. Both embrace you closely.

NICKY

Telegram.

Stavka. 4 October, 1915.

Sincerest thanks for dear letter; I have so far had no opportunity for writing. Thanks also for telegram. We had a little review, with a moleben [Te Deum], on the occasion of the Convoy's holiday. Baby had lunch with the others and is going to church this evening. We are together for the first night, it is very cosy. Both are in thought and in our hearts with you.

NICKY.

Telegram.

Stavka.   5 *October*, 1915.

Thanks for good wishes. To-day in church we were in prayer with you and the girls. Yesterday evening I gave him your presents. He was delighted, especially with the big knife, which he took with him to bed. He is very cheerful, and is ready to take part in everything. It would be better if you arrived a few days later, as you wrote. Both kiss you tenderly and fondly.

NICKY.

Telegram.

Stavka.   6 *October*, 1915.

My heartfelt thanks to you for your dear letter and to our Friend for his greetings. In thought I am always with you. We have both been very busy, replying to telegrams and thanking for congratulations. The weather is good, somewhat calmer. The news is good. Both kiss you fondly.

NICKY.

Mogilev.   6 *October*, 1915.

MY PRECIOUS LITTLE BIRD,

My warmest thanks for your loving letter; I am in despair at not having written once since we left, but really, I am occupied *here* every minute from 2.30 to 6. And the Little One's presence takes up part of my time too, for which, of course, I am not sorry. His company gives light and life to all of us, including the foreigners.

It is very cosy sleeping side by side. I say prayers with him every night since the time when we were on the train; he says his prayers too fast, and it is difficult to stop him. He was tremendously pleased with the review; he followed me, and stood the whole time while the troops were marching past, which was splendid. I shall never forget this review. The weather was excellent and the general impression astounding.

Life here goes on as usual. Alexey lunched in his room with Mr. Gilliard only on the first day, and after that he begged hard to be allowed to lunch with all of us. He sits on my left hand and behaves well, but sometimes he becomes inordinately gay and noisy, especially when I am talking with the others in the drawing-room. In any case, it is pleasant for them, and makes them smile.

Before the evening, we go out in a car (in the morning he plays in the garden), either into the wood or on the bank of the river, where we light a fire and I walk about near by.

I am surprised at the amount he is able, and wishes, to walk, without complaining of being tired ! He sleeps well, as I do too, in spite of the bright light of his lampadka [ikon lamp]. He wakes up early in the mornings, between 7–8, sits up in bed and begins to talk quietly to me. I answer him drowsily, he settles down and lies quietly until I am called.

Paul is very charming and modest; we have had some delightful talks. He knows about his wife's letter and is displeased with it.

God bless you, my Sunny, my beloved Wify ! I kiss you and the girls tenderly. A. as well.

Always yours

NICKY.

Mr. GILLIARD : Pierre Gilliard, a gentle and affectionate Swiss, not lacking in shrewd observation, tutor to the Tsarevitch, and loyally devoted to the Imperial Family. In 1917 he bravely accompanied the family to Tobolsk, and was separated from them at Ekaterinburg by the Bolsheviks. His book is one of the best which has been written on the last days of the Romanovs, and contains photographs of extraordinary interest. His kindly nature made him a general favourite.

Mogilev. 7 October, 1915.

MY DEAR, PRECIOUS WIFY,

My warmest thanks for your dear letter. You have suddenly numbered your last two letters No. 465 and 466, running ahead by a whole hundred—the last before these was No. 364. Agoosenki ! Please thank all the girls for their letters.

There is no sun to-day for the first time—it has become grey and dreary; my report was finished earlier than usual, and I went into the little garden where Alexey was marching about, singing loudly, and Derevenko was walking on another path, whistling. I had not been there since the day of our arrival. His left hand hurts him a little, because yesterday he worked in the sand on the river bank, but he pays no attention to it and is very cheerful. After lunch he always rests for about half an hour, and Mr. Gilliard reads to him, while I write. At the table, he sits on my left : George is usually his neighbour. Alexey loves to tease him. It is extraordinary how he has lost his shyness ! He always follows me when I greet my gentlemen, and stands still during our zakouska.

You must save up your strength now, to be able to stand the fatiguing journey here ! Please.

The news which comes from all our fronts is good—with the exception of the vicinity of Riga, where our troops have abandoned their advanced positions too quickly. Three Generals will pay for this—I gave Rouzsky orders to dismiss them and to replace them by better ones; they are *my* first victims, but deservedly so.

The little Admiral had not answered my letter then, but now he asks for leave to go to Kislovodsk for a short cure.

Well, my little bird, it is time to finish, as the train is leaving earlier than usual. God bless you and the girls !

With warm good wishes and most ardent love always, my precious darling,

Your loving old
NICKY.

DEREVENKO : a sailor orderly who was one of the attendants of the Tsarevitch. He deserted the family at the time of the Revolution.

Sir J. Hanbury-Williams (p. 231) gives a pleasant account of Alexey's life at the Stavka. During the time of the zakouska (hors d'œuvres, eaten standing at a side table) " every conceivable game went on, a ' rag,' in fact, ending most likely with a game of football with anything which came handy. . . . The devoted tutor was almost in despair, and it generally ended with the intervention of the Emperor."

On the day following that on which this letter was written, the enemy was ten miles to the east of Riga, and the withdrawal to which

H

the Tsar here refers was absolutely necessary. The present editor has been unable to trace the names of the generals who were to be disgraced, nor is there any record of dismissals at this time.

Telegram.

Stavka. 8 October, 1915.

Thanks for dear letter. The news is good. Our attack on Baranovitchi yesterday was successful; we have taken a great number of prisoners. I have again no time to write. It is cloudy, cold. . . .

Telegram.

Stavka. 9 October, 1915.

Hearty thanks for letter and postcards : I think them very good. I hope that you are not too tired. Admiral Phillimore appeared here to-day, dined and brought me a letter from Georgie. It is cold, dull. The hand is well. Both kiss you fondly.

NICKY.

PHILLIMORE : Admiral Sir Richard Fortescue Phillimore, K.C.B. He commanded " Inflexible " at the Battle of the Falkland Islands in 1914, and also at the bombardment of the Dardanelles forts. He was a Beach Master at Gallipoli. From October 1915 to December 1916 he was attached to the Imperial Stavka.

Mogilev. 9 October, 1915.

MY BELOVED SUNNY,
I do not know how to thank you for your sweet letters, which bring me daily so much joy ! It seems that the trains are running better now—-the courier leaves here at 2 o'clock after midday—and that is why I have no time to write. After lunch there is always some one who has to be received, while Baby is resting. At 2.30 I go out, because the days after dinner have become short.

On Sunday, the day after to-morrow, we are going to Berditchev, where old Ivanov is stationed. I should like to see him, and perhaps review some troops, if there should be any in the neighbourhood, while the Ray of Sunshine is with me, and return here on Tuesday—at the latest on Wednesday—it depends on the day of your arrival here. I hope you will approve of this trip. I telegraphed on purpose. Paul is going to Tsarskoe Selo, also on Sunday.—This is the reason:—

I am sure that you remember my wish of old, to collect our Guards into one group as a *personal* reserve. It took a whole month to fish them out of the fighting lines. Besobrazov will be appointed chief of this group, which will consist of two Guard Corps : the 1st (already existing) and the 2nd, composed of our Rifles and those of Warsaw—of the Guard Division. Gen. Olokhov will command the latter, and I offered the first to Paul, who accepted with joy and gratitude. That is why he is returning, in order to prepare himself for a long period of absence !

I am sure that he will carry out his duties well—he will keep them in hand, and they will all help him—their former commander !

When I informed Paul of this intention of mine, he wept, and nearly suffocated me—he is so keen on taking part in the war !

Well, my little bird, my precious darling, I must finish. May God bless you and your journey ! I love you tenderly and kiss you passionately.

Ever your old

NICKY.

Telegram.

Stavka. 10 *October,* 1915.

Thanks for dear letter and news. Thursday will be quite convenient. It will be best not to write again. The news is still good. To-morrow, in the course of the day, I am going away for two days; the details are in my last letter. Paul is in bed—his old illness again,—he will have to stay here. . . .

Telegram.

Jlobin. 11 *October,* 1915.

Many thanks for telegram. We are travelling well. The weather is sunny. Alexey and I embrace you closely.

NICOLAI.

Telegram.

Berditchev.   12 October, 1915.

We are going for several hours to Rovno with General Ivanov. We wish you a happy journey with all our heart. We embrace you closely.

NICKY. ALEXEY.

This was the first visit of the Tsarevitch to the front. Ivanov joined the train at Berditchev, and General Broussilov joined the party at Rovno. After inspecting the troops, the Tsar and his son paid a surprise visit to a dressing-station after nightfall. It was a little building, faintly lit by torches. The wounded men could hardly believe that the Tsar was among them, and one of them raised his hand and touched his coat as he passed, to assure himself that it was no dream. Alexey was " profoundly moved " (Gilliard, p. 126).

Telegram.

Kiev.   14 October, 1915.

Yesterday we spent an unforgettable day among the troops. The impressions are of the very best. We thank you for the last letters. We look forward to our meeting to-morrow, and embrace you.

NICKY.

Telegram.

Reval.   28 October, 1915.

I have arrived safely. All the morning I drove round the fortifications in a car, saw lots of troops, among them the regiment of Sherekhovsky and the artillery from Osovetz. All look splendid. Bright, cold weather. I thank you tenderly for the news and kiss all.

NICKY.

Telegram.

Venden.   29 October, 1915.

Yesterday, in the early afternoon, I visited our and the English submarines. Interesting in the highest degree— splendid young men. Then two factories, docks, and the naval hospital. To-day it is much warmer. I shall tele-graph in the evening. . . .

Telegram.

Venden. 29 October, 1915.

Inspected three regiments of various Siberian troops and the cavalry behind Riga.   It is warm, rainy, no snow.   Went to a large, beautiful hospital.   Heard firing in the distance. The impressions are very good. . . .

Telegram.

Orsha. 30 October, 1915.

Am very grateful for letters and telegram.   In Vitebsk I inspected the wonderful fighting Division.   Am extremely satisfied with its magnificent appearance.   Alexey accompanied me everywhere during these days.   To-day we are spending the night in the train, as we are travelling behind time.   All is well.   Both embrace you closely.

NICKY.

Mogilev. 31 October, 1915.

MY PRECIOUS SUNNY,

Here we are again in our old rooms, which are well arranged and put in order.   The weather is luckily dry and bright—8° of warmth.   This is very pleasant after the terribly cold day in Reval.

For the rest, the time spent there has proved very successful and interesting.

All the morning Baby and I drove about the neighbourhood in a car, getting out to inspect our troops near their positions and defences, which are skilfully hidden in the woods or placed in the open fields.

I was amazed at the amount which has been done during the war, but much more remains to be done in order to complete all that is necessary.   In spite of a closed car, and the fact that we were warmly clad, we all felt cold, and returned joyfully to have lunch in the train.   At 2 o'clock we continued our tour, and visited the old "Europe," which is now the senior of our English submarines.

Fancy, they are all commanded by the little Podgoursky ! I was so pleased to be on board and to speak to the English officers and sailors. I thanked them all on the deck, and rewarded some of them with decorations for their last exploits ("Prince Albert" and "Undine"). Our people praise them highly, and they have become great friends—real comrades!

Alexey climbed everywhere and crept into every possible hole—I even overheard him talking freely to a lieutenant, asking him questions about various matters! Then we drove to two new naval factories, a shipbuilding yard and one for engines—very interesting! Paid a short visit to the naval hospital—250 sick, and only 4 wounded sailors. It was dark already when we returned to our train. From tea till dinner-time I listened to Admiral Kanin's long report —in the presence of Grigorovitch. All the naval authorities and four English officers dined with us, and at 9 o'clock we left Reval, after spending a strenuous but instructive day. We travelled all night through a snowstorm, and arrived in Venden on Thursday morning, where Gen. Gorbatovsky met us and came into the train. At 1 o'clock we passed through Riga, and stopped at a little station outside the town.

Here Gen. Radko-Dmitriev was waiting for us, beside a magnificent Guard of Honour composed of the 4th Ekaterinoslav Dragoon Regiment. The parade-ground was not far off, where an inspection of two mixed regiments of Siberian Rifles took place; among them were Mamma's and Alexey's regiments. They looked very well. The booming of the guns reached us from the distance—our successful attack was being launched at that very moment. On our way back to the train, we went into a large hospital full of seriously wounded, poor souls.

As we had started with an hour's delay, we passed Pskov at 12.15 at night, and I had to receive Rouszky for about an hour, so that I did not succeed in going to bed before 2 o'clock. Slept splendidly till 10.30 on Friday morning.

The weather was warm, but it rained in torrents.

At 2 o'clock we arrived at Vitebsk and went straight to the inspection of the 78th Infantry Division. It poured with rain, and the field was covered with pools of water, to Baby's great delight.

This Division distinguished itself in the Carpathian battles. When it arrived here a month ago it numbered only 980 men—this for a division ! Now it has again reached the complement of 15,000. Above 3000 have returned to their regiments—all with Crosses of St. George. They had a magnificent appearance—like the Guards. On our way to the station we went into the cathedral, which was packed with people. We arrived at Mogilev after dinner, but spent the night in our cosy train. This morning at 10 we moved across. Alexey ran into the garden, and I went to hear the report, which naturally proved to be a long one. To-day it was quiet along the whole of the front—only perestrelka [cross-fire]. All our foreign friends met us with cordial faces—Alexey and his fat Belgian smiled at each other across the table. We had our usual drive in the car, walked and kindled a fire by the roadway.

Now, my beloved darling, it is time for me to finish. I am *so* grateful to you for your letters ! Tenderly, tenderly I kiss you and the girls. God bless you !

Ever your hubby
NICKY.

PODGOURSKY : a Captain in the Submarine Section of the Baltic Fleet. GRIGOROVITCH : Admiral Grigorovitch, the Minister of Marine. GORBATOVSKY : General V. N. Gorbatovsky, commanded in succession the 3rd Grenadier Division, the 19th Army Corps, the 1st, 12th and 6th Armies. He was dismissed after the February Revolution.

The " fat Belgian " was Baron de Ricquel, the Belgian military attaché at the Stavka. He was the special friend of the Tsarevitch, and used to take part in the improvised games of football.

Telegram.

Stavka. 1 *November*, 1915.

Thanks for dear letter and news. I have heard nothing about Roumania, but Greece is becoming very suspicious. The little arm has been aching a little since yesterday. Charming, warm weather. Both kiss you fondly.

NICKY.

Mogilev. 2 November, 1915.

MY DEAR LITTLE BIRD,

Many, many thanks for your sweet letters. What a pity it is that you are again feeling worse and that your heart is enlarged! Take care of yourself and rest well. But I know that this is useless advice, as it is impossible to live near the capital and not to receive anybody.

When we arrived here by train in the evening, Baby played the fool, pretended to fall off his chair, and hurt his left arm (under the arm-pit); it did not hurt afterwards, but swelled up instead. And so the first night here he slept very restlessly, kept on sitting up in bed, groaning, calling for you and talking to me. Every few minutes he fell off to sleep again—this went on hourly till 4 o'clock.

Yesterday he spent in bed. I explained to every one that he had simply slept badly, and myself as well—and so it was.

Thank God it is all over to-day—except for paleness and a slight bleeding at the nose. For the rest, he is exactly as he usually is, and we walked together in the little garden.

At 4 o'clock in the afternoon we went to the theatre, where we were shown a cinematograph—among other things, pictures of your stay here.

On the 5th, on Thursday evening, we are starting on our tour to the South. It will last a week, and then we shall return here.

I am afraid that it will be difficult for me to communicate everything to you in detail by telegraph—but perhaps I shall find time to write to you, as the distances between these towns and little places are not great, and we shall come to a stop at some of the stations—so one must suppose. I have just received your last letter of the 1st November, in which you speak of your conversation with Khvostov. I had no idea that Drenteln was his brother-in-law. I cannot understand what worries Khv. in this story about a letter. I could wish, indeed, that you paid a little less attention to such trifles. I told you several days ago that I had offered Drent. the command of the Preobraj., and I cannot retract it.

Please receive General Murray before his departure for England.

Well, I must finish, as I have to read through a great pile. Baby has gone to bed. God bless you and the girls. Good-bye, my own dear Sunny ! I kiss you fondly and long for you terribly.

Your hubby
NICKY.

Preobraj. : the celebrated Preobrajensky Regiment of the Guard, in which Drenteln was a colonel.

MURRAY : General Sir Archibald James Murray, K.C.B., a distinguished soldier. He was Chief of the Imperial General Staff in 1915, and General Officer Commanding (1st Class) in Egypt in 1916–17.

Telegram.

Stavka. 4 November, 1915.

Both thank you sincerely for your dear letters. It snowed here too during the night, but now it is clear. It has all disappeared. In thought we are always together. Both kiss you fondly.

NICKY.

Mogilev. 4 November, 1915.

MY BELOVED SUNNY,

Thanks for your sweet letters, which arrive here again in the evening. I hope your poor heart will soon be all right again. I hate separation at such moments, and understand well that a depressed condition is natural at those times when one is suffering from internal pain.

Yesterday we arranged a Te Deum for dear Olga's sake—the church was full of generals, officers and men—mostly those living here. I ordered this thanksgiving moleben [Te Deum] for Baby and myself. A great number of people are being invited to table now (it is at N. P.'s suggestion)—in this way they all come under one's eye. Some of the foreigners have gone to the front, others to Petrograd. The tall Montenegrin is returning home, as he is wanted by the King. To-morrow we are going away for a week, and I am glad that we are going to the South, and especially that I shall see my favourite troops, which I have not seen since the beginning of the war. In Odessa we shall see the Gvard. Equip., who will join the rest of the Guards, who [the latter] are being also sent there—to Bessarabia—in about 3 weeks' time.

I shall explain to you later on what measures will be adopted in case Roumania does not allow our troops to pass through that country.

Is everything quiet on our front? Ask General Murray what his opinion is concerning our affairs—it will interest you, as he has seen and heard much during his tour on our front.

My own little one, I love you so tenderly, am so in need of you!

5 November.

Yesterday, Alexeiev, Ivanov and I conferred about Roumania and Greece. We came to the conclusion that, so far, it is wiser to leave the first alone, and not to send Kyrill. France and England have apparently understood, at last, that Greece must be made to behave decently towards them and the poor Serbs!

It is time for me to finish. May God bless you, my treasure, and the girls, and may He keep you! . . .

Ever your old hubby
NICKY.

Telegram.

Stavka. 5 November, 1915.

Thanks for news. I am afraid the letter will arrive after I have seen him. I am starting at midnight. Rain, wind. Both embrace you closely.

NICKY.

" Him " refers to A. A. Khvostov, the Minister of Justice.

Telegram.

Odessa. 7 November, 1915.

Warmest thanks for news. I have spent a very satis-factory day. Inspected several transports and a hospital ship. After lunch, a brilliant inspection of our fine fellows, and others. Cold, windy, sunny weather. Complete order reigns in the town. Both kiss you fondly.

NICKY.

" Our fine fellows "—the Gvardeisky Equipage.

Telegram.

Reni. 9 November, 1915.

Thanks for telegram. After the inspection of our troops we visited a church, all the institutions and Veselkin's flagship. He has done an astonishing amount here, and done it well. The weather is cold. We embrace you closely.

NICKY.

Telegram.

Balta. 10 November, 1915.

Many thanks for letters. I have just made an inspection of the Nijegorodtzi, Severtzi and the Khopertzi. All presented themselves in ideal condition. 4 deg. of frost. Fog. I was glad to see many acquaintances, to whom I have given your greetings. Now we are going further. . . .

Telegram.

Novopoltavka. 11 November, 1915.

I thank you sincerely for the telegram. To-day it was warm at last. In the morning a magnificent inspection of a division at Kherson, and, during the day, of another at Nicolaievo. The impressions are most gratifying. To-morrow night we are returning to the Stavka. I embrace all tenderly.

NICKY.

Telegram.

Mogilev. 12 November, 1915.

Have just arrived. I shall spend the night in the train. Excellent impressions from the whole tour. Tender thanks for the file of letters, received on my return. You had better write again. Give her my greetings. The weather is calm, much snow. I hope that your health will soon improve. . . .

Mogilev. 12 *November*, 1915.

MY BELOVED DARLING,

Here we are again at the Stavka, after an absence of exactly one week—hour for hour. It makes me feel nearer to you, somehow, as the letters come on the following day, whereas during our tour we received them only on the third.

I cannot say yet when we are coming home, but I think it might happen in about six days. That will be a happy moment—how much there will be to relate !

Well, thank God, our journey has passed off and ended splendidly ! A whole rainbow of impressions ! Only, alas ! the weather was unfriendly—we hoped to meet a little warmth, but the South received us very coldly, with a piercing wind. The only sunny day we had was in Odessa. There we were met by Kyrill, Boris and Shcherbachev. The streets were crowded with young soldiers, cadets, students from the military schools and the people—it reminded me so much of my visit there in the spring. But this time I had our Treasure with me. He sat with a serious face, saluting all the time. Through the tumult of the crowd and the shouts of " hurrah ! " I managed to hear women's voices calling out : " The heir, the angel, the pretty boy ! " Exceedingly touching ! He heard them too, and smiled at them. Having visited the cathedral, we drove to the port and went on board a large French ship which has been converted into a floating hospital; on the new cruiser " Prouth "—formerly " Medjidye "—a very fine ship, almost entirely refitted; then on the korabl-priyut [home-ship] for boys whose fathers are at the war, under Alexey's patronage (the pretty Mme. Sosnovskaia is at the head of it); and lastly, on one of the seventy transports, under the command of Admiral Khomenko. Before the evening a grand inspection took place. What a magnificent appearance the Gvard. Equipage presented ! I addressed a few words to Poloushkin and Rodionov when driving past them, but have not said good-bye to them, as I hope to see them when the Guards are collected together.

There were many troops, so that the inspection lasted a long time, and it was already dark when we returned to the station. I had a long conversation with Shcherbachev, whom I promoted to the rank of Adjutant-General.

The following morning, the 8th November, I inspected a whole Army Corps, very close to the train, by a village called Eremeievka. The troops seemed to me splendid, well trained, well equipped, and so on. I lunched in the train on the way to Tiraspol, where we were together on the day of our trip to Kishinev. Here we looked at another corps, at present stationed at Odessa—this one appeared even better. Then we travelled all night to Reni, arriving there on the morning of the 9th, at 9 o'clock. Here the permanent way is old and terribly jolting, the train rocks as though on the sea. The Danube is a powerful, broad river, between handsome wooded banks, reminiscent of the English lakes [literally, ponds]. Our fat friend Veselkin met us in the early morning, in order to explain thoroughly everything beforehand. What we saw was interesting in the highest degree. I must admit that he possesses the gift of good organisation, and knows how to make people of different stations work hard in complete agreement with each other. To describe all this in a letter would take too long !

Here I inspected the 3rd Turkestan Rifle Brigade—they looked, and marched past, absolutely like our very best Guard regiments. We visited also several of the recently equipped heavy batteries, which cover the river Prouth—flowing into the Danube. They are very well placed. Again we travelled all night, and arrived at Balta on the 10th of November, after breakfast. 4° of frost, and fog. That was a pity, because the country looks charming. After a quarter of an hour's drive in a car, we arrived at the place [appointed] for the inspection of the Caucasian Cavalry Division. All the four regiments were amazingly beautiful ! How sorry I was that you could not admire them !

I delivered your greetings to all the officers of the three Dragoon regiments. On our way to Kherson we met many trains full of young soldiers, whom we inspected at the stations where we stopped. The inspection of the 2nd Finland Rifle Brigade took place in this town, and, after midday, of the 4th Finland Rifle Brigade in Nicolaievo. It had become warmer at last, and my fingers ceased aching when I was riding. Alexey has borne the strain of this week astonishingly well, only occasionally he suffered from a little bleeding at the nose. He was in excellent spirits all the time. Everything is well with the old man. He is now and then very pale before meals, and at times says foolish things across the table, but feels no fatigue from what we are doing and from much walking.

13 *November.*

We returned home at 10 o'clock in the morning. Found the rooms excellently ventilated and cool, and, in a way, fresh. Alexeiev's report lasted a long time—each had much to tell to the other. To-morrow I shall give him the newspapers you sent me.

I woke up with a shocking cold in the left nostril, so that I am thinking of spraying it with cocaine. Apart from that, I feel strong—heaps of energy! The time-table for the trains has been altered here. They are coming in at 11 in the morning and leaving at 6 in the evening, which is more convenient—at least for me. I greatly hope that your poor heart will get better and will not cause you so much pain. I am always sorry for you, my dear Wify, when I hear that your health is not good and when you suffer physically. . . .

Everybody here has learnt with sorrow of Eshappar's death. Such a capable and energetic man! What a loss!

Well, my treasure, I must finish. God bless you and the girls! With countless kisses

Your old hubby

NICKY.

POLOUSHKIN: Captain A. S. Poloushkin of the Gvardeisky Equipage. RODIONOV: Lieutenant N. N. Rodionov, also of the

Equipage. ESHAPPAR : General F. V. Dubrail-Eshappar, formerly
an officer in the Empress's Own Uhlan Life-Guards.   He was Master
of the Household to the Grand Duke George Mikhailovitch.

Telegram.

Stavka.   13 *November*, 1915.

Both thank you sincerely for dear letters.   It is sad not
to be together to-morrow—the day of our wedding, for
which I am sending my heartiest wishes.   Both kiss you
fondly.

NICKY.

Telegram.

Stavka.   14 *November*, 1915.

I am much touched with the little frame and the wishes
for this day.   Hearty thanks for the letter.   I am leaving
on Tuesday.   I have been to church to-day.   Snow, 5 deg.
of frost.   I kiss you tenderly.

NICKY.

Telegram.

Stavka.   16 *November*, 1915.

I thank you sincerely for dear letter.   Lovely sunny
weather.   I am counting the hours till our meeting.   We
both send you all our warmest greetings.

NICKY.

MY BELOVED,

It is hard to part again, having spent barely 6 days
together.   *Duty !*—that is the reason.   Please take care of
yourself, do not overtire your poor heart.   I love you so
truly !   In thoughts and prayers I am nearly always with
you, and especially in the evenings, when we are accustomed to be together !   I hope that that time is not behind
mountains and that nothing will distress you.   God bless
you and the dear girls !

I kiss you tenderly and love you infinitely.   Always, my
Sunny,

Your old hubby

NICKY.

24 *November*, 1915.

" I hope that that time is not behind mountains " is a popular
Russian saying. It means " I hope that such a good time has not
gone for ever," implying, of course, the hope that it may occur
again.

Telegram.

Stavka. 25 *November,* 1915.

Thanks for dear telegram. We have arrived safely. It
has been thawing since the morning. It is strange and
lonely here. We both kiss you fondly.

NICKY.

Telegram.

Stavka. 26 *November,* 1915.

Hearty thanks for dear letter and congratulations. The
review and festival have passed off excellently, though quite
differently from usual. The weather is spring-like, but
rainy. We both send you all, and her, our gratitude and
warm greetings.

NICKY.

Stavka. 26 *November,* 1915.

MY BELOVED WIFY,

The journey was dull and quiet; we both felt so sad
without you and the girls. We were met by Alexeiev,
several of the Generals from the Staff and old Pilz, and
drove to our house.

Then I was bothered with petty questions concerning
to-day's festivities. Baby slept well; his legs and arms
did not hurt. It was warm and damp. Feodorov was
rather anxious about the review and the slippery ground.
Thank God, everything has passed off well, and touchingly.

At 10 in the morning we both came out. All the officers
who had come from the army stood to the left of the porch,
and opposite them a wonderful company of non-commis-
sioned officers and ensigns, with two, three and four Crosses
of St. George, and all the medals, on their breasts. Then,
with their backs to the street, a grand gathering of wounded
men who have been sent to serve at the Stavka, and, still
further, our soldiers and Cossacks, police, gendarmes, etc.

After a thanksgiving moleben [Te Deum], they all marched past, with the generals and officers at their head. I addressed a few words to them, and then went to the report. At 12 we visited the dinner which had been arranged for everyone, and I drank their health in kvas. After this Alexey went home, and I with the others to the Gorodskaia Duma. We lunched in two high halls—170 men altogether. When we rose, I spoke with every officer, which took an hour and a half—but I did not mind that, as it was most interesting to listen to their answers. At the end, I promoted them all, each to his next rank. The effect was tremendous! Among the officers I noticed, and spoke to, Navrouzov and Krat, and gave them greetings from you and the girls. Nic. Pav. is leaving to-morrow to take over the command of the Gvard. Equip. from Poloushkin.

God bless you, my darling Wify! I kiss you and the children tenderly.

Ever your old hubby

NICKY.

Please forward my letter to Malcolm.

The "wonderful company" was the Battalion of St. George, consisting of men who had been decorated with the Cross of St. George, an award for conspicuous bravery in the field.

Gorodskaia Duma, the Town Duma or Town Council, which sent representatives to the central or State Duma in Petrograd. The reference here is to the Duma building or Town Hall.

NAVROUZOV: Captain T. B. Navrouzov of the 17th Nijegorodsky Dragoons. Nic. Pav.: N. P. Sablin. MALCOLM: Sir Ian Malcolm, K.C.M.G. He has held many diplomatic and political appointments, and was British Red Cross Officer during the war in France, Switzerland, Russia and America. He was private secretary to Mr. Balfour at the Peace Conference in 1919.

Telegram.

Stavka. 27 November, 1915.

Warmest thanks for letter and news. To-day is the holiday of my Nijegordtzi. Navrouzov and Chavchavadze came to lunch; they hope to see you soon. N. P. has said good-bye; I am glad, for his sake. A slight frost. I kiss you tenderly.

NICKY.

I

Stavka. 28 *November*, 1915.

DARLING SUNNY,

My warmest thanks for two dear letters. I have again been busy all the morning and after dinner, and could scarcely snatch a quarter of an hour for writing a few words.

Grabbe asks you to send 70 ikons here for our 4th Kouban sotnia, who are soon going off to the front.

This very moment Voeikov has brought me the paper with the time-table for our tour. We are starting on the 3rd of December for Jmerinka, and shall spend the 4th, 5th and 6th with the Guard Divisions. I am glad that it has fallen out thus, and that I shall spend my namesday among them.

Excuse this terribly hasty writing, but I have only a few minutes left.

Silaiev has just looked in—he looks radiant. He has given me the girls' greetings, for which I thank them very much.

I send you Georgie's reply—keep it.

I hope that your poor heart will soon be better; I am *so* sorry for you! God bless you, my dear little bird, my treasure, my dear Wify! I kiss you and the children lovingly.

Always yours

NICKY.

SILAIEV: Colonel I. Z. Silaiev of the 13th Erivan Grenadier Regiment, attached to the Imperial suite during the war.

Stavka. 30 *November*, 1915.

MY DEAREST WIFY,

My warmest thanks to you for your letters. I always look forward to them with a beating of the heart. Having opened the envelope, I push my nose inside and breathe in your scent!

With a view to inspecting the Guards with more comfort both to them and to ourselves, we are starting on Thursday the 3rd, and will return here either on the 7th or the 8th of December. The troops are now on the move, and we shall therefore see them nearer the frontier than we originally expected.

Drenteln is taking leave here on the day of our departure, and is going straight to Petrograd, for family reasons. The same with Nic. Pav., who is returning from Odessa for ten days. I am not sure whether I can see the Gv. Equip. again, as they must stay as long as possible in that town. What a pity !

That French gentleman—Paul Doumer—whom I received on the last day of my stay at home has arrived here this morning. He lunched, and then I had a talk with him.

I have just received your dear letter No. 398, for which I thank you very much, my treasure !

In one of your previous letters you mentioned Spiridovitch. But it seems to me that I told you before my departure that Khovstov talked to me about it, and asked that he should not be appointed to Obolensky's post, with which I entirely agree. Khovstov then said that, in his opinion, our Veselkin would be a very suitable man. But there is no hurry, as Obolensky is remaining for the present. As for the old men and children from East Prussia, who are now in Siberia, I have made arrangements to have them sent to Germany. The report has been a short one this morning, so that before lunch I could at last take a walk with our Little One. He marched about with his rifle, and sang loudly.

God bless you, my Sunny, my darling. I love you tenderly and kiss you.

Your hubby
NICKY.

PAUL DOUMER : Deputy, at one time Governor-General of French Indo-China, President of the Budget Commission and President of the Chamber of Deputies. Then on a political mission to Russia. SPIRIDOVITCH : A. I. Spiridovitch, of the Gendarmerie. He was attached to the Court Commandant (Voeikov) for duty, and accompanied the Tsar to the Stavka. He succeeded Doumbadze as Mayor of Yalta. OBOLENSKY : Prince A. N. Obolensky, President of the Committee of Supplies till November 1916.

Telegram.

Stavka. 1 *December*, 1915.

Hearty thanks for letters. I am sorry for Sonia. The weather is again frosty. Thank her sincerely for letter and present. I kiss you tenderly.

NICKY.

SONIA : Princess Orbeliani, lady-in-waiting to the Tsaritsa.

Telegram.

Stavka. 1 *December*, 1915.

I am terribly shaken at Sonia's sudden death. I feel for you, but for her it is a true release. I implore you not to tire yourself. Both embrace you and kiss you fondly.

NICKY.

Telegram.

Stavka. 3 *December*, 1915.

God bless you. My heart and soul are with you. Alexey has had rather a bad cold since yesterday. It will be disappointing if he has to stay in the train and see the troops. Give Trina my condolences. We are starting now. Both embrace you tenderly.

NICOLAI.

TRINA : Mlle. Schneider, the Tsaritsa's " reader." She was one of the small company of friends and retainers who went with the Imperial Family to Siberia in 1917. Killed by the Bolsheviks.

Telegram.

Stavka. 3 *December*, 1915.

Owing to his cold, Alexey has had bleeding at the nose at intervals the whole day. Have decided, on Feodorov's advice, to return to the Stavka. I shall be very glad if you come to spend the 6th of December together. I embrace you closely.

NICOLAI.

The Tsarevitch, as is commonly known, was a hæmophiliac, and bleeding of any kind had the most serious consequences. In the present case, his life was in actual danger. It was the Tsar's intention to visit the Guard regiments in Galicia, and he and the Tsarevitch were already in the train when, during the night, Alexey's condition became alarming. At three o'clock in the morning Professor Feodorov decided to wake the Tsar and to advise him to return immediately to the Stavka. They got back to Mogilev on the same day, but Alexey grew rapidly worse, and it was decided to take him to Tsarskoe Selo (Gilliard).

Telegram.

Stavka. 4 *December*, 1915.

We have arrived safely; are remaining in the train. As his temp. rose to 39, I decided to return home at once. I am leaving to-day at 3; hope to arrive to-morrow at 11 in the morning. He slept fairly well, is cheerful; the bleeding is considerably reduced; seldom coughs. Hearty thanks for letter. Both kiss you.

NICKY.

Telegram.

Stavka. 4 *December*, 1915.

Thank God, he is better now. Temp. 37·5. The bleeding has stopped, though it might easily begin again from moving or coughing. He has no headache. Eats, on the whole, well. I shall telegraph in the evening. Warmest thanks for second dear letter. I am so glad that I shall soon see you at home.

NICKY.

Telegram.

Vitebsk. 4 *December*, 1915.

Has spent the second half of the day well. At 8 o'clock the temp. was 38·11. In excellent spirits, and rather astonished at our going home. Please let there be nobody on the station to-morrow. Both kiss you fondly.

NICKY.

According to Gilliard, the journey was "agonising." The train had to be stopped several times in order that the dressings might be carefully renewed. The boy had two attacks of syncope during the night, but towards the morning there was a slight improvement. He was taken to the palace with infinite precautions, and the wound was cauterised. It was on this occasion that the Tsaritsa attributed her son's escape from death to the timely presence of Rasputin (Paléologue, Vol. II, p. 138).

Telegram.

Semrino. 12 December, 1915.

I have made inquiries about the frost-bitten Cossacks. It has turned out to be an absolute lie from some doctor. . . .

Telegram.

Kiev. 14 December, 1915.

Have arrived safely. One degree of warmth. Thanks for news. Ksenia, Sandro and Olga spent a little time with me after tea, and we had a pleasant talk. . . .

Telegram.

Podvolochisk. 15 December, 1915.

All three reviews have passed off very successfully. The appearance of the troops is magnificent. The weather is warm—2 deg. I am leaving now; I remembered Alexey in these places. I embrace all closely.

NICKY.

Telegram.

Bakhmach. 16 December, 1915.

At present I am under the delightful impressions of all that I saw yesterday. I thank you very much for letter. I am glad that health is better. There are 4 deg. of frost here. . . .

Stavka. 17 December, 1915.

MY DARLING SUNNY,

Here I am again, and full of the happiest impressions. First of all, my tenderest thanks for your four dear letters : two I received on the way, and two on my arrival here.

Ksenia and Olga kiss you; we spent two pleasant hours in the train, Sandro as well. That very night it became quite warm, and I opened the window into your coupé and the doors into mine—so that I slept well. On the 15th I got up early, because the first inspection—of the 1st Cavalry Guards Division—was due to begin at 8.30. The weather was lovely, exactly as with us in the spring, in April; only it was terribly muddy on the fields and roads. Great was my happiness at seeing the dear regiments, which I had not seen since the very beginning of the war ! Two Cossack regiments were here also, and three batteries of horse artillery, and all marched past very well. I invited all the commanding officers into the train, and fed them on the way to Volochisk. Among them were Dmitry and Linevitch, who, according to his own words, feels much better.

At Voloch, quite close to the train, the second review—of the 3rd Guard Division (Varshavskaia)—took place. Our Rifles, grown into a whole division, the fine battalion of the Gvard. Equip., the sappers and their artillery. The appearance of the troops was *brilliant.* They did not march past, owing to the deep, thick mud—they would have lost their boots under my very eyes. The generals, Kyrill and N. P., lunched in my train—after which I promoted him. Later, we moved on to Austrian territory. The last inspection, which began at 3.30, took place within two versts of the station of Podvolochisk, as I had been detained at the previous inspections. Here were present the 1st and 2nd Infantry Guards Divisions with their artillery. It was already getting dark, so that I again rode twice along the ranks from the front to the rear, after which Shavelsky held a moleben [Te Deum] in the centre of a huge square in complete darkness. Having sat down in the car, I shouted " Good-bye " to the troops, and from the invisible field rose a terrible roar, which accompanied me to the train. Here the last party came to dinner. On that day I inspected 84,000 soldiers—Guards alone—and fed 105 commanding officers !

Alas, I must finish !

God bless you and the dear children ! Tell the Little One that I miss him terribly.

Accept tender kisses from

NICKY.

LINEVITCH : Colonel A. N. Linevitch, A.D.C. to the Tsar.

It was after one of these tours of inspection that the Tsar remarked to Sir J. Hanbury-Williams that he had been " doing a bit more of the publicity and photography business ! " (p. 70).

" I promoted him," N. P. Sablin to a command in the Equipage.

Telegram.

Stavka. 18 *December,* 1915.

Thanks for dear letter and list of New Year's greetings. During the day I am busy, but it is very lonely in the evenings and at night. Thank her for her letter. I embrace and kiss you fondly.

NICKY.

Stavka. 18 *December,* 1915.

MY BELOVED SUNNY,

Heartfelt thanks for your dear letter and for sending me the list of the New Year's telegrams. Thank the Little One and the girls for their letters.

Beletzky, among others, dined here to-day; he told me how Masha V. behaved herself before and after her departure from town, and how she was received on her sister's estate.

I have some hope of being able to return home precisely for the Christmas holidays. This is my plan: I leave to-morrow night, the 19th, for the Western Front (Everth), and arrive, via Minsk, at the little station of Zamirye, not far from Baranovitchi. Here I shall stay for two days, and hope to inspect a great many troops. For Tuesday morning I shall arrange an inspection at Molodechno, and for Friday another at Vileiki, whence I shall at once go back through Minsk and Orsha—home, where I hope to arrive on Thursday at 5.30, so as to be in time for the evening service. That would be splendid!

There is very little news from the south, as a thick fog interferes with our artillery fire; none the less, some of the infantry regiments went up, or crawled up, to the wire entanglements of the Austrian positions, and even took the first lines in several places. But this must not yet be spoken of—do me the favour.

I have no more time to write, so I must finish.

The old man's health is excellent; the other day he succeeded in persuading me to allow him to lead in the march past at the head of his squadron of Cavalry Guards— on horseback, but at a walking pace. He was tremendously happy after it.

God bless you my darling, my little bird. . . . I kiss the dear children.

With my tenderest love I remain

Ever your old hubby

NICKY.

BELETZKY : S. P. Beletzky, a Privy Councillor and Senator, Assistant Minister of Internal Affairs from September 1915 to February 1916. MASHA V. : Marie Vassilchikova, a maid-of-honour, who remained in Austria after the beginning of the war and was instrumental in conveying peace overtures from the Germans. She was dismissed from her appointment and met with general disapproval in society. EVERTH : General A. E. Everth. After the battle of Lyublin he took over the 4th Army from Baron Salza, and was later promoted to the post of Commander-in-Chief of the Western Front. His task was perhaps more difficult than that of any of the other generals, and it is to his credit that he was not conspicuously unsuccessful. Dismissed during the February Revolution in 1917.

Telegram.

Stavka. 19 *December,* 1915.

Warmest thanks for dear letter. I am glad that the Little One is on his feet again. Fancy, Georgie has promoted me to Field-Marshal of the British Army. I am leaving to-day at 10 in the evening. You will find the explanation in my second letter. I kiss all fondly.

NICKY.

Sir Hanbury-Williams tells us that the Tsar's appointment as a Field-Marshal of the British Army, of which he heard on New Year's Day, caused him " real satisfaction and pleasure."

Telegram.

(*Place not given.*)   20 *December,* 1915.

Thanks for news. In the morning I held a grand inspection. I was very pleased with the brave and healthy appearance of the troops. The weather is not cold. The roads are good. I embrace you all closely.

NICKY.

Telegram.

Army in the Field. 21 *December,* 1915.

Hearty thanks for dear letter. To-day I have driven round the fighting front of two corps, in a place which is known to me. I received the most pleasant impressions from the troops. Real thawing weather. I embrace you closely.

NICKY.

Telegram.

Army in the Field. 22 *December,* 1915.

I thank you with all my soul for letter. Congratulate you on Anastasia's namesday. In the morning I inspected the troops of the army in this place, saw our Caucasian friends. All sections look remarkably well. . . .

Telegram.

Army in the Field. 23 *December,* 1915.

This morning I made the final inspection of the army on the Western Front. The troops look splendid. . . .

Telegram.

Stavka. 31 *December,* 1915.

I have arrived safely, could not sleep. The weather is the same. Hearty thanks for dear letter. In thought we are always together. I kiss you fondly.

NICKY.

Stavka. 31 *December,* 1915.

I thank you with all my heart for your sweet letter, which you gave to Teter., and which I found as a surprise when I was going to bed ! My warmest thanks for all your love and kindness during the six days we were together. If you only knew how it supports me and how it rewards me for my work, responsibilities and anxieties, and so forth ! Indeed, I do not know how I could have endured it all, if God had not decreed to give you to me as a *wife and friend !*

I speak in earnest. At times it is difficult to speak of such truths, and it is easier for me to put it down on paper—owing to stupid shyness.

Yesterday, after having parted from you, I received the fat Khvostov—for an hour and a half. We had a good serious talk. After tea I took up this book—" The Million-aire Girl "—and read a great deal. Extremely interesting, and soothing to the brain; it is many years since I have read English novels !

I slept badly, or, more correctly, little, as I could not get off to sleep, my feet were so cold, and at last I crept with my head under the sheets, and in this manner warmed the edge of the bed—this at length improved matters !

On my arrival here this morning I found the weather just as cold as at home—10 deg. Now the cold is less severe, there is no wind, a lot of snow, After a lengthy report, the usual lunch with all the foreigners. I passed on Alexey's greeting to them, and they asked a great deal about him, and were sorry not to see him now.

Our prayers will meet to-night—the moleben [Te Deum] will take place in the church at 11.45.

God bless you, my darling, and the dear children !

Eternally, my dear Sunny,

Your old hubby,

NICKY.

TETER. : N. C. Teteriatnikov, a valet.

" The Millionaire Girl," a novel by A. W. Marchmont.

Telegram.

Stavka. 1 *January,* 1916.

I thank you heartily for dear letters and wishes. I have at once ordered the repeal of the prohibition concerning the tramways. Have always thought it unjust. I hope you are not tiring yourself. I kiss you tenderly.

NICKY.

" Concerning the tramways." Soldiers were not allowed to ride on the trams, and this was considered, naturally, as a most unjust restriction.

Stavka. 2 January, 1916.

MY OWN BELOVED, DARLING SUNNY,

I thank you with all my heart for both dear letters. I am distressed by your ill health, and live in anxiety when I am parted from you. My loneliness is nothing compared to this. My dear, be prudent and take care of yourself.

I send you these telegrams to read, and then tear them up.

You ask me how I greeted the New Year. We too had a moleben [Te Deum] in the church at midnight. O. Shavelsky spoke very well, and to the point.—I had a headache and lay down immediately after.—On New Year's Day I felt quite well again. At 10 o'clock I received several pleasant people from the town, and later went to church.

A few papers have come, as well as a number of telegrams, mostly family and foreign ones, which are always more difficult to answer. Of the regiments, the Erivantzi alone telegraphed.

I must confess that the book I am now reading is absolutely fascinating. When I have finished it I shall send it on to you. You will probably guess which parts interested me most.

The foreign officers asked my permission to telegraph to Alexey, and were greatly touched by his well-composed reply.

Tell him that they always finish their zakouska in the little room, and remember him.

I also think of him very often, especially in the garden and in the evenings, and I miss my cup of chocolate.

The weather is pleasant, mild, 3°, and quantities of snow, but there has been no sun since the day of my arrival here. —The days have become much longer.

I must finish.

May God preserve you, my dear Wify !

I kiss you and the children tenderly.

Your old

NICKY.

MY DEAREST,

Up to now I have not received a single letter. The train is six hours late, owing to a violent snowstorm.

A storm has been raging here too since yesterday, and in the night the wind howled down the chimney like that terrible tremolo in the " Ahnfrau." I am very grateful for your dear telegram. I am glad that your headache has nearly gone; but the naughty heart persists in being disobedient !

To-day I can write to you and the children, as no papers have come in. I telegraphed to Ania yesterday, and received a very becoming reply.—Nobody remembered this anniversary, so that I reminded Fred. and Voeikov about it. Valia is in bed : he has a high temperature, I have only just visited him. He is feeling better, but his face is swollen up and red with the cold.

A great deal of snow has come down during the night. I was glad to find a wooden shovel in the garden, and have cleared one of the pathways.—That is a very useful and pleasant occupation for me, as at present I take no exercise. And then I do not miss the Little One so much.

The morning reports are short nowadays, because everything is quiet at present, but on the Caucasus our troops have begun an offensive, and fairly successfully. The Turks had not expected it to take place during the winter. In Persia we are also dealing heavy blows to those accursed gendarmes, who are under the leadership of German, Austrian and Swedish officers. Among the rest, I have received a very cordial telegram from Harding, the Viceroy of India, in the name of the Government, the princes and the people. Who would have thought it ten years ago ?

I was touched by the flower sent by our Friend.

Farewell till our next meeting, my darling Sunny. God guard you.

I kiss you tenderly and love you infinitely.

Eternally your

NICKY.

" *Die Ahnfrau,*" a drama by Franz Grillparzer. In the last act the family ghost (*die Ahnfrau*) rises from the grave to receive a member of the household who is dying. The wind is supposed to be howling outside the house, and, when the play is given with incidental music, the orchestra reinforces the effect with an appropriate tremolo. This drama was popular with Russian audiences.

VALIA : Prince V. A. Dolgorouky, Marshal of the Court, attached to the Tsar at G.H.Q. He was a charming and gallant man. He went with the Tsar to Tobolsk, and was murdered, together with General Tatishchev, at Ekaterinburg in 1918.

Telegram.

Stavka. 3 *January,* 1916.

Tender thanks for dear letter. I have only just received it now, as the train was late, owing to snowdrifts. The weather is warm. [But] it is beginning to freeze again. I hope you will soon recover your strength. I kiss you tenderly.

NICKY.

Stavka. 4 *January,* 1916.

MY DARLING SUNNY,

Hearty thanks for dear letter, which arrived yesterday evening after mine had already been dispatched.

The train was again late to-day, but the wind has died down and it is snowing.

I sincerely hope that your headache has gone and that the poor heart feels better.—I read out aloud, with pleasure, your long New Year's telegram to old Gorem. It is very well composed.

All is quiet on our front. Our offensive is developing successfully in the Caucasus, but slowly, because of the deep snow. Our troops are fighting courageously, and have taken many prisoners, equipment, stores and so forth.—As far as I can judge by what Alexeiev read to me this morning, Nicolasha is confident and satisfied.

My dear, I am longing for you. . . . Just *here,* away from

Ministers and strangers, we would have plenty of time to talk quietly about various questions, and spend a few cosy hours together. But what is to be done? You have said very justly, in one of your last letters, that our separation is *our own* personal sacrifice, which we are making for our country in this sorrowful time. And this thought makes it easier for me to bear it.

The kind old General Pau is a delightful neighbour at the table. I like his simple, sound outlook on things and his straightforward talk.

I am still getting masses of postcards from various English regiments. Sir Williams gave me an enormous quantity of them for Alexey; I shall gradually forward them to you— and let them be kept in order.

Farewell till our next meeting, my dear child! I must finish, as the courier is due to leave!

God bless you and the dear children! I kiss you passionately and them tenderly.

Your old hubby
NICKY.

Telegram.

Stavka. 4 January, 1916.

Thanks for news. The train is again very late. It will come in at about 9 o'clock. It is rather cold. I have written. Hope you are feeling better. I kiss you tenderly.

Telegram.

5 January, 1916.

Have only received your dear letter this morning, for which I thank you very much, also for the telegram. 15 deg. of frost. Bright, sunny weather. I am feeling well. . . .

Stavka. 5 January, 1916.

MY BELOVED DARLING,

There were no letters yesterday, but to-day, as a recompense, I have received two [literally, a whole two]. One in the morning and the other soon after during the day. My heartfelt thanks for both.

Tell Alexey that I am glad he has begun writing his diary. It teaches one how to express one's thoughts clearly and concisely.

How sad that you are not feeling better, and that the beastly headache persists !—It is very fortunate that Mamma was pleasant to N. P.—Perhaps we shall manage to see the others—Kogev., Rod., and so forth, when they come for a short leave ?

To-day the weather is clear but cold—15° with wind. I hope it will be warmer to-morrow; then it will be more pleasant to attend [when I attend] the consecration of the waters on the river near the big bridge.—This morning, after service, O. Shavelsky went all over the house and sprinkled everything with holy water, beginning with my blue room, where he read several prayers !—The foreigners will have to eat fish and mushrooms to-day, but they assure us that they like it.

I think incessantly about a successor for the old man. In the train I asked the fat Khv. what was his opinion of Sturmer. He praises him, but thinks that he is too old also, and that his head is not as clear as formerly. Incidentally, this old Sturmer has sent me a petition to allow him to change his surname and adopt the name of Panin.— I replied, through Mamant[ov], that I could not grant permission without the previous consent of the surviving Panins.

The little Admiral is well, but angry with Manus, who desires to receive the name of Nilov. What do you think of this ?

I must finish, my precious Wify. God keep you and the children ! I kiss you and them tenderly, and remain

Your faithful hubby

NICKY.

Kogev., Rod. : L. V. Kogevnikov and N. N. Rodionov, Lieutenants in the Gvardeisky Equipage. "The old man"—Goremykin. Sturmer : B. V. Sturmer, formerly Governor of Yaroslav (where he distinguished himself by his persecution of the Liberals), a Master of Ceremonies at the Court and an extreme Conservative. He was appointed President of the Council of Ministers in succession to Goremykin. Later, he became the Minister of Foreign Affairs. His character seems to have been well summarised by Count V. N. Kokovstov, a former President of the Council, who described him to Paléologue as " an incapable and vain man, but who has astuteness and even finesse when his personal interests are at stake." His election was due to the influence of Rasputin and the Tsaritsa; but he was so ill fitted for his duties, or, indeed, for any duties, that he was removed from office by the Tsar at the end of the year. Sturmer was the *bête noire*, not only of his own colleagues, but also of all the Allied ambassadors. Mamantov : V. I. Mamantov, a member of the Council of State and head of the Petitions Department. Manus : I. P. Manus, a Councillor of State, and the conductor of dubious transactions on the exchange. He was accused of being in close touch with enemy financiers, and it was rumoured, though perhaps with little foundation, that he paid large sums of money to Rasputin.

Stavka. 6 January, 1916.

My dearest,

Hearty thanks for dear letter No. 420, and for the brilliant idea of deputing George and Tatishchev to see how the prisoners of war are kept in Siberia. I shall do it.

The blessing of the waters to-day went off well. When I got up there were 15° of frost; towards the time for the blessing of the waters the temperature rose to 7, and now to 5—curious fluctuations. The sun is already beginning to warm in a spring-like fashion.

The kind Bishop Constantine officiated in our church, and thence the procession of the Cross made its way down to the river.

All the troops which are stationed in the town were lined up on both sides, the battery saluted 101 times, and two aeroplanes hovered over our heads. Masses of people, and exemplary order. On the way back I left the procession near the house where the Staff is quartered, as I had to go

K

to the report. The crowd cheered me.—The old man insisted on being allowed to accompany me during the
ceremony, as he was feeling well.—The little Admiral was
more cautious, and stayed at home, because he has a cough.
Both throw themselves at your feet !

On Friday I am arranging a cinematograph for all the
school-boys, and shall take advantage of this opportunity
too !

I have just received your telegram, saying that Anastasia
is suffering from bronchitis; how tiresome ! I hope that it
will soon pass over.

I have finished my book, and shall certainly read it aloud
to you and the children when I return home—exceptionally
interesting, and quite proper.

I must finish this letter, my own precious Wify.

May God bless you and the children ! I press you passionately to my heart . . . and remain

Eternally your faithful

NICKY.

CONSTANTINE : Archbishop of Mogilev and Mstislav.

Stavka. 7 *January*, 1916.

MY DEAR TREASURE,

The train is late again, so that I have received neither
letters nor newspapers.

I am receiving Trepov and Naoumov, who have arrived
from Kiev, and later General Belaiev from the War
Ministry—I do not know on what matter.

I shall tell the latter about the German prisoners of war,
the day of Wilhelm's birthday, and so forth. I mean to
send George a telegram in cipher dealing with what he is to
pay special attention to when visiting the prisoners of war,
in addition to other details which I wish to depute him to
investigate.

To-day I asked Fredericks to write very sternly to Maximovitch about the clubs, and to [tell him to] watch all that goes
on in them. He must cut short any gossip and criticism
which he hears personally, and warn those who wear the

golden uniform or aiguillettes that they will be deprived of
them if they persist in behaving in this way.

I forgot to thank you for dear Baby's photograph, which I
think charming. It stands opposite me on the writing-table.

Somebody has taken away the shovel from the garden—
actually there is nothing more to be cleaned up there. I
prefer to walk there alone, which I am accustomed to do, as
it gives me a chance of thinking quietly, and good ideas
often occur to me on my walks. I keep on racking my brains
over the question of a successor for the old man if Sturmer
should really not be young enough or sufficiently up to
date.

Our troops are attacking very successfully in the Caucasus,
and are not far from Erzerum, the only Turkish fortress
there. I think the black sisters must feel very depressed over
the fate of their unhappy country.

May God guard you and the dear children! I kiss you all
tenderly, my dear ones. I kiss you tenderly and ardently,
my beloved Sunny.

Eternally your
NICKY.

TREPOV : A. F. Trepov was Minister of Ways and Communications. He succeeded Sturmer as President of the Council. A
capable and honest man with Conservative tendencies. He was a
staunch monarchist, but, in common with other honest men, strongly
opposed the Rasputin clique. In consequence of this he became,
inevitably, an object of the Tsaritsa's hatred. NAOUMOV : A. N.
Naoumov, Minister of Agriculture. BELAIEV : General M. A.
Belaiev, Assistant Secretary of State for War. MAXIMOVITCH :
General C. C. Maximovitch, assistant to the Commandant of the
Imperial Headquarters.

The " black sisters " were Princess Anastasia of Montenegro,
married to the Grand Duke Nicolai Nicolaievitch, and Princess
Melitza of Montenegro, married to the Grand Duke Peter Nicolaievitch.

Telegram.

Stavka. 7 *January*, 1916.

At last your dear letter has arrived. I am sincerely grateful. The weather is dull, it is thawing. I have received

two Ministers who have arrived from Kiev—Trepov and Naoumov. A very important meeting. I kiss all tenderly.

NICKY.

Stavka. 8 *January,* 1916.

MY DEAR, BELOVED WIFY,

I thank you heartily for your dear letter, which I received after lunch. Then I had to read through the papers, had a walk for about half an hour, and now have sat down to write a few lines to you. The cinematograph for the boys begins at 4 o'clock.

I am *happy* every time that you see N.P., especially now, when he is leaving for God knows how long ! You ask me where Misha is ? I am sure that he has returned to Gatchina, after having spent a fortnight in the country. Why do you not see him at once ?—True, you have not been feeling well enough to receive.

I always tear up A.'s letters into small pieces after having read them, so that you need not worry. None of her letters will be preserved for posterity.

My dear, there is nothing of interest which would be worth while writing about—I repeat to you only the old story, which you have known for 22 years—that I love you, that I am devoted and faithful to you to the end !

I love you passionately and tenderly, my own Sunny ! May God guard you and the children ! I kiss you all fondly.

Eternally your old

NICKY.

Greetings to A.

Gatchina : one of the Imperial Palaces, the former summer residence of the Dowager Empress, near Leningrad.

" A's letters." The Tsaritsa had expressed anxiety about their conservation, and begged the Tsar to see that they were always destroyed.

Telegram.

Stavka. 9 *January,* 1916.

Many thanks for dear letter. I am glad that everyone is getting better. Give her my greetings. . . .

Stavka. 9 *January*, 1916.

My BELOVED DARLING,

My heartfelt thanks for dear letter No. 423.

How vexatious and boring that the little ones are not quite well, and that you, poor dear, are not even well enough to go upstairs to see them ! I sincerely hope that this state of affairs will soon come to an end.

The weather is disgusting; it snows, it rains, and a strong wind is blowing—exactly as it was with you. I am beginning to arrange programmes for short tours—of course only for the inspection of troops.

A great number of cavalry and Cossack divisions, who are resting and getting into order, are stationed along the line of Orsha, Vitebsk and further towards Dvinsk. I shall let you know the moment I decide upon anything finally. As to St. coming *here*, I consider that inconvenient. I receive here exclusively people who have some connection or other with the war. His arrival, therefore, would only serve as an occasion for various rumours and suppositions.—I desire that his appointment, if it does take place, should come like a clap of thunder. For this reason I shall receive him at once on my return.—Believe me, it is better so.

Ella has written to me, asking me to give the next award to Basilevsky. He has already had one conferred upon him, last year, at the New Year. But I intend to reply to her that the 1st of January has already passed, and that it would be better to wait until Easter, which will be here in three months ! He is, of course, a very excellent man and a good worker, and is, according to what she says, very useful to her committee.

I have heard or read nothing about Samarin, which is rather strange ! Only you mentioned him in your last letter.

I must finish. God keep you and our chicks ! I kiss you tenderly and passionately, and remain, my precious Wify,

Your loving old hubby

NICKY.

BASILEVSKY : P. A. Basilevsky, Chief Equerry, a Councillor of State and a Guardian of the Dowager Empress's institutions in Moscow. He was Marshal of the Nobility in Moscow.

Stavka. 10 *January,* 1916.

MY DEAREST,

Thank you tenderly for your sweet letter No. 424.—
I am happy to hear that all our invalids have a normal
temperature, as you telegraphed to me.—Feodorov told me
that all sorts of children's ailments are prevalent here in the
town, so that from this point of view it is a good thing for our
Ray of Sunshine not to be here. The walks round the garden
are boring me to distraction; I never stay there above 50
minutes, as otherwise I should not be able to read and write
and finish all by 5 o'clock, because the train leaves at 6
o'clock.

Later on, when the weather gets better, I shall alter the
disposal of my time, as it is extremely necessary for me to
get enough fresh air !

To-morrow I hope to inform you of my plans. Possibly
towards the end of the week I might come home ! !

My sincerest thanks also for the sweet flowers, which
reached me quite fresh.

Give A. my kind greetings, and tell her that I think
of her !

I am writing in a terrible hurry, because there is much for
me to look through, so excuse this short and uninteresting
letter.

May God preserve you and the dear children !—In thought
I shall be with you on Tatiana's namesday !

I kiss you tenderly, my beloved, darling Sunny.

Your

NICKY.

Telegram.

Stavka. 10 *January,* 1916.

Sincerest thanks for letter and news. I am glad that
everybody is feeling better. The English General, Callwell,
has come about several matters. . . .

CALLWELL: Major-General Sir Charles E. Callwell, K.C.B.
Retired, after service in the Afghan, Boer and South African Wars, in
1909. He was Director of Military Operations at the War Office,
with temporary rank of Major-General during the first seventeen

months of the war, and was afterwards employed on special missions. He wrote, among other books, " The Experiences of a Dug-Out."

                                          Stavka. 11 *January*, 1916.

MY DARLING WIFY,

I thank you tenderly for your dear letter. It is always such a joy to get them. I breathe in their perfume and re-read every page with delight. I hope sincerely that you are better, and that you will feel stronger when I return. Try to lie on the balcony every day, or to drive in the park. Anyhow, you must know that fresh air in conjunction with rest are undoubtedly the best cure for you. That is true— true !! The weather is very changeable—frost at night, and in the morning everything thaws in the sun. The streets and the paths in the garden are terribly slippery.

At four o'clock I must go to the cinematograph, which is being arranged for the other half of the schoolboys. I shall sit in the middle box with old Fred., who is totally deaf.— We cannot converse, as I have no wish to answer all his questions with a roar amidst the deadly silence of the theatre !

This very second Tet-v has brought me your dear letter No. 425, as well as Tatiana's and A.'s letters. I kiss you fondly for all that you write, my beloved. Pitirim is coming to-morrow. Beletzky has informed Voeikov about it. General Callwell is a very quiet and clever man. He has brought me a letter from Georgie. There is a whole English colony here now. It is quite amusing to listen to the English conversation at the table.

Farewell till our next meeting, my tenderly beloved Sunny. May God keep you and the children ! I kiss you and them fondly and remain

                    Your faithful hubby
                                          NICKY.

Telegram.

                                          Stavka. 12 *January*, 1916.

Sincerest thanks for letters and the little bottle. I send Tatiana my best wishes. I am sorry that we are not together. I have just had a friendly talk with our Metropolitan. It is damp and warm. . . .

" Our Metropolitan "—Pitirim, formerly the Exarch of Georgia, Archbishop of Kartalia and Kakhetia. Appointed through the influence of Rasputin.

Stavka. 12 *January*, 1916.

MY DARLING,

My hearty thanks for your dear letter, and for the little bottle and the flowers from our Friend.—I drank the wine straight out of the bottle to His health and happiness; drank it all, to the last drop.

This happened after lunch—the young Ravtopoullo lunched with us as well. He has been sent here from his regiment to obtain boots and all sorts of warm things. I was very glad to see him and talk to him. He congratulated me on Tatiana's namesday, and requested me to give his respects to you and the girls. I congratulate you also !

During the day I received Pitirim. He spoke of the Synod, the clergy and especially of the Gos. Duma. This surprised me, and I should like to know who influenced him in this matter. He was very glad to be received and to be able to speak out freely.

Now I must finish; I have no time.

God guard you, my beloved darling. I kiss you and the dear children fondly. Give her my greetings and thank her for her letter.

Eternally your old

NICKY.

Gos. Duma : Gosoudarstvennaia Duma, the State Duma.

Stavka. 13 *January*, 1916.

MY PRECIOUS WIFY,

My plans are now settled. To-morrow—on Thursday —I get into the train, and on Friday morning shall hold the inspection of the Trans-Baikal Cossack Division in Bobrouisk. —The same day I am returning here, and am spending the night in the train.

On Saturday morning there will be my usual report, and

then I shall leave immediately for Orsha.—Three Cossack divisions will be drawn up in the neighbourhood—the 1st and 2nd Koubanskaia and Ouralskaia—after which I shall continue my journey home, and shall arrive at Ts. S. on Sunday at 12 o'clock.—Alas, I shall miss the church service ! Perhaps I shall manage to spend 8–9 days at home—that would be splendid !

My dear little Sunny, I am burning with impatience to see you as soon as possible, to hear your voice, to look into your eyes . . .

I think that separation actually makes love stronger and mutual attraction greater. I hope that you will feel quite well and strong by then.

Tatiana's namesday was celebrated in the town with great solemnity. There was a concert, a play and living pictures in the theatre. Apparently it was crowded with people and very successful, but lasted from 9 till 1.30.—The Governor was unable to tell me how much had been collected during the whole evening.—Tatiana's portrait with her autograph was sold together with the programme.

Feodorov has had slight pains in the left side of the abdomen and a slight temperature for the last two days, so that I asked him to lie down. He looks, as he always does, cheerful. At this moment—2.30—your dear letter No. 427 has been brought to me.

I kiss you fondly and thank you for all that you write.— May God bless you and our dear children !

Your deeply loving old hubby

NICKY.

Stavka. 14 *January*, 1916.

MY PRECIOUS,

This will be my last letter. Yesterday a great many generals and other persons of high rank arrived here to take part in the commission under Alexeiev's presidency for the discussion of the questions about supplies, coal and other things. Pr. Ouroussov, who works in the Red Cross, as well as in connection with the organisation of the begentzi, together with Gen. Ivanov, have arrived; then, to my great astonishment, the Mayor of Moscow, Chelnokov, the President of the Soius Gorodov, and several other distinguished persons from various other ministries. I invited them to dinner.—A few minutes before dinner I received Chelnokov privately—he presented to me a warm address from Moscow, in which he thanks the troops for the good reception which was accorded to the delegation sent for the distribution of presents to the soldiers.—He breathed heavily, and jumped every second from his chair while he was speaking. I asked him whether he was feeling well, to which he answered in the affirmative, but added, that he was *accustomed* to present himself before Nicolasha, and had not at all expected to see *me* here. This reply, and his general bearing, pleased me this time !

Poor Alexeiev sat with them yesterday evening from 9 to 12. And to-day again.

Now, after Feodorov, Voeikov has fallen ill with influenza : foolish man, two days ago he had a fit of shivering, and when he took his temperature it was 39°. I persuaded him with difficulty to stay in bed this morning, but now he has got up again. Our Poliakov put 17 cuppings on his chest and back, which helped him considerably, otherwise he might have got inflammation of the lungs !

I thank you and kiss you heartily for your dear letter No. 428, which has only just arrived.

Well, farewell. God guard you, my beloved Sunny, my precious darling ! I kiss you and the dear children tenderly. In 2 days, God willing, we shall be together again.

Your

NICKY.

OUROUSSOV : Prince N. P. Ouroussov, a Member of the Council, an Equerry, and Marshal of the Nobility in the province of Ekaterinoslav. CHELNOKOV : M. V. Chelnokov, the Mayor of Moscow. He was a Liberal, and his audience with the Tsar had for its object the representation of public opinion. That, no doubt, accounted for his nervous demeanour.

Soius Gorodov : the Union of Towns.

POLIAKOV : Dr. S. P. Poliakov, an assistant physician, attached to Headquarters.

Telegram.

Stavka. 14 *January*, 1916.

Am very grateful for dear letter.   In the evening I go over to the train, leave for Bobrouisk during the night.   Warm, greyish weather.   I embrace all tenderly.

NICKY.

Telegram.

Bobrouisk. 15 *January*, 1916.

I have just held the inspection of the Zabaikaltzi.   Am very pleased.   Thanks for yesterday's telegram.   The weather is sunny, windy. . . .

Telegram.

Stavka. 15 *January*, 1916.

Tender thanks for letter and telegram.   Have just returned.   It is frosty; terribly windy.   You must at all costs recover towards Sunday.   I embrace you closely.

NICKY.

Telegram.

Orsha. 16 *January*, 1916.

Hearty thanks for letter.   I have returned, very pleased with the inspection.   The weather is propitious.   My invalids, V. and F., are better. . . .

Stavka. 28 *January*, 1916.

MY OWN DARLING,

Again I must leave you and the children—my home, my little nest—and I feel so sad and dejected, but do not want to show it.   God grant that we may not be parted for long —I hope to return on the 8th of February.   Do not grieve and do not worry !   Knowing you well, I am afraid that you will ponder over what Misha told us to-day, and that this question will torment you in my absence.   Please let it alone !

My joy, my Sunny, my adorable little Wify, I love you and long for you terribly !

Only when I see the soldiers and sailors do I succeed in

forgetting you for a few moments—if it is possible ! With regard to the other questions, I am going away this time with greater peace of mind, because I have unlimited confidence in Sturm.

God guard you ! I kiss you all fondly.

Always your

NICKY.

Telegram.

Vyshki Rwy. 29 January, 1916.

Many thanks for letter yesterday evening. I am very pleased with the inspection. Have seen many troops. My company of Kabardintzi was in the Guard of Honour. . . .

Telegram.

Army in the Field. 30 *January,* 1916.

Have just finished a big inspection. Saw Tatiana's regiment. Found them all in splendid condition and order. The weather is warm. I embrace all closely.

NICKY.

Telegram.

Army in the Field. 31 *January,* 1916.

To-day there was a splendid review of two cavalry divisions. Am very grateful for yesterday's letter, and for the second, just received. . . .

Telegram.

Stavka. 1 *February,* 1916.

I thank you heartily for dear letter, Olga as well. Left the train in the morning. It is not cold : 3 deg. It is snowing a little. So far I am very favourably impressed by the reviews. I kiss all tenderly.

NICKY.

Stavka. 1 *February,* 1916.

MY OWN BELOVED SUNNY,

At last I have found a free evening to talk to you quietly. I long for you intensely. First of all I hasten to thank you for your three dear letters. They came, of course, very irregularly, because the train travelled backwards and forwards on the line, as it was near Dvinsk, where bad birds fly. A great deal of snow has fallen for the last three days, which makes it hopeless for them !

The inspection of the 1st Army was held not far from the little station of Vyshki. To my great joy a company of the Kabardinsky Regiment was stationed there, but it contained only one officer of my acquaintance, and several men who were in Livadia ! Among numbers of cavalry regiments were two regiments of Mamma's and Ksenia's (I could not find Gordinsky). But your Alexandrovtzi and my Pavlovtzi were not present. Such a pity ! They had only just been sent to the trenches, to relieve the infantry. Good Lord !—what does your poor Plehve look like ? As green as a corpse, blinder and more bent than ever, and scarcely able to move his legs. Sitting on horseback, he threw himself so far back that I thought he felt giddy. He assured me that he rode very often ; but I doubt it.

The troops were in excellent condition, the horses also. After lunch I had a talk with Plehve. He reasons quite soundly and normally ; his head is fresh and his thoughts clear, and when he is sitting down he seems all right, but he presents a grievous sight when he gets up.

I spoke severely to him about Bonch-Brouievitch—that he was to get rid of him, and so forth. Then I had a good walk along the main road. At 6 o'clock we passed through Dvinsk. There is the usual lighting in the streets of the town. I saw only one searchlight illuminating the dark horizon !

We spent the night somewhere near Polotzk, and on the morning of the 30th of January returned to Drissa. There I was met by Everth and Gen. Litvinov of the 1st Army, and three cavalry divisions—the 8th, 14th and one of the Siberian Cossacks. Tatiana's Uhlans looked fine fellows, as did all the other troops. So tidily, cleanly and well dressed and equipped, such as I have seldom seen, even in peace time ! Truly excellent ! They all look so well in their grey papakhi [Caucasian fur caps], but at the same time they so resemble one another that it is difficult to tell to which regiment they belong.

Yesterday, the 31st Jan., the last inspection was held, at which the 6th and 13th cavalry divisions were present. They are just as fine fellows as they used to be in former times. The weather is not at all cold—3-4° of frost—and it is again snowing. Of course the old man rode again on horseback, and was very proud of it—he talks to everyone about it, which drives Nilov to fury !

After lunch, the train left the station of Borkovitchi; at 3 o'clock we passed through Vitebsk and Orsha, and arrived here at 11 o'clock in the evening. The air was lovely, so that Voeikov, Grabbe, Kedrov and I took a refreshing walk before going to bed. To-day at 10 in the morning I moved into my quarters and spent two and a half hours with Alexeiev.

In Mogilev I found Sergey, who has already installed himself here, but none of the foreigners, except Williams, as they have all gone to Odessa for a time. During the day I walked in the garden, because there was not enough time to drive out. I had to settle down to my papers, and only finished with them towards dinner.

It is late now, I am very tired, so that I must wish you good-night, my darling Wify, my only and my all ! Why is it that you cannot sleep, my poor dear one ?

2 February.

I have only just finished lunch with all the foreigners; they arrived yesterday evening.

This morning I went to church, and later had a long conversation with Alexeiev concerning the retiring of Plehve and Bonch-Brouievitch. It transpires (apparently) that the latter is hated by everyone in the army, beginning with the highest generals !

To-morrow I shall have to find a successor for him (Plehve). Your dear letter No. 436 and telegram have been received. I thank you tenderly. How troublesome that you have pains in your face, and even a swelling ! My dear, I am so sorry for you ! The water in Mogilev has again had a bad effect on my stomach; in every other respect I feel well. I thank you also for the charming flower.

Now I must finish, beloved.

God guard you and the children ! I embrace you closely and kiss you tenderly.

Eternally your old hubby

NICKY.

" Bad birds "—enemy aeroplanes.—PLEHVE : General P. A. Plehve. He had been Chief of the Moscow Military District, and at the beginning of the war commanded the 5th Army. He was promoted to the command of the North-west Front. A fine strategist and one of the most efficient of the Russian commanders. He died in 1917. BONCH-BROUIEVITCH : General M. D. Bonch-Brouie- vitch was Chief of Staff to General Plehve. He went over to the Bolsheviks during the Revolution. LITVINOV : General A. I. Litvinov. Commanded the 6th Corps at the beginning of the war, and in November 1914 succeeded Rennenkampf in the command of the 1st Army. He held this appointment until the Revolution. KEDROV : Rear-Admiral M. A. Kedrov, an A.D.C. and member of the Imperial suite before the war. In November 1915 he was appointed to the battleship " Gangut," and in February 1916 he was summoned to G.H.Q. in order to give explanations in regard to dis- turbances in the Fleet. His accounts were satisfactory, and he was made commander of the mining division of the Baltic Fleet, and promoted to Rear-Admiral in the autumn of 1916. SERGEY : the Grand Duke Sergey Mikhailovitch. He was Inspector-General of Artillery, and extremely conservative in military matters. Polivanov applied to the Tsar for his removal from this post, and he was re-. placed by General Manikovsky. Brutally murdered by the Bolsheviks in July 1918.

Telegram.

Stavka. 3 February, 1916.

Have only just received the news that Erzerum has been attacked and taken. Thanks be to God ! Have sent the petition to the Minister of War, with the order to send this man to the front. I saw Alek, who demonstrated anti-gas masks. . . .

The capture of Erzerum, with 13,000 prisoners and 323 guns, was an important military success.

" The petition " is referred to in the Tsaritsa's telegrams : " What have you done with the petition which was sent to me by Schulen- berg ? . . . Can the young man be sent to the army ? " Schulenberg was the director of a home for crippled soldiers and of a Red Cross train dedicated to the Tsarevitch.

Stavka. 4 *February,* 1916.

MY DARLING SUNNY,

My warmest thanks for dear letter. I read with interest the extract you sent me from N.P.'s letter.

I am very happy about our great success in the Caucasus —I never supposed that Erzerum would be taken so soon. It appears that our troops, after attacking the forts, had to stop [were ordered not to advance further]; but their on-slaught was so impetuous that they broke through to the rear of the Turks, and in this way occupied the town.—This information came to me from Tiflis from N. in 7 minutes, just as we were getting up from the table.

Alek was calm and not excited. He made a long report, and then offered to show me some experiments with asphyxiating gases.—Three officers and two chemists in various masks went into a carriage and stayed there over 30 minutes. I could watch them through the windows— how they stood and walked about in those terrible yellow fumes. Even in the open air the horrible stench could be detected. Strange people! They make these experiments with delight—like a sport!

Now, about my plans.—I want to return in order to be present at the opening of the G. Duma and the G. Soviet. Please do not speak of this as yet. I am leaving on Satur-day, to hold an inspection of the wonderful 1st Siberian Corps, and arrive at Tsarskoe on Monday, the 8th.—Shall stay there for two days, and hastily return here, because I have ordered our military conference for Thursday the 11th, with the participation of all the Commanders-in-Chief. I intended to do this from the very beginning, but somehow it could not be arranged.

I shall be *very happy* to see you and the children—if only for 2 days—it is better than nothing. Now, my darling, my dear, swollen-cheeked Wify, I must finish.

God guard you all! I kiss you and the children fondly.

I remain

Your faithful and tenderly devoted

NICKY.

" N."—the Grand Duke Nicholas. " G. Duma and G. Soviet," the State Duma and the Council of State.

Telegram.

Stavka. 5 February, 1916.

I thank you heartily for dear letter; Olga, and her, as well. Also for the news. I have had a drive and a good walk. I kiss you tenderly.

NICKY.

Stavka. 6 February, 1916.

MY BELOVED WIFY,

I thank you sincerely for your last two letters. I cannot understand what was the matter with you—I am speaking of the pains in your face. I hope that they will be gone by my return, and that both of Alexey's arms will be better. Kiss him tenderly for me.

After a lengthy and complicated discussion with Alexeiev, I have decided to appoint Kouropatkin in Plehve's place.—I know that this will provoke a great many rumours and criticisms, but what can one do, if there are so few good men? So that I sent for him and told him about it yesterday.

You ask me about Rouszky. He wrote a little while ago, complaining of his health, and saying that ever since the month of October he has been unable to get rid of the polzouchy plevrit [literally, creeping pleurisy]. I hope that, with God's help, Kouropatkin will be a good Commander-in-Chief. He will be directly under the Stavka, and in this way he will not have on his shoulders the same responsibility which he had in Manchuria. You can be quite sure that the armies under his command will welcome the appointment. He spoke very well and judiciously of his new position, and will come back here to the military conference.

The sums received and spent by your sklad [Red Cross depot] are enormous—I should never have thought that they could reach such dimensions.

I look forward with impatience to to-morrow's review,

L

at which I hope to see the first eight Siberian regiments, with mine at the head.

It is snowing to-day, and a strong wind blowing.—If it would only stop for Sunday !

May God guard you and the children ! And so, in a day's time, I shall be able to press you to my heart, my dear child, my Sunny. I kiss all fondly.

Always your

NICKY.

KOUROPATKIN : General A. N. Kouropatkin was Minister of War in 1904 and Commander-in-Chief during the Japanese War. In view of his poor reputation as a leader the present appointment was certainly not a wise one. He was succeeded by General Dragomirov.

Telegram.

Polotzk. 7 February, 1916.

Thanks for news. I am delighted with the inspection of the Siberian Rifles. The road was very difficult [in very bad condition]. Lots of snow. Am therefore two and a half hours late. I embrace you closely.

NICOLAI.

Telegram.

Stavka. 11 February, 1916.

Arrived at 4 o'clock. Was met by all the commanders. The conference will begin at 6 o'clock. Clear, cold, sunny weather. Many thanks for dear letter yesterday evening. I embrace you tenderly

NICKY.

Stavka. 12 February, 1916.

MY DEAREST,

I thank you most warmly for your dear letter—the first that I received here. I am returning you the French book ; I am reading the new English one with avidity, when there is leisure. The journey was absolutely quiet. I insisted on our train not making more than 40 versts an hour. Four commanders-in-chief met me here on the platform. I saw Alexeiev for a minute, then, at 6, went to the

Staff quarters, where the conference dragged on till 8, and was continued immediately after dinner till close on 12.30. Poor Plehve looked like a dead man ; he was so pale. To-day he is lying down in his sleeping carriage, unable to move— probably over-fatigued !

On the whole I am quite satisfied with the results of our long conference.—They disputed much among themselves. I asked them all to speak out plainly, because, in these important problems, truth is of the utmost significance.— I prefer not to write on this subject, but will tell you about it all when we meet.

It is very cold and windy.

I must finish. God keep you, my dear ! I kiss you and the dear children affectionately.

Eternally your old
NICKY.

Telegram.

Stavka. 12 *February*, 1916.

I am very grateful for letter and telegram. The conference came to an end after midnight. Am satisfied with the result. It is cold, windy. I kiss you tenderly.
NICKY.

Stavka. 13 *February*, 1916.

MY BELOVED SUNNY,

The courier has not yet arrived. I have finished with my papers, and therefore have more time for my letter.

To-day is the regimental festival of my Uhlans—they are resting somewhere in southern Galicia. In honour of the day I have promoted Zamoisky to be Wing-Adjutant [A.D.C.]. I have inherited him from Nicolasha ; he was attached to him as orderly.

There has been a lot of bother all these last days, especially for me. First of all, the conference, which lasted for 6 hours. At the same time I had to speak seriously to some of the generals, to receive Sandro with a long report, Boris after his review, Polivanov and Admiral Phillimore, who has returned from Arkhangelsk. Yesterday Dmitry appeared unexpectedly on his way through for a ten days' leave. I shall see him for a little time at my leisure to-day.

Sandro is in excellent spirits. He is going home for five days—try to see him.

Olga writes that she is leaving Kiev for a few days in order to visit her regiment, as she has not so much to do at the present time.

When free from work, I enjoy reading the book, " The Room of Secrets." It reminds me in some ways of a book which we read together.

For the last two days the weather has been very unfavourable for long walks—a strong wind has been blowing, with frost and snow, so that I was compelled to walk in the tiny garden ! ! ! Poor little one ! ! !

They have just brought me your dear, scented letter, and Olga's.—I thank you heartily for them and for the interesting news from Victoria's letter. This scent excites and brings forth wonderful memories; it quite drew me to you ! I must finish now. I hope that you are feeling better.

May God bless you and the children ! I kiss you tenderly
Your old
NICKY.

Give her my greetings.

ZAMOISKY ; Count A. S. Zamoisky, Cornet in the Life-Guard Uhlans (His Majesty's Own).
" The Room of Secrets," a story by William le Queux.

Telegram.

Stavka. 13 February, 1916.

Hearty thanks for letter. I have only just returned from church. Dmitry had tea with me before his departure for home. I kiss all tenderly.

NICKY.

Telegram.

Stavka. 14 *February,* 1916.

I am very grateful for dear letters. I had no time to-day to write to Sossy. Had a good walk out of the town. A cold, bright, sunny day. . . .

Sossy: the identity of this lady is by no means clear. According to the Russian editor, she may be Queen Sophia of Greece. But it is quite conceivable that the name is due to a false transcription, and should read "Sunny."

Stavka. 15 *February,* 1916.

MY OWN DARLING,

I thank you sincerely for dear letter—my old heart beats faster every time when I open and read them. Everything is absolutely *quiet* here now. All the plans for the approaching offensive [the word offensive is omitted in the text] are prepared, and are now being put into execution—hence, Alexeiev has proposed to me to go home [*i.e.,* has suggested that I might go home].—I shall start during the day on Wednesday, and hope to reach home on Thursday at 11 o'clock in the morning.—I shall stay for a week and a half. Will this not be splendid, darling?

Just now, after lunch, I found your letter No. 446 on my table, and thank you most warmly for it. How annoying that you have a cough and a temperature of 37·3! Why?

This morning, after having got up, I allowed Botkin to sound and examine me all over.—He asked to be allowed to do it here, as there is more time here—he had not overhauled me like this since I was in the Crimea. He found everything in order, and the heart even better than last time! Strange!

George has arrived, but I have not yet seen him, because his train was late. To-morrow Sir Arthur Paget is coming, and will present me with the Field-Marshal's baton. I have asked all the English officers who are staying here to be present at this little ceremony.

I received Georgie's letter before—it was brought by Gen. Williams, who saw Paget in Petrograd.

Now, my dear Wify, I must finish this, my last letter.

God preserve you all!

I kiss and embrace you fondly.

Your old

NICKY

PAGET : General the Right Hon. Sir Arthur Fitzroy Paget, eldest son of General Lord Alfred Paget. He commanded the forces in Ireland from 1911 to 1917.

Telegram.

Stavka. 16 *February*, 1916.

Hearty thanks for dear letters. I have just received Sir A. Paget with the baton. Saw a cinema for girls in the theatre. It was charming. I embrace all tenderly.

NICKY.

Telegram.

Stavka. 3 *March*, 1916.

Have arrived safely. It was fairly cold during the night. Here it is moderately warm. I have finished the book to-day. I feel lonely, but well. I kiss you tenderly and passionately and thank you for the telegram.

NICKY.

Stavka. 3 *March*, 1916.

MY PRECIOUS DARLING,

Your telegram, in which you inform me that you had slept well and that your face had not ached much, consoled me greatly, as I felt worried at leaving you in such a condition !

The journey was good, but I felt so tired yesterday in the train that I remained lying down in my coupé till tea-time, and after dinner I read this interesting book.—Having slept yesterday for 10 hours, I feel well again to-day.

This morning, passing through Orsha, I inspected an echelon of the Guards of the Litovsky Regiment, which is going to the north ; they jumped out of the carriages, and I went round them twice. Such fine fellows !

I arrived here at 2.45, and was met by the usual public [people], among them the new Governor—Yavlensky—who made a good impression on me. From 3.15 till 5.15 I was occupied with Alexeiev, who thanks you very much. He showed me that nearly everything is ready for our offensive.

I talked for a long time with Gen. Palitzyn, whom Nicolasha has sent here. He understands quite well that we
cannot spare our troops for the Caucasus.

Now, my dear, I wish you a good night and pleasant
dreams.

4 *March.*

Only three of the foreigners appeared at dinner; old Pau
is laid up with rheumatism, and the others have gone away.
George arrived here a few hours before me. Sergey is not
here.

There was 1° of frost last night; it thawed during the day.
The weather is the same as at home, and everything is
covered with a light mist. Last night I played dominoes
for an hour; the Admiral was very charming and modest
this time!

Only this very moment, having come back from lunch, I
have received your dear letter with the pretty postcard and a
letter from Marie. Now I am going for a drive in the car
along the main road. It is thawing and dull.

Be well. God guard you, my beloved Sunny!

I kiss you and the dear children tenderly. Give A. my
greetings.

Eternally your old hubby

NICKY.

" The new Governor "—of Mogilev.—PALITZYN : General F. F.
Palitzyn, a Councillor of State, and formerly Chief of the General
Staff.

Telegram.

Stavka. 4 *March,* 1916.

Sincerest thanks for dear letter, also for Marie's long letter.
I have written. Had a nice walk. The weather is mild,
dull. I kiss all tenderly.

NICKY.

Stavka. 5 *March,* 1916.

MY OWN,

My heartfelt thanks for your long letter, with the
details of your talk with N.P., as well as for Olga's and

Alexey's letters. They have arrived very punctually to-day. I am very grateful to you for writing to me about all this beforehand, and thus preparing me for the conversation with him and Kyrill.—Why are you again anxious about A., now that everything is in St.'s hands? On Monday, I hope, his appointment will be made public. Khv. has written a long letter to me; speaks of his devotion and so on, *does not understand* the reason, and asks to be received. I forwarded this to St. with an endorsement [to the effect] that I had never doubted his loyalty, but shall receive him later, if, by his good behaviour and tact, he deserves to be received. It is a damnable story!

Sergey has come back to-day. Poor old Pau is laid up with rheumatism in the knee, so that Feodorov visits him from time to time. As far as I know, he is quite at ease in regard to the battle at Verdun. The French have lost 42,000 men, but the German losses must be at least four times as great!

The courier has to leave in a quarter of an hour. I have finished the book with regret, and shall re-read it aloud with delight.—May God guard you, my beloved Sunny!

I kiss and embrace you and the children affectionately.

Eternally your old

NICKY.

"His appointment"—the appointment of Sturmer to the post of Minister of Foreign Affairs.—Khv.: A. N. Khvostov, the Minister of the Interior, was dismissed because of his attitude towards Manouilov, one of Sturmer's protégés, and a man of worse than doubtful character. "Does not understand the reason"—for his dismissal.

Telegram.

Stavka. 5 March, 1916.

I thank you, Olga and Alexey tenderly for letters. It is warm, foggy. Have only just come back from church. I embrace you closely.

NICKY.

Stavka.   7 March, 1916.

MY PRECIOUS SUNNY,

I thank you most warmly for your dear letters.   I
was greatly vexed at not being able to write to you yesterday, but indeed I was very busy.   I received all day long,
and was left in peace only at 10.15 in the evening.   Gen.
Callwell has come from England, together with another very
interesting man—Major Sykes, who has travelled all his life
in Asia Minor and Mesopotamia, and knows the Turks and
Arabs well.   He has told me many strange and noteworthy
things.   To-day he has already started for Tiflis, in order to
give N. all necessary information.   Callwell is also going there
soon, as Georgie has commissioned him to present the highest
English Order to Youdenitch.   Yesterday dear old Pilz
went to Petrograd, to the place of his new appointment.
He was fêted here, and all the people saw him off in a remarkably warm and touching manner.   Taking leave of me in
my room, he wept, and begged me to be careful concerning
the story about our Friend—of course with the best intentions, and for our own good.

The weather is getting gradually warmer, but it is dreadful
that we never see the sun !

I am glad that you saw old Sturmer, and now know his
opinion of some of the Ministers and of things in general.   I
cannot understand why you think that the Admiral has a
bad influence on V.   They meet only at the table, and say
very rude things to one another.   The Admiral is deeply
attached to Feodorov; I had a long, thorough talk with the
latter.   I must finish this letter.

May God guard you, my darling, and the children !   I kiss
you all tenderly (her as well).

Eternally your old

NICKY.

SYKES : Brigadier-General Sir Percy M. Sykes.   His travels in
Persia and Baluchistan are well known.   In 1916 he raised the
South Persian Rifles, and was G.O.C. in Southern Persia till the end
of 1918.   He is the author of important books on Persia and Central
Asia.   YOUDENITCH : General N. N. Youdenitch.   Before the war
he was Chief of Staff in the Caucasian Military District, and at the

beginning of the war commanded the Caucasian Army. He was then serving with the Grand Duke Nicholas.

Stavka. 9 March, 1916.

MY BELOVED SUNNY,

I thank you most warmly for your dear letters, and for the love which enriches every one of your lines ! I rejoice in them, drinking in each word of the letter, breathing its perfume, and pressing to my lips the paper which has been touched by your hands.

How strange that the weather with you has suddenly changed, and that severe frosts have set in ! Whereas here it is thawing rapidly—that is the chief reason why our offensive is beginning in a few days. If we wait another week, the trenches in many sectors of our front will be flooded with water and the troops would have to be taken very far back. If that happened they would be deprived of the chance of moving forward for a month or a month and a half, till the roads got dry.

Then the Germans would undoubtedly attack us with an enormous mass of heavy artillery, as they did last summer. For this reason, therefore, it has been decided to take the initiative into our own hands, taking advantage of the onslaught at Verdun. May God guard and bless our valiant troops ! I beg you not to tell *anyone* of this.

Yesterday I went to a cinematograph which was particularly interesting, because we saw many photographs of Erzerum immediately after its fall. The high mountains are amazingly beautiful; covered with deep snow, glistening in the sunlight.

After this we saw two amusing pictures with Max Linder in the chief part—this would probably have appealed to the children.

I am glad that you have found a new book for us to read aloud [for our reading aloud]. Have those two books from Marshton [Marston] come yet from England ? So far I have no time to read for my own pleasure, although I play dominoes in the evening every other day.

Well, I think it is time for me to finish my letter. God

guard you, my darling Wify, and our children! I kiss and embrace you all tenderly.

Your old hubby

NICKY.

"Our offensive is beginning in a few days." In connection with this offensive (preceding the great offensive of Broussilov) the following passage from Ludendorff is worth quoting: "From the 18th to the 21st of March the situation of the 10th [German] Army was critical and the numerical superiority of the Russians overwhelming. On the 21st they won a success on the narrow lake sector which affected us gravely, and even the attack west of Postovy was only stemmed with difficulty" (p. 211). By the end of April, however, the 10th Army had regained the ground which it had lost between Lake Narotch and Lake Vishniev.

Stavka. 10 *March*, 1916.

MY BELOVED,

I thank you warmly for your dear letters—they are my consolation in my loneliness here. The days seem to fly; I have lots of work to do, see crowds of all sorts of people, and yet do not feel tired. Unfortunately I have not even time for reading!

Your lovely lilies of the valley smell deliciously—many thanks! I was very glad to see N.P. Kyrill and he dined with me yesterday and lunched to-day—now they have gone. Last night I talked with them for a long time, and agreed to leave the battalion at its present strength—4 full companies; it ought not to be reduced by one man till the end of the war. To-day Kyrill spoke to me about the "P. Zvezda." I told him that it had been agreed between Mamma and me to appoint Lialin, but that he should ask her again, if he wished, although I doubted very much whether she would change her decision. Shir.-Shikh. is an excellent man, but he has not been on any ship for many years.

I have at last found a successor for Polivanov—it is Schouvaiev, whom I can trust absolutely. I have not spoken to him yet. Further, I intend to attach old Ivanov to my person, and to appoint Broussilov or Shcherbatchev to his post—probably the former. After P.'s removal I shall sleep in peace, and all the Ministers will feel relieved as well.

11 *March.*

The morning work with Alexeiev occupies all my time till lunch, but now it has become of absorbing interest. Cold weather has set in here as well—at Riga the frost reaches 10° at night—it is terrible for the poor wounded, and for the troops, who are posted on many sectors of the front in the snow, opposite the enemy's wire entanglements.

May God bless you and the children, my dear ! I kiss you all tenderly. I thank A. for her charming letter.

Eternally your old hubby

NICKY.

" The battalion "—of the Gvardeisky Equipage.—" P. Zvezda "— " Poliarnaia Zvezda," " Polar Star," one of the Imperial yachts. LIALIN : Captain M. M. Lialin of the Equipage, described as the senior wardroom officer. SHIR.-SHIKH. : Prince S. A. Shirinsky-Shikhnatov, a captain in the Equipage. SCHOUVAIEV : General Schouvaiev, who succeeded Polivanov as Minister of War, was an amiable and conscientious but totally inefficient man. The dismissal of Polivanov, whose bluff manners made him personally distasteful to the Tsaritsa and her friends, was, in the words of Sir Alfred Knox, " a disaster." He was " undoubtedly the ablest military organiser in Russia." The Tsar had never liked him. The statement that " all the Ministers will feel relieved " shows very clearly that extraordinary and fatal ignorance of opinion which was so often apparent in the Tsar's words and conduct.

Telegram.

Stavka. 10 *March*, 1916.

I thank you and Marie heartily. Saw Kyrill and N.P. together. This question is now definitely settled. 3° of frost. A strong wind. I embrace you closely.

NICKY.

Telegram.

Stavka. 11 *March*, 1916.

I thank you and Shvybzik warmly for letters. A very busy day. Things are going well on the whole. It is much warmer. I kiss you tenderly.

NICKY.

SHVYBZIK : a pet name for his daughter Anastasia. It has no particular meaning.

Telegram.

I am very anxious about your incessant pains in the face. I thank you heartily for your dear letter, Tatiana as well. I had again no time to write, am very sorry. A beautiful sunny day. I long to be more in the open air. There is no special news. . . .

MY BELOVED WIFY,

For the last 3 days there was no time whatever to write to you; I was very busy with the military operations and the redistribution [of the troops]. I had to write to Pol. and explain why I was dissatisfied. I am quite certain that kind old Schouvaiev is just the right man for the post of Minister of War. He is honest, absolutely loyal, is not at all afraid of the Duma, and knows all the faults and short-comings of these committees. Then I had to receive and read my beastly papers—all in such a hurry !

The Ministers are beginning to arrive here now, one after another—the first was Naoumov, then Shakhovskoy, and so on. To-day I had a conversation with General Manikovsky —the commander of the chief Art[illery] Dept. He told me that he would like to send in his resignation, as Pol.'s behaviour to him was quite impossible. When he heard that P. is dismissed and Schouv. appointed, he crossed himself three times. Old Ivanov will be replaced by Broussilov. You see that your hubby has been working during these days —many changes have already been made, and more will take place—including Rongin as well.

How sad that you have pains in your face and eye ! Is it due to nerves? I am so sorry, my dear, that I cannot be with you and console you when you are suffering !

Things are moving very slowly at the front; in several places we have sustained heavy losses, and many generals are making serious blunders. The worst of it is, that we have so few good generals. It seems to me that during the long winter rest they have forgotten all the experience which they acquired last year. Lord ! I am beginning to complain, but that is ne nado ! I feel firm, and believe absolutely in our final success. May God bless you, my own, my all, my treasure, my darling ! I kiss you and the children fondly. Greetings to A.

Eternally your old hubby

NICKY.

Pol. : Polivanov. SHAKHOVSKOY : Prince S. Shakhovskoy, the Minister of Trade. He became Minister of Public Welfare in the Provisional Government of 1917. RONGIN : Major-General S. A. Rongin held the post of Assistant to the Chief of Communications on the General Staff before the war. During the war he was Chief of Communications and was attached to the Stavka.

" Ne nado ! " An expression frequently used in the Imperial Family. There is no exact corresponding phrase in English; it is akin to the French " *ça ne fait rien.*"

Telegram.

Stavka. 14 *March,* 1916.

Many thanks to you and Olga for dear letters. It is colder to-day. At last I have written to you. I hope that you are feeling better and that the pains have gone. I embrace you closely.

NICKY.

Stavka. 15 *March,* 1916.

MY TREASURE,

I thank you tenderly for your dear letters. I cannot tell you how I sympathise with you when you are oppressed by those terrible pains in the face, and how I long to be near you at those times in order to comfort you ! It is quite impossible for me to decide when I shall be able to come home for a few days—perhaps not for some time, and perhaps in about a week !

What I was afraid of has happened. Such a great thaw has set in that the positions occupied by our troops where we have moved forward are flooded with water knee-deep, so that it is impossible either to sit or to lie down in the trenches. The roads are rapidly deteriorating; the artillery and the transport are scarcely moving. Even the most heroic troops cannot fight under such conditions, when it is impossible even to entrench oneself. In consequence, our offensive had to be stopped, and another plan will have to be worked out. In order to discuss this, I am thinking of summoning three Commanders-in-Chief to the Stavka, which will give me an opportunity for seeing Broussilov before his new movement.

You write that you have heard it seems there is much talk in town of the losses among some of the Guard regiments. That is an invention, as they are 50 versts from the firing line, and I still hold them in reserve in the extreme rear. They have moved forward a little towards Dvinsk—that is all. I agree with your opinion about M. P. Sablin. It would be excellent if Eberhardt took him to himself as Chief of Staff, but I never insist upon this sort of appointment, because the Chief of Staff must give absolute *satisfaction* to his commander. A little while ago Admiral Eberhardt went to Batoum and had a long conversation with Nic. concerning the plan of the combined military [and naval] operations against Trapezound [Trebizond]. Our dear *plastouni* will have to play a big part in them.

As far as I know, all loyal and right-thinking people applaud the appointment of Schouvaiev.

Now, darling, I must finish. May God bless you and the children! I kiss and embrace you tenderly, and sincerely hope that your pains will soon and completely disappear.

Eternally your old hubby

NICKY.

M. P. SABLIN : a naval officer, the brother of N. P. Sablin. EBERHARDT : Admiral A. A. Eberhardt, commander of the Black Sea Fleet till June 1916.

Telegram.

Stavka. 15 *March*, 1916.

I thank you heartily for precious letter, as well as Marie and Alexey. Thick fog, fairly warm. In thought we are always together. I kiss you tenderly.

NICKY.

Telegram.

Stavka. 16 *March*, 1916.

Many thanks to you and Anastasia for letters. The terrible fog persists. The break-up of the ice on the river has begun; the water has risen very high. I also have received a letter from the energetic sailor in the Far North. I embrace you tenderly.

NICKY.

"The energetic sailor"—referred to in the following letter and telegram as "R." M. S. Rostchakovsky, a retired naval officer, who had become an intimate friend of the Court circle during the Japanese War. During the Great War he appears to have been a supervisor of various undertakings on the Murman Coast.

Stavka. 17 *March*, 1916.

MY BELOVED SUNNY,

This letter will be handed to you by Schouvaiev—so I hope that you will soon receive him.

I also return R.'s letter, which is very like the one sent to me by him a few days ago through Admiral Phillimore. I will show it to you when I return home. For three successive days we have been sitting in a thick fog, and that has a truly depressing effect. The spring is coming rapidly; the Dnieper broke up yesterday and has risen considerably; but so far there are no floods in this district. Yesterday I had a drive in a car, and took one of my last year's favourite autumnal walks, in the direction of the bank, to the place which Baby had liked so much too. The view was truly magnificent—the whole river was covered with blocks of ice; they moved swiftly but noiselessly, and only occasionally could be heard the sharp sound of the clashing of two large ice-blocks. We all stood for a long time admiring this spectacle. Only think, it is for the first time in my life that I have seen such an aspect of nature—with the exception, of course, of the Neva—in town—which is, naturally, quite a different thing.

Perhaps it will soon be possible to go out in boats!

Can you imagine—the other day the little Admiral asked

Grabbe to put at his disposal a quiet Cossack horse for riding !
He is delighted, enjoys his rides, feels very well, and sleeps
better. But he always sets out and returns in such a way
that we shall not see him on his jaunts; queer fellow !

Now I must go to the Report.

Fancy, Alexeiev told me that I could go home for a week !
All the Commanders-in-Chief are coming here about the 30th
or 31st, as I have, perhaps, written before. I am *very glad*
of this unexpected luck. May God bless you, my Sunny, my
beloved dear Wify, my little child ! I kiss you and the
children tenderly.

Eternally your old hubby

NICKY.

Telegram.

Stavka. 17 *March,* 1916.

I have replied to R. Am very pleased with his work. My
hearty thanks for dear letters. I can leave to-morrow, and
shall be at home on Saturday in the evening. Please receive
Schouvaiev after 12. He is leaving to-day with a letter from
me. Happy to see you. I embrace you tenderly.

NICKY.

Telegram.

Stavka. 18 *March,* 1916.

Many thanks to you and Olga for dear letters. Cold, rainy
weather. Am happy to be coming home. Delighted with
the charming flowers. I kiss all tenderly.

NICKY.

Telegram.

Jmerinka. 28 *March,* 1916.

Thanks for telegram. It is absolutely spring-like here.
Dmitry is touched and, with me, embraces all of you.

NICKY.

Telegram.

Kamenetz-Podolsk. 29 *March,* 1916.

I have returned from the review near Khotin. The troops
presented themselves in excellent condition. Saw our

M

Kouban Cossack Squadron. Wind, rain, hail. Have visited two hospitals. I embrace all closely.

NICKY.

Telegram.

Kamenetz-Podolsk. 30 *March*, 1916,

A fine warm day at last. Held a fine inspection of a Trans-Amur division. Visited two hospitals. Am leaving now. . . .

Telegram.

Mena. 31 *March*, 1916.

Hearty thanks for two dear letters. I hope to be in Mogilev this evening The weather is excellent. I embrace you closely.

NICKY.

Telegram.

Stavka. 31 *March*, 1916.

Have arrived safely. My sincerest thanks for yesterday's dear letter. Mild weather. Good-night, sleep well.

NICKY.

Stavka. 31 *March*, 1916.

MY BELOVED SUNNY,

At last I have snatched a minute to sit down and write to you after a five days' silence—a letter is a substitute for conversation, not like telegrams.

I thank you tenderly for your dear letters—your first seems to have come so long ago ! What joy it is to get several in one day, [as I did] on the way, coming home !

During the journey I read from morning till night—first of all I finished " The Man who was Dead," then a French book, and to-day a charming tale about little Boy Blue ! I like it ; Dmitry does too. I had to resort to my handkerchief several times. I like to re-read some of the parts separately, although I know them practically by heart. I find them so pretty and true ! I do not know why, but it reminded me of Coburg and Walton !

I am very pleased with my tour. Thank God, all has passed off well ! You can imagine how agreeably surprised I was when, riding round the troops at a big review, I saw our dear Cossacks, who smirked and smiled broadly, beginning with Joukov, and down to the last soldier—among them Shvedov and Zborovsky. I gave them greetings from you and the girls. They had only just returned from the trenches. The weather was beastly—a strong wind, with sun, hail and rain. Unfortunately I did not see your Krymtzi !

The Staff of the 9th Army prepared a simple lunch for me in the little town of Khotin, where I also visited two hospitals. That day we spent 9 hours in the open air. In Kamenetz-Podolsk the generals dined with me in the train. I had much conversation with Keller, and gave him your greetings. He has not changed at all. The next day, that is yesterday, I inspected the recently formed division—the 3rd Trans-Amur Infantry Division. It made an excellent impression — magnificent, tall fellows, real guardsmen. During the review we heard our guns firing at Austrian aeroplanes which were dropping bombs on both of our bridges over the Dniester. Then I visited 2 more hospitals and [saw] Lechitzky; he is beginning to recover, but is still lying down. I left Kamenetz-Podolsk after lunch; the weather had by then become warm and clear, and I arrived here to-night at 9.30. I went to bed rather late, as I had to prepare myself for the military conference.

1 *April.*

A warm, grey morning after a night's rain—just the right weather for a prolonged conference [literally, sitting]. It began at 10 o'clock and lasted till lunch-time, and will be resumed immediately.

Dmitry is leaving this evening; he will spend three days at home and then return to his regiment. I asked him to go to see you. I forgot to tell you that I saw Misha twice at Kamenetz-Podolsk. He left before me for his division, which is stationed not far from Kamenetz-Podolsk.

Now, my angel, my tender darling, I must finish. May
God bless you and the children !

I kiss you and them fondly.

Eternally your old hubby

NICKY.

" The Man who was Dead," a story by A. W. Marchmont.—
" Little Boy Blue "—the hero of " Through the Postern Gate," a
once popular novel by Florence L. Barclay. This book seems to
have appealed profoundly to the Tsar and the Tsaritsa, and there
are several pathetic and playful allusions to it in their correspondence.
The choice of such a book and the impression which it made are
facts of some significance, and help us to realise vividly the tastes
and proclivities of the royal couple.

Walton : Walton-on-Thames, where the Tsar (then Tsarevitch)
stayed with Prince Louis of Battenberg in 1894. See further reference, and note thereto, in letter of 8th June.

JOUKOV : Colonel A. S. Joukov of the Imperial Escort. He committed suicide on the 9th June. See letter of 12th June. SHVEDOV
and ZBOROVSKY, junior officers of the Cossack Escort (or Convoy).
Krymtzi : Crimeans. A cavalry regiment of which the Tsaritsa was
the Colonel-in-Chief.

Telegram.

Stavka. 1 *April*, 1916.

Hearty thanks for dear letters. From 10 in the morning
till the evening I have been at the sitting. Am terribly
weary. A delightful spring-like day. I embrace you
closely.

NICKY.

Telegram.

Stavka. 2 *April*, 1916.

I thank you all heartily for this evening's greetings, as
well as for the dear letter and the ikon. Wonderful weather.
I embrace you closely. Good-night.

NICKY.

Telegram.

Stavka. 3 *April*, 1916.

I am very grateful for dear letters, flowers and book.
Lovely warm weather. I hope that you are feeling better.

I have received Vyshinsky, who will visit you before his departure. . . .

VYSHINSKY : Major-General E. E. Vyshinsky, formerly commanded the 13th Life Grenadier Erivan Regiment, afterwards Assistant Quartermaster-General on the staff of the Grand Duke Nicholas in the Caucasus.

Stavka. 3 *April*, 1916.

MY BELOVED,

I thank you tenderly for your dear letters; now that I no longer see any troops they are my sole consolation. Many thanks also for the little ikon—I have fastened it to my chain. Now I shall at least wear *something* from you ! Here are three flowers which I found on my walk yesterday.

Again I have no time for writing. I am continually besieged by crowds of people who wish to see me and make endless reports. I hope I shall be left in peace during Holy Week.

Thank you for sending me the new book. My dear, I love you greatly, even more than ever; I long for you so much, especially at the present time !

I must finish now. May God bless you and the children ! I kiss you and them tenderly.

Eternally, my dear Wify, your old hubby

NICKY.

The ukase is splendid.

Stavka. 4 *April*, 1916.

BELOVED WIFY,

I thank you tenderly for your letter and for all that you write in it ; for the dear words of love which console and calm me so much in my loneliness. Of course I go to church every morning and evening. O. Shavelsky takes the service so well; exactly an hour. Alexeiev and many others of the Staff go to Communion on Thursday. I am sorry that I cannot go to Communion together with them, but I do not want to change my confessor ! I forgot to choose and bring here Easter cards and eggs to send to you and the children ! For the others, I have a sufficient quantity of china eggs.

It rained this morning, and as I had to read and sign much before Easter I did not go for a drive in the car, but just walked for a little in the garden, and am now writing to you. The view from there is truly magnificent—the river has become an enormous lake, with a whole lot of houses in the mjddle. The current here is very strong. Yesterday the Admiral ordered two sailors to try to row in one of the boats, and they could with difficulty row up the river ! It is a pity, as I intended to try myself, although I have not yet given up the idea.

There is a lull in the military operations at present, but in the Caucasus, along the shores of the Black Sea, our troops pursue the Turks, and I hope that Trapezound [Trebizond] will soon be ours. The fleet helps a great deal in these land operations. I have forgotten to mention my recent conversation with Misha at Kamenetz-Podolsk. He asked to be recalled in June and to be appointed to the Stavka. Then I began to preach to him about our father, about the sense of duty, example to others, and so on. When I had finished, and we had said good-bye to each other, he again asked me coldly and quite calmly not to forget his request, as if I had not spoken at all. I was furious !

But I must finish now. May God bless you and the children ! I kiss you all tenderly, and remain
Your faithful hubby
NICKY.

My dear, I love you so deeply and ardently !

Telegram.
Stavka. 4 *April,* 1916.

I am very grateful for dear letters and two telegrams. Delightful weather, rather cool. In thought we are constantly together. I am amusing myself with a little puzzle, as I have been reading a lot. I embrace you, kiss you.
NICKY.

Stavka. 5 April, 1916.

MY OWN DARLING SUNNY,

Thanks be to God, our valiant troops, working with our Black Sea Fleet, have occupied Trapezound ! I received this information from N. when I was already sitting in the car ready to drive out. Such a success, and in such a week ! After that, I drove as far as the weir, and went up the river in a beautiful large motor launch with comfortable cabins. The current is very strong, but we made good progress none the less, and reached the places where Alexey had often played last autumn. It is practically impossible to recognise the locality : so completely is everything flooded. The morning was lovely, but, of course, as soon as I was on the river a thunderstorm burst out; it rained in torrents and became colder. But I was very pleased to have been on the river and to have seen the two fine sailors from the " Razvedchik " and the " Dozorny " by the weir with our dear dvoika [dinghy].

The courier is leaving, and I must make haste and finish this scribble. To-morrow you are going to confession. I beg you, my dear, to forgive me if I have hurt you in any way. I shall think of you particularly to-morrow and on Thursday morning; I always think of you, but at such times —particularly. May God bless you and the children ! I kiss you and them tenderly. I long for you all terribly.

Eternally your hubby

NICKY.

Give A. my greetings.

The capture of Trapezound (Trebizond) was of some importance. The Grand Duke was also pressing the enemy to the west of Erzerum.

Telegram.

Stavka. 5 April, 1916.

Hearty thanks for dear letter. I am very happy, now that Trapezound has been taken. I hope that you are not feeling worse after your fall. Good Lord ! what carelessness ! I kiss you tenderly.

NICKY.

Stavka. 6 April, 1916.

MY PRECIOUS SUNNY,

Many thanks for dear letter, in which you tell me of Dmitry's visit. I fail altogether to understand how people can say—and particularly Voeikov to A.—that I am coming home for three days. Now, in Holy Week, or later? I have not yet made any plans, and have therefore not spoken a word to anyone. Yes; I am thinking of appointing Alex. Adjutant-General. Old Freder. is quite hale and hearty, only he occasionally forgets in a conversation what has been said to him before; I hear—at least with half an ear—what goes on at the other end of the table—sometimes most amusing misunderstandings! He rode perfectly at both reviews.

You wish my adjutants [A.D.C.'s] to be on orderly duty with me—I quite agree with you, but you know there are not many of them left. Some of them have been promoted, others it would be undesirable to have here. A list of them is always under my eyes. Do you know who ought to get the Erivantzi? Silaiev! Vyshinsky gave me this good idea; he thinks that he is just the right man. V. has found out about the ugly incidents which have been taking place in the regiment—the intrigues of the senior officers (native-born), especially against S.—but now that is all over, and they will be removed. Yesterday I questioned S. about it for the first time, and he confirmed every word of the former commander. Then I told him of the impending appointment, which made him very happy.

I do not feel so lonely now, as I have much work to do, and when I am at leisure I refresh myself with a good book. I have just had your dear letter No. 475 brought to me—many thanks for it and for the Easter postcards. I do not feel in the mood for going to confession to Shav., because I am afraid that instead of bringing peace and calm to my soul it might bring the contrary! Spiritually I feel well. I shall think particularly earnestly of you to-morrow morning. How boring that A. has a bad arm! I hope that it will soon be better. Kiss him tenderly for me. May God bless you, my Sunny, my only, my all! I kiss you and the girls tenderly. May the receiving of the Holy Sacrament bring you peace and comfort !

Eternally, my dear,

Your

NICKY.

Silaiev refused the command of the regiment, on the grounds of ill health.—" Native-born "—Georgian.—" A." here refers to Alexis.

Telegram.

Stavka. 6 April, 1916.

Many thanks for letter and postcards. I hope that your arm and his are better. Lovely weather. Had a very pleasant sail up the river—a desperate fight with the current. In thought we are together. I embrace you closely and bless you.

NICKY.

Stavka. 7 April, 1916.

MY DARLING,

I am writing only a few lines, because I have no time again, owing to the Ministers having sent me mountains of papers—presumably [so that I might deal with them] before Easter. I have made a note on the petition of the wounded Jew from America, " to be granted universal domicile in Russia," and have sent it on to Sturmer.

Tender thanks for your dear letter and for the little eggs. I hope that Baby's arm will not hurt for long. This morning I thought a great deal about you in our little church. It is very quiet and peaceful here; many Staff officers with their families came to Communion. On the days when I cannot go out for walks the sun shines invariably, whereas when I drive or row the sky becomes overcast, so that I cannot get sunburnt !

To-morrow is the 8th; my prayers and thoughts will be with you, my girl, my own Sunny. At that time I fought for you, even against yourself ! ! !

Like the little Boy Blue, only more stubbornly.

May God bless you and the children! I kiss you and them fondly.

Eternally your

NICKY.

The album which I am sending to Alexey is from the English military photographer.

" Universal [unrestricted] domicile in Russia." The domicile of Jews was restricted to certain towns and areas, except by a special permit from the police.

" At that time I fought for you," refers to the time of the Tsar's courtship, when he persuaded his future wife (then Princess Alexandra of Hesse-Darmstadt) to become a member of the Orthodox Church.

Telegram.

Stavka. 7 *April,* 1916.

Thank you and Tatiana heartily for dear letters. I am very pleased with the eggs which you have sent. Misha— the ass—has sent a telegram with the notification of his second daughter's engagement to Georgie Bat. I shall reply for both of us. Good-night. I embrace you tenderly.

NICKY.

" The eggs "—Easter eggs.

GEORGIE BAT. : Prince George of Battenberg, now the Marquis of Milford Haven, and at that time a midshipman in the Royal Navy. He was engaged to Nadejda, the second daughter of the Grand Duke Michael, whom he subsequently married.

8 *April,* 1916.

Christ has risen!

I send you, my darling, my precious Sunny, my sincerest, loving Paschal greetings.

It is still harder to be separated at such a time!

May God bless you in all your undertakings!

I love you tenderly and cover your dear face and hands with passionate kisses.

Always your

NICKY.

" Christ has risen ! " The traditional Russian greeting on Easter morning—" Christos voskres ! "—to which the person thus greeted

replied, " Voiestino voskres ! " (" Verily He has risen ! "). The
Tsar sends the greeting on Good Friday, in order to be sure that it
may arrive in time for Easter.

Telegram.

Stavka. 8 April, 1916.

I thank you heartily for telegram and letter. In thought
I am inseparably with you. Warm, rainy weather. I am
going to church now. Tell Ella I think that the work is
very well done. I kiss you tenderly.

NICKY.

Stavka. 8 April, 1916.

MY DEAR BELOVED,

I must begin my letter to-day with reminiscences of
what happened 22 years ago ! As far as I remember, there
was a concert in Coburg that evening and a Bavarian band
was playing; poor Uncle Alfred was rather exhausted by
the dinner, and constantly dropped his stick with a clatter.
Do you remember? Last year, too, we were not together
on this day—it was just before the journey to Galicia ! !

It is indeed hard to be separated in Holy Week and at
Easter. Of course I have not missed a single service. To-
day, on both occasions, Alexeiev, Nilov, Ivanov and I
carried the Plashchanitza. All our Cossacks and crowds of
soldiers stood round the church along the route of the procession of the Cross. It rained all day long, and I hardly
went out, seeing that the church service was to begin at 2.30.

Rostchakovsky suddenly appeared this evening at dinner;
I shall receive him to-morrow evening. He has grown older,
and reminded me in some way of Pimenov and Beskrovny.
He has become much calmer. I told him that you would
be glad to see him on his way back.

You have asked me several times in your telegrams what
to say to Ella? I simply looked through the inscriptions
on the pictures, and had not the least idea what I was
supposed to say, so I wrote that I thought the work splendidly done ! But what work I meant I do not know myself.
Ha ! ha !

My beloved, I want you very much. . . . Now it is time to go to bed. Good-night, my dear, beloved darling, sleep well—pleasant dreams—but not of Catholic priests !

9 April.

I am finishing this letter after lunch. Have only just received your dear letter, with the book-marker out of the tiny eggs, for which I thank you tenderly.

I shall hang the little ikon and the egg opposite the place where I stand. There were lots of people in the church to-day, and children, who were taken to Communion. These latter stared at me and bowed many times, bumping against each other ! Now I must finish. May God bless you, my treasure, and may He send you a happy and peaceful Easter ! I kiss you and the children fondly.

Your loving and devoted hubby
NICKY.

" What happened 22 years ago "—at the time of the Tsar's betrothal at Coburg. " Uncle Alfred," Duke Alfred of Coburg.
Plashchanitza : a winding-sheet, representing that in which Christ was wrapped, carried in the Good Friday ceremonies.

Telegram.

Stavka. 10 *April,* 1916.

Verily He has risen ! In thought I greet all of you on Easter Day. I thank you once more for my Easter presents. A very fine midnight service ended at a quarter to two, after which all the higher ranks broke their fast at my house. I kiss you tenderly.

NICKY.

" Verily He has risen ! " The answer to the Tsaritsa's Easter greeting, sent by telegram. Breaking the fast (Rasgovliatsia) concluded the seven weeks' fast of Lent by the eating of food which had been blessed in the church.

Stavka. 10 *April,* 1916.

MY DEAR SUNNY,
I thank you once more for all the pretty things which you sent me for Easter—they made my two rooms look homely and have brightened them up.

Think of it! I can get away on Tuesday and be at home on Wednesday. This will be a great joy and happiness to me. To-day the weather is beautiful, without a single little cloud; the birds sing merrily and the bells are chiming. At 10.30 I exchanged Easter greetings with the whole of my household, the Escort, the Staff and the priests. Everything passed off smoothly, but, for the first time in my life, I had to distribute the eggs myself! To-morrow, some time during the day, it is the turn of the Cossacks and the soldiers. This will take place in the open air, outside the town, near the barracks.

On my way back I shall hold an inspection of the Guards. Yes, Silaiev has been promoted—but this always comes too late—I mean to say, the appointment.

The foreigners came to offer their congratulations as well, and each received an egg.

I prefer those eggs with initials only to the former sort; moreover, they are easier to prepare.

I have only just returned from a delightful trip on the river; it made me feel supple in all my limbs. This time I rowed in the dvoika [dinghy] from the " Standart."

It is 5 o'clock already; I must go to vespers. May God bless you, my angel, my dear girl, darling Wify! I kiss you all tenderly.

Eternally your hubby
NICKY.

" Easter greetings." The ceremonies of Easter were observed with great joy and piety by all Russians. " Christosovatsia," or Easter greetings, in which all took part, included three kisses— one on each cheek and one on the lips. Eggs were presented to friends and relatives, and these were specially prized if they had been taken to church and blessed before the presentation. The eggs given and received by persons of high rank or of wealth were often of immense value, made of gold encrusted with jewels, and containing elaborate trifles worth many thousands of pounds.— " Standart "—The Royal yacht.

Telegram.

Stavka. 10 *April*, 1916.

I thank you heartily for dear letter and his sketch, which I like very much. Wonderful weather. I hope that you are not tired. I have had a delightful row on the river. . . .

"His sketch"—a portrait of Alexey by the artist I. B. Striedlov.

Telegram.

Stavka. 11 *April,* 1916.

I thank you heartily for dear letters. To-day I exchanged Easter greetings with nearly 900 soldiers. Beautiful warm weather. I shall try to bring her with me. George M. has come back from the front. I kiss you tenderly.

NICKY.

Telegram.

Malaia Vishera. 24 *April,* 1916.

It is hot and dreary in the carriage. In thought I am with you. I am reading. Embrace all closely.

NICKY.

Telegram.

Stavka. 25 *April,* 1916.

Have arrived safely. Everything is covered with delicious verdure, it smells so good. I have finished a delightful book with tears in my eyes. I long for you greatly. I kiss you tenderly.

NICKY.

Stavka. 25 *April,* 1916.

MY BELOVED,

It was terribly hard to part and again leave you and the children. I ran into my coupé, as I felt that, otherwise, I should not be able to keep back my tears ! Your dear letter has calmed me, and I re-read it a great many times.

When we were passing the Alexandrovsky Station I looked out of the window and saw a hospital train overcrowded with the unhappy wounded, doctors and sisters. At first it was terribly hot in our carriages—23°—; towards the evening it became bearable, and to-day the temperature is ideal, as it rained the whole morning and has become cooler.

I read with avidity that delightful book, " The Rosary," and enjoyed it. Unfortunately I have finished it already. But I have some Russian books left.

I gave Voeik. orders to work out a plan for our joint tour in the South. I shall speak of it more fully to Alex. I noticed with pleasure that he looks well and has become sunburnt.

The tent is being put up in the garden. The trees and bushes are turning green, the chestnuts will burst into bud in a day or two—everything shimmers and smells good ! The river has gone down to its normal level. I hope to be able to row a little to-morrow.

Igor is behaving well, and seems to be on splendid terms with everybody. I have just received your second telegram. I am very glad that N. P. and Rodion. dined with you. Their presence has such an invigorating effect—particularly now !

Now it is time for me to go to bed. So good-night, my dear Wify, sleep well, pleasant dreams !

26 *April.*

A lovely morning; I got up early and walked for half an hour in the garden, then had breakfast and went to Alex. As usual, the first report was very lengthy.

I must finish, as it is time to go rowing on the river.

God guard you and the children, my darling Sunny ! I kiss you and them tenderly.

Eternally your hubby

NICKY.

" The Rosary," a story by Florence Barclay, at one time a " best seller " of an ultra-sentimental type.

IGOR : Prince Igor Constantinovitch, captain in the Ismailovsky Guard Regiment. Murdered by the Bolsheviks in 1918.

Telegram.

Stavka. 26 *April,* 1916.

Many thanks for letter and telegram. Lovely weather. Had a row in the dinghy. Boy Blue loves and misses you. I kiss you tenderly.

NICKY.

Stavka. 26 *April*, 1916.

MY DEAR SUNNY,

Tenderly, tenderly do I thank you for your dear letter. If you only knew what joy they bring me, and how excited I become when I see them on my table ! The one I received to-day begins with the words " Boy Blue." I was so touched by that ! It will be delightful if you bring that book with you !

The weather is beautiful to-day, and I enjoyed my trip down the river. We went in three dinghies; Igor, Feodorov and Dm. Sher. followed in a large motor launch. The first of them cannot row—he says that after a few strokes he begins to cough and spit blood ! For the same reason he cannot walk quickly—poor boy ! And he is only 22 years old.

We rowed half-way back as well, under the burning sun, but then changed over into the motor launch. Here Feodorov began to test our pulses for fun—after strenuous rowing against the current Valia's was 82, mine 92, Voeik.'s 114 and Kira's 128. Upon that, we began to chaff him about his abstention from meat, and told him that it seemed to do him little good, at any rate to his heart ! Ten minutes later Feod. again took our pulses—Valia's and mine were normal, but in the case of the other two it was still beating fast. If you come here on a fine day you must go for one of these trips with all the children—you would greatly enjoy the fresh air after the heat in the train !

George has arrived from Moscow; he saw Ella, who sent me a very pretty ikon of the Holy Mother of Vladimir, which she had just visited. Try to see mother. It seems that she is leaving on Saturday. Give her my love.

Ah ! this morning, when washing by the open window, I saw two little dogs between the trees opposite, chasing each other. . . . Is not this a truly spring-like scene?—and I made up my mind to tell you about it. I saw that the sentinels were equally amused by the sight.

27 *April.*

It has become very much fresher; it rained heavily in the morning. I am sending you two itineraries to choose from—I naturally prefer the one which will bring you here sooner and quicker. May God guard you, beloved! I kiss you tenderly and warmly.

Your old
NICKY.

KIRA : Colonel K. A. Narishkin, A.D.C. to the Tsar.—"The Holy Mother of Vladimir "—see note to letter of 23rd May.

Telegram.

Stavka. 27 *April,* 1916.

The cornet of the 8th Loubensky Hussar Regiment is alive and well, and is present here in person. It is colder to-day and drizzling with rain. I embrace you closely.

NICKY.

Stavka. 27 *April,* 1916.

MY BELOVED WIFY,

I thank you tenderly for your dear letter with the enclosed letters from Olga and Alexey. The Little One begins thus : " I count the days—why, you know yourself." Very charming ! It rained all the morning, and suddenly became cold—only 10°—after the heat of the previous days.

The French Ministers have arrived, with several officers —they had a prolonged conference with Alexeiev, Belaiev, Sergey and others ; then they had dinner, at which meal they were both my neighbours; in this way I avoided the necessity of talking to each separately.

I think your idea, which you write about, of raising another large internal loan, a very good one—please speak about it to Sturmer, and even to Bark. I am sure that the latter will be extremely flattered and touched, and at the same time he will be able to show you how it is done, and wherein lie the difficulties, if there are any.

Before my departure I gave the Ministers orders to work out a comprehensive plan for many years ahead for the construction of new railways, so that this new money loan would just help to bring it into practice.

N

I have just received the following telegram : " La cen-
tenaire met aux pieds des Vos Maj. sa profonde reconnais-
sance, sa fidélité à un passé toujours présent.—Leonille
Wittgenstein."
Very prettily expressed, I think.
I enclose Olga's letter, which please return to me. Poor
girl ! it is only natural that she should suffer—she hid her
feelings for so long that she had to give them vent at last.
She aspires to real personal happiness, which she has never
had.

28 April.

Thank heaven, a lovely warm day ! It was very cold
during the night, only 4°, so that I was even compelled to
shut the window ! I thank you and Tatiana for your dear
letters.
I hope that your face will not trouble you much. God
guard you, my darling Wify ! I kiss you and the children
tenderly, and thank them all for their letters.

Eternally your hubby

NICKY.

I have not been able to fix the date for my departure to
the Guards, for several reasons, which I shall explain.

" The French Ministers "—Viviani and Albert Thomas. They
had been presented to the Tsar about a week previously at Tsarskoe
Selo by M. Paléologue. BARK : P. L. Bark, the Minister of
Finance. LEONILLE WITTGENSTEIN : Princess Leonille Ivanovna
Sayn-Wittgenstein (née Princess Bariatinskaia), born in 1816.—Olga :
The Tsar's sister.

Telegram.

Stavka. 29 April, 1916.

I am very grateful for dear letters and telegram. Have
received one from her. Bright weather. I kiss all tenderly.

NICKY.

Stavka. 29 April, 1916.

MY OWN,
    Yesterday I was very busy, and could not, as usual,
begin writing to you before going to bed.

I sent Boris a written reprimand for his behaviour to his Chief of Staff—Bogaievsky.

In the course of the day I watched the experiments carried out with burning spirits of wine and kerosine, which were being projected to a given distance ! After that I enjoyed with the others a row on the river in our three dinghies. In the mornings and evenings it is always clear here, but towards midday the sky becomes overcast, which annoys me, as I want to get sunburnt, and not to be like all, or, at any rate, most of the Staff officers !

Your dear letter No. 486 has arrived—I thank you heartily. I am glad that you have decided to come here at 2 o'clock. I shall order Voeikov to work out the itinerary of our journey. The general outline of it is as follows : we leave Mogilev on the 7th, and on the 9th stop for a few hours in Vinnitza. Then we make for Kishniev, where the new division is quartered, and back to Odessa, where I shall inspect the Siberian troops—probably on the 11th. Thence to Sevastopol, for as many days as you wish. On the way back we can go together as far as Koursk, and part there, to go simultaneously to Ts. Selo and here ! Probably the 17th or 18th of May !

Now, my darling Sunny, I must finish. God preserve you and the children ! I kiss you and them tenderly. I long for you madly.

Eternally your hubby

NICKY.

I thank you very much for the charming blue flowers.

Stavka. 30 *April*, 1916.

MY BELOVED WIFY,

I thank you fondly for your dear letter. I am again very busy, and must receive a lot of people. These receptions take away much of my free time, which I usually employ in reading the newspapers and writing letters. At present I do not look through any newspapers or illustrated journals and do not play dominoes any more in the evenings. Indeed, only three of those who played dominoes are left here now. I am very disappointed that I did not succeed in seeing the Guards, but I could not possibly get away, as an incessant correspondence was being carried on between Alexeiev and Everth concerning future plans, which affect the Guards as well. Because of this, Besobrazov had to be sent for. I shall explain the reason on your arrival here.

Poor S.'s imprisonment troubles me very much. Khvostov (Justice) warned me that this would probably have to take place by order of the senator in whose hands the case is. I told him that, in my opinion, it was unjust and unnecessary; he replied that it was done in order to prevent S. from escaping from Russia, and that somebody was already spreading rumours to that effect, so as to stir up public opinion! In any case, it is disgusting.

Now I must finish this letter, my beloved. God keep you and the children!

I kiss you passionately and the children with (fatherly) tenderness.

Eternally your hubby

Boy Blue

NICKY.

" An incessant correspondence between Alexeiev and Everth." According to von Falkenhayn, the Russian attacks of March and April were " bloody sacrifices rather than attacks." " There was no doubt," he says (p. 241), " that these attacks by the Russians were simply carried out under pressure from the Western allies and for the sake of helping them."

" Poor S.'s imprisonment." The imprisonment of Soukhomlinov, regarded by the Tsar as a grave injustice.

1 *May*, 1916.

I thank you heartily for dear letter. Yesterday I was very busy; to-day too. So I could not write a long letter. The weather is getting better, though it is still very cold. It snowed a little this morning. I count the days until our meeting!

God guard you and the children! I kiss all tenderly.

Your loving

NICKY.

Stavka. 1 *May*, 1916.

MY OWN DARLING,

I thank you tenderly for your dear letter No. 488. Here is the month of May, and the nearer the date of your coming approaches, the more impatient I become ! I only hope that the weather during your stay here may be fine and warm.   As far as I remember, there was no sun at all during your last stay at Mogilev.   But that is quite another matter.

We shall stay at Odessa for 24 hours—I think you will have time to look over everything you wish to.

Boris immediately [and] very amiably replied by telegraph, so that the reprimand has done good ! Very likely Plen is mixed up in all this business.

Veselkin appeared to-day, thin and sad.   He told me that there was a set of people who were trying to break his neck by spreading libels about him.   I had heard something, and was very glad to learn that everything has turned out to be an invention; he left me completely reassured—I mean to say that he felt very much relieved when he had told me everything straight out.   His work is going on well and smoothly.

Please tell Paul, when you see him, that his appointment will take place on the 6th of May.   Besobrazov is coming here to-morrow—I shall talk it over with him once more.

Now, my beloved, it is time to go to bed, as it is late. Good-night !

2 May.

The weather is undoubtedly getting better and warmer. I have only just returned from the report.   I forgot to tell you that Romanovsky dined here yesterday—he is now on his way to France, where he is being sent with two others. He has become thinner, but looks well.

This is my last letter !   God guard you and the children ! I wish you a quiet and pleasant journey !

God grant that in three days' time we shall be together. I kiss you tenderly, my beloved Wify.

Your old hubby

NICKY.

PLEN : Colonel I. M. Plen of the Cavalry Guards, at one time attached to the Grand Duke Boris.

The appointment of the Grand Duke Paul was to the command of the Guards.

ROMANOVSKY : presumably General Romanovsky, Quartermaster-General of the 9th Army.

Telegram.

Stavka. 2 *May*, 1916.

Hearty thanks for dear letter. I have written my last letter. Beautiful weather, strong wind. I rowed on the river; was tossed from side to side on the waves, very amusing. Thought of the Little One. I embrace all closely.

NICKY.

Telegram.

Stavka. 4 *May*, 1916.

Thanks for dear telegram. I quite agree. May God bless your journey. I kiss you fondly.

NICKY.

" I quite agree." The Tsaritsa had telegraphed : " I forgot to tell you that in my opinion it would be an excellent thing to send George to Nijni, as I consider that at such a national festival, especially in war time, a representative of our family ought to be there, and George is the most suitable."

Telegram.

Gloushkovo. 17 *May*, 1916.

It feels empty and sad without you. I have finished the book. I thank you heartily for letter. Alexey and I embrace all tenderly.

NICKY.

Stavka. 18 *May*, 1916.

MY OWN DARLING,

I thank you tenderly for your sweet letter, which I had not in the least expected ! Oh, how I miss you . Our mutual journey and the time spent on the Black Sea have passed like a dream. It is a consolation for me that the

Ray of Sunshine has remained with me. I love you with an eternal love which grows continually. May God bless you, my darling !

Your
NICKY.

I kiss you and them tenderly.

" The time spent on the Black Sea." The Tsar and Tsaritsa had spent about ten days together in the Crimea.—" The Ray of Sunshine " —Alexis, who had come to the Stavka with his mother and was remaining there.

Telegram.

Stavka. 18 *May,* 1916.

Hearty thanks for telegram. I hope you have arrived safely. The weather here is fine and warm. Since yesterday we have been to play on the sands. Both are perfectly well. I miss you terribly. I kiss all tenderly.

NICKY.

Telegram.

Stavka. 19 *May,* 1916.

Am deeply touched by the sweet letter. Best wishes to Tatiana's Uhlans, and to yours. . . .

19 *May,* 1916.

MY OWN DARLING,

I thank you fondly for your dear letter, which was such a delightful surprise ! Thank God that you do not feel fatigued after our journey ! To-day the weather has suddenly become cold, with bright sunshine. We both slept excellently, side by side. Yesterday we played happily on the sand. May God guard you and the girls ! I kiss you tenderly, my dear Sunny, and them also.

Always yours
NICKY.

Stavka. 20 *May,* 1916.

MY DEARLY BELOVED WIFY,

Thank you for your dear letter, written before your arrival at Tsarskoe; I had not in the least expected to get it so soon. It was terrible seeing you go away with the girls—Baby and I immediately went into our train, and we left Koursk ten minutes after you. I took him into your coupé and let him smell your pillow and the right-hand window curtain; he was absolutely amazed at recognising the smell of your perfume, and shyly remarked that he felt sad without you. Then I kissed him, and told him to go and play " Nain Jaune," promising to take him for a little walk with me at the next station. Of course I was occupied with my beastly papers. I could begin my new book only in the evening, after he had said his prayers. It was very cold during the night, but luckily the weather cleared up and became warmer when we arrived here. We had a drive in the motor car to-day, and found a lovely place with soft sand, where he played happily. Yesterday the weather suddenly changed and it became cold—4° in the night; but the sun warmed the air, and the temperature rose to 10° in the shade. For our second drive we chose a little road along the river, and stopped about three versts below the new bridge. The sand there was as white and soft as on the seashore. Baby ran about there, shouting : " Quite like Evpatoria "—as it was very warm. Feodorov allowed him to run about barefoot—naturally he was delighted ! I took a little walk along the river up to the bridge and back, and thought of you all the time, and of our walk on the first day of your arrival here. At present it seems just a dream !

I am fairly busy now in the evenings, as the Ministers and other people wish to see me. We dine at 8 o'clock, in order to have more time after tea. So far I have no desire to have dinner in the tent—the evenings are very cold.

Alexey behaves much better at table, and sits quietly by my side. He brings much light and animation into my life here, but none the less I long and yearn for your tender love and caresses !

Separation teaches much !

When one is so often absent one begins to appreciate that which passes unnoticed, or which one does not feel so strongly, [when] living quietly at home !

Now, my dear, I must finish. God guard you and the dear girls! I kiss you all fondly. I long for you very much.

Always your

NICKY.

" Nain Jaune "—a card game, usually known as Pope Joan.

Telegram.

Stavka. 21 *May,* 1916.

Hearty thanks for dear letters. To-day is Georgie's birthday. It is again very warm. Both kiss you and the girls tenderly.

NICKY.

" Georgie's birthday "—the birthday of King George V.

Stavka. 21 *May,* 1916.

MY BELOVED WIFY,

I thank you tenderly for your dear letter. They arrive now before 12 o'clock. To-day the weather is warm, the barometer is falling—possibly there will be a thunder-storm.

How good that you have seen Yedigarov and the others!

I have received Trepov, who has just returned from the Caucasus. He visited the front at Trapezund and saw Nicolasha. He left with a good impression of him and of the whole country generally. The local inhabitants told Tr. that the native tribes have become much more loyal than they were before, and they *attribute this to the influence* of the august cousin. If that is so, so much the better. I shall receive Sturmer this evening. I have put all the questions down in writing. Yesterday I received Naoumov, who has been travelling in the East and South.

Laguiche is going to town, as he has been replaced—more correctly, he and old Pau—by the new General, Janin, Joffre's favourite. Old Pau has to undergo a cure before returning to France. We all wanted him to go to Sevastopol, but he is afraid to go *so far.* Then there is nothing else left for him but Staraia Russa.

Now it is time to finish. May God guard you and the girls! My dear, my only and my all, my tenderly beloved Wify, I kiss you passionately and tenderly. . . .

Always your

NICKY.

YEDIGAROV : Captain D. S. Yedigarov of the 17th Nijni Dragoon Regiment.—" The august cousin," the Grand Duke Nicholas. JANIN : General Janin, the French military attaché at the Stavka. " Staraia Russa "—a town in the province of Novgorod, celebrated for its clinical mud-baths.

Telegram.

Stavka. 22 *May,* 1916.

Hearty thanks for dear letters. Lovely weather. We have begun dining and lunching in the tent. Had a splendid row down the river to the new bridge. I kiss you tenderly.

NICKY.

Stavka. 22 *May,* 1916.

MY BELOVED SUNNY,

I thank you tenderly for your dear letter with the two pansies—I gave one to Baby. Now, at last, the weather has become fine and warm. Yesterday evening, when Alexey was already in bed, a thunderstorm broke out; the lightning struck somewhere near the town, it rained hard, after which the air became delightful and much fresher. We slept with the window open, which he approved of greatly. Thank God, he looks well, and has become sun-burnt!

I assume that you will have received from Grigorovitch the details of the naval battle; if not, ask him to tell you all he knows. The English have acknowledged the loss of the " Queen Mary," the " Invincible " and the " Warspite," and of 6 torpedo boat destroyers. The Germans must have lost quite as much—at any rate, more than they have published so far! Of course this is sad—but think of what we lost at Tsoucima 11 years ago!! Nearly the whole fleet!

To-night we have begun the bombardment of the Austrian

positions a little to the north of Rovno. May God bless our troops, who are so eager to begin the attack !

The naval expedition on the Black Sea has succeeded splendidly—a new division has disembarked to the west of Trapezound !

Good-bye, my love, my Sunny, soul of my soul ! May God keep you and the girls ! I kiss you tenderly.

Yours eternally

NICKY.

" The naval battle "—the Battle of Jutland. Tsoucima : the Russian fleet was annihilated in the Straits of Tsu-shima on the 27th May, 1905—the anniversary of the Tsar's coronation and of the disaster at the Kremlin, when hundreds of people were crushed to death. Of the thirty-six ships which went into action under Rojdestvensky, twenty-two were sunk, six were captured and six interned. Thus the Japanese fleet, led by Admiral Togo, won the most complete naval victory of modern times.

" Eager to begin the attack." Broussilov's great offensive began on the following day, and led to a series of brilliant victories on the Carpathian front.

Telegram.

Stavka. 23 May, 1916.

Hearty thanks for dear letters. Beautiful dry weather. I am happy about our first success in the south-west. I kiss you tenderly.

NICKY.

Stavka. 23 May, 1916.

MY DEAR WIFY,

I thank you sincerely for your dear letters. I have handed the papers concerning Mlle. Petersen over to Fred., —she will receive the 2000 Rb. He made inquiries as to why she had been sent away—it transpires that she has two brothers serving in the German army, and that she had been corresponding with them through prisoners of war, and in spite of Nicolasha's order to desist, she nevertheless persisted—that is the reason !

I gave Shavelsky orders last evening in the garden to

write for the Mother of God of Vladimir to be sent here.   I hope she will be brought in time, before the coming of our days of trial.   This morning I heard good news about the beginning of our offensive in the South-west.   So far we have taken yesterday several guns and over 12,000 prisoners, mostly Hungarians.   God grant that it may go on in this way.

You can see, from this, that I cannot absent myself from here, and, unfortunately, shall not be able to visit the Guards. This is very disappointing; the more so, as it may happen that they will be sent into action, and I have not inspected them since the month of December.

You will receive this letter on the eve of your birthday. I am distracted at not having a present for you, my beloved. Please forgive me.   I can only offer you my unbounded love and fidelity, and am terribly sorry that I shall be parted from you on this day.   The only consolation lies in the fact that *duty* to the Fatherland demands this sacrifice.   May God bless you and the girls !   I kiss you and them tenderly, my darling Sunny, my little Wify.

All yours

NICKY.

Mlle. Petersen : it appears from the Tsaritsa's letters that this lady was destitute.

The Mother of God of Vladimir : the Ikon or Image of the Holy Virgin from Vladimir, one of the ancient capitals of Russia.   The province of Vladimir borders that of Moscow to the east.   It must be remembered that the Orthodox religion was, at that time, a vital force in the life of Russia.   Certain ikons were believed to possess miraculous powers, and their presence gave confidence and courage both to the leaders and to the troops.—" Our offensive in the South-west."   Broussilov's energetic advance compelled a general retreat of the Austrian forces.

Telegram.

Stavka.   24 *May,* 1916.

I am very grateful for dear letters.   We both send you our very best and tenderest wishes and blessings.   Wonderful weather.   I embrace you closely.

NICKY.

Stavka.   24 *May*, 1916.

MY DEAR,

I thank you heartily for your dear letter.   I enclose a letter from Olga which Sandro brought from Kiev.   To-day is your birthday; my prayers for you and my thoughts of you are more heartfelt than ever !   May God bless you, and may He send you all that for which I pray daily to Him with all my heart !

I cannot express in words how sorry I am that it is impossible for me to spend these two days with you and to rest in your tender embrace !

Thank God, the news continues to be good !—our troops have captured, in all, 30,000 prisoners and many guns and machine guns.   Our dear Crimean Rifles bore themselves like real heroes, as usual, and have taken several Austrian positions at the first assault !   If our offensive develops, our cavalry may break through to the enemy's rear.

I have received a very amiable reply from Georgie, in answer to my telegram which I sent him after the naval battle.   It appears that only their cruisers fought the battle with the whole of the German fleet, and that when the English Grand Fleet came on the scene the Germans hastily retired to their harbours.

Please let Betsy Sh. know that, of course, there is no need for her to go to Germany.   I had her in view because she is such a capable and good woman.   Of course, Mak. is entirely unsuited for the post of Minister of Internal Affairs.   I wonder where these rumours originate.

Now, my love, my darling Wify, I must finish.

May God bless you !

I kiss you and the children tenderly, and hold you in a close embrace.

Eternally your

NICKY.

Betsy Sh. : Mlle. Schneider.   MAK. : A. Makarov, who had been Minister of the Interior, 1911–13.

Telegram.

Stavka. 25 *May*, 1916.

Sincerest thanks for your letter. Once more we both send you, with all our heart, our best wishes. I long for you terribly. The loss of Lord Kitchener must indeed be very distressing for Georgie. I kiss you tenderly.

NICKY.

The " Hampshire," with Lord Kitchener on board, had been lost a week previously.

Telegram.

Stavka. 26 *May*, 1916.

Many thanks for dear letters. To-day there are over 50,000 prisoners, counting from the beginning. Ideal weather. I have received her photographs. Shall I send them to you ? I kiss you tenderly.

NICKY.

Stavka. 26 *May*, 1916.

MY TREASURE,

I thank and kiss you tenderly for your dear letter. I found this " lucky bit " on a lilac bush in the garden on your birthday—I send it to you for remembrance ! The feelings I lived through yesterday were of a very mixed nature—the joy at our successes fought against the sorrow called forth by the sad news about Kitchener. But such is life; especially in war-time ! You know, of course, from the newspapers, how the number of prisoners and other trophies captured by our troops is growing. I told the Italian General that, in my opinion, their losses were counterbalanced by the victories of the Russian army, which is avenging them. He readily agreed with me, and said that the Italians would never forget our help. He is stupid, and our other foreign officers do not like him. Old Pau has at last consented to go for his cure to Essentouky before his return to France. Gen. Janin gives the impression of a well-informed military man, bears himself modestly, and is, for the most part, silent.

George has returned from the Crimea; all three brothers were together for two days. Sandro has gone to Kiev to-day. This morning I received with Baby the deputation from the 1st Life Grenadier Ekaterinoslav Regiment of the Emp. Alexander II, as to-day is the anniversary of the day on which I became their Colonel-in-Chief at the grand review in Moscow, after the coronation—20 years ago. There are only two Lieutenant-Colonels left from that time!

The old man is going away for 10 days, and I have asked Benckendorf to come here for that period. Now it is time to finish this letter, my beloved. May God bless you and the children! . . .

Eternally your
NICKY.

A " lucky bit " is a lilac bloom with five or more petals instead of the usual four. It is particularly efficacious if the finder eats it. " The Italian General " : the Italian military attaché at the Stavka, Colonel (not General) Marsengo. BENCKENDORF : General P. C. Benckendorf, Chief Marshal of the Court.

Telegram.

Stavka. 27 May, 1916.

I thank you heartily for dear letters and charming flowers. Have you found my letter of yesterday in the large envelope? In thought I am always with you. Very good news. I kiss you tenderly.

NICKY.

Stavka. 27 May, 1916.

MY BELOVED,

I thank you tenderly for your dear letter. Benckendorf has just arrived, and has given me by word of mouth the latest news of you. What a pity that it was not you yourself! Thank God, the news continues to be good!

The Staff has reckoned that the total number of German and Austrian prisoners taken by us reaches 70,000 men and a thousand officers! And the word " victory " has been used for the first time in the official communications. N.

has sent me—from himself personally—a very cordial telegram.

I understand perfectly what you mean about A. I beg you, my dear, be first of all your *own mistress*—[mistress] of your own time, and plan it out in accordance with your own duties and wishes. It is quite sufficient if you reserve for her some time after lunch or in the evening, but not both the one and the other. I sincerely wish her well, but, of course, I think that you can act with a clear conscience as you find best, according to your own habits!

Alexey and I have just received a deputation from the peasants of the Kherson Gov. (Odessa). Fancy, these dear [touching] folk have presented me with 600,000 R. from the entire population [of the province] for military requirements! Think out [some cause] to which we might devote this colossal sum; and would it not be better for me to send it to you? I have not yet decided how to spend it.

The weather is lovely and very warm, even hot, and the perspiration is streaming off my face—we shall go to the river.

The Ikon is arriving from Moscow to-morrow. A solemn reception will be prepared for it.

I must finish now. May God bless you and the children, my dear Sunny!

I kiss you and the children tenderly, and remain eternally
Your
NICKY.

Stavka. 28 *May*, 1916.
MY OWN DARLING SUNNY,

I have no time whatever to write properly. Everything is going splendidly with us. To-day the Holy Ikon of the Vlad. B. M. will be brought into our church. I am quite convinced that its blessing will be of great help to us. I love you and long for you terribly.

Gen. Williams thanks you very much for the flowers. May God bless you, my beloved! Thousands of tender kisses from
Your
NICKY.

" Vlad. B. M."   Vladimirskaia Bogia Mater—The Mother of God of Vladimir.

Telegram.

Stavka.   28 *May*, 1916.

Hearty thanks for letter and telegram.   The ikon was brought to-day and set up in our church.   Masses of people accompanied it.   Here too the heat is terrible.   Both kiss you tenderly.   God bless you !

NICKY.

Stavka.   29 *May*, 1916.

MY BELOVED WIFY,

I thank you tenderly for your dear letter.   In thought I go back to the event which took place 19 years ago, on the farm in Peterhof !   May God bless Tatiana— may God grant that she will remain as good, loving and patient a girl as she is now, and be our consolation in old age !

I have again no time at all to write.   The heat is frightful, and my hands perspire terribly.   Yesterday the soldiers carried the Ikon along the streets ;   that reminded me of Borodino.   To-morrow it will be taken to the front, to the troops which will soon begin the attack on the German positions !   Later, it will be brought here.

Thank God, the news is very good !—our troops are attacking and pressing the enemy.   The number of prisoners exceeds 100,000 men and one general—I have not found out his name yet.

I must finish now, my treasure.   May God bless you !   I kiss you tenderly.

Eternally your

NICKY.

Telegram.

Stavka.   30 *May*, 1916.

It is clear and cool now, after a very rainy morning. Very many thanks for dear letters.   I have only just

O

returned from the cinematograph. The news is still good. I kiss you fondly.

NICKY.

Stavka. 30 May, 1916.

MY BELOVED,

I thank you tenderly for your sweet letter. The heat was terrible here too for the last few days, but yesterday, after heavy rain and a real storm, the temperature has luckily dropped to 13°, and now we can again breathe easily. It seems strange that even I should suffer from the heat; our rooms were terribly stuffy—19° in the bedroom !—hence I slept rather badly. This morning it rained in torrents, and in such rain we had an exceedingly long moleben [Te Deum] in front of our house, in the presence of the troops and an enormous crowd of people. Then everybody came up to kiss the Ikon. Some time to-day it will be taken to the front, whence it will be brought back here in a week or two. Our heads and necks got thoroughly wet, to Baby's delight. After having kissed the Ikon I went to the Report, but he stood for a long time under the porch, watching the crowd ! At 12.30 it was all over—the people and the soldiers had begun to assemble as early as 10.30. The night's storm has greatly damaged the telegraph wires, for which reason we received incomplete news from the South-western front, but those which got through are highly satisfactory. So far we have taken over 1600 officers and 106,000 men. Our losses are not great on the whole, but, of course, not the same in all the armies. I am glad that you have seen N. P., and would very much like to visit them myself, but at present this is quite impossible !

New regiments are being formed now, in order to be sent to France and to Salonica. . . .

May God bless you and the girls ! I kiss you tenderly, and many, many times.

Eternally your

NICKY.

Telegram.

Stavka. 31 *May,* 1916.

We both thank you warmly for your dear letters. Beautiful weather. I was very busy. Good-night. I embrace you closely.

NICKY.

Stavka. 31 *May,* 1916.

MY DARLING WIFY,

I thank you tenderly for your dear letter. The weather is lovely at present, after yesterday's downpour. The rooms are quite cool again. I took a long walk in the woods and fields with Valia D., while Baby played by the side of the main road. Then we went to the cinematograph, which was very entertaining. To-day we are going for a trip [literally, walk] on the river, after having inspected several passing regiments at our station.

On the whole, our successes are everywhere satisfactory, with the exception of one place, just in the centre of both of our attacking flanks. The Austrian troops and some of the German divisions are making desperate efforts to break through in this place, but without result. All necessary measures are being taken for the support of our corps, and new reserves are being brought up. Here we naturally suffer heavy losses; but what is to be done! These troops have carried out their duty valiantly—they had to attract the enemy's attention, and in so doing help their neighbours.

I have heard nothing of your Crimeans! I hope that Keller will distinguish himself in some way with his cavalry; perhaps he will succeed in occupying Chernovitzi. Then our Cossacks and our 1st Koubanskaia will move towards that town.

My dear, I long for you so much! Ever since our arrival here I have not been able to touch the new book, which I should like to read; there is no time. May God bless you, my beloved Wify! I kiss you passionately and the girls tenderly.

Eternally your old

NICKY.

Chernovitzi : Czernovitz.

"The new book"—yet another story by Florence Barclay : "The Wall of Partition." It is referred to by the Tsaritsa in her letters, and later by the Tsar.

Telegram.

Stavka. 1 *June,* 1916.

Hearty thanks for dear letters and telegram. Dreary, wet weather. Good news. I kiss you fondly.

NICKY.

"Good news." During the fighting at Lokachi and Kolki in the Lutsk sector 31,000 prisoners were claimed.

Stavka. 1 *June,* 1916.

MY OWN DARLING SUNNY,

I thank you tenderly for your dear letter. Bencken-dorf has come in just at this moment, and has brought me a letter from Miechen. She is staying [literally, sitting] at Minsk, and has sent Etter with this letter and with the Pologenie concerning the organisation of her institutions. I sent Etter to Alexeiev, because this is too serious a matter to be sanctioned with one stroke of the pen ! Thank God that she has not put in an appearance in person !

Owing to hurry, I forgot to mention, last time, our visit to Pourishkevitch's train. It is not a hospital train—it consists of 3 carriages, with a library for officers and men and a field medical store, very well fitted out, and calculated to serve three army corps. He dined with us, and told us many details of interest.

Wonderful energy and a remarkable organiser ! This train has no sisters, only men. I inspected the train when it stood at our platform, where I had inspected the troops which were going to the South.

If the Guards should be moved it will be only in order to bring them a little nearer to the front. The whole of the cavalry has already moved to the West to replace the 7th Cavalry Corps, which is attacking. The weather changes continually—to-day it is colder and is raining.

My own girl, I long for you so much—it is already more than a fortnight since we parted! God guard you all! I kiss you and the girls tenderly. . . .

Eternally, beloved,
Your
NICKY.

MIECHEN: the Grand Duchess Marie Pavlovna, widow of the Tsar's uncle, the Grand Duke Vladimir. She was the daughter of the Duke of Mecklenberg-Schwerin. ETTER: A. S. von Etter, an Equerry and Councillor of State, in the service of the Grand Duchess Marie Pavlovna.—Pologenie: a draft scheme for regulations or statutes. POURISHKEVITCH: V. M. Pourishkevitch, an excitable but highly intelligent member of the Duma. He belonged to the group of the Independent Right. His name will be preserved in history as that of the man who organised the murder of Rasputin and who played the decisive part in the murder itself.

Telegram.

Stavka. 2 *June,* 1916.

Sincerest thanks for dear letters. It is very warm. At times it pours with rain! Give her our greetings. Both kiss you tenderly.

NICKY.

Stavka. 2 *June,* 1916.

MY DARLING,

I thank you tenderly for your dear letter No. 506 (only think, what a big number!). Every evening, before saying prayers with our Ray of Sunshine, I tell him the contents of your telegrams, and read all his letters aloud to him [*i.e.*, the letters received by Alexis]. He listens, lying in bed, and kisses your signature. He is beginning to be talkative, and inquires about many things, because we are alone; sometimes, when it is already getting late, I have to urge him to say his prayers. He sleeps well and quietly, and likes the window to be left open. The noise in the streets does not disturb him.

I send you several of the last photographs.—The first shows the arrival of the miracle-working Ikon, the other the Te Deum under the pouring rain. Choose the one you like best !

I received Bark yesterday; he is working out the railway loan in which you are interested. In a week's time he is going to England and France.

To-morrow I shall receive Mamantov, after which, I hope, the influx of people who come here to try my patience will temporarily cease.

I have less time for reading since the coming of the spring, because we spend much more time in the open air—usually from 3 to 6 o'clock; when we return home we drink tea, and Baby has his dinner.

Now, my joy, it is time to finish. God guard you and the girls ! I kiss your dear little face and love you ardently.

Eternally, Wify mine, all yours

NICKY.

Stavka. 3 *June*, 1916.

MY OWN DARLING,

I thank you tenderly for your dear letter No. 508. What a joy it is, on my return from the Report, to find on the table an envelope bearing your beloved writing ! I run with it into the garden after lunch, and quietly enjoy your letter all by myself. To-day a band is playing in our neighbourhood in the public gardens. It gave everybody great pleasure listening to the music during lunch—they are playing still, and crowds of people are listening. I ordered the commander of the local regiment to march through the town with the band—it has such a heartening effect ! They have already passed several times.

I have heard nothing about the wounding of Zborovsky; I only know that their division has not been moved anywhere. I shall surprise you by what I am going to say now : our front [line] railways have been working much more effectively during the last weeks.

The transport of troops from North to South was accomplished much quicker, and with better order, than formerly. The transporting of one army corps usually took about a fortnight; whereas each corps was recently transported within a week or six days! So that yesterday I addressed a few amiable words to Rongin and his subordinates! One must be just.

My beloved angel! How I long for you, thirst to see you, to kiss you and to talk to you!

I feel that I shall soon ask you to come here for a few days, to enliven us all with your charming presence. God keep you and the girls! I press you tenderly to my breast and cover you with countless kisses, my dear old Wify.

Yours eternally
NICKY.

Telegram.

Stavka. 4 *June,* 1916.

I am very grateful for dear letters and delightful photograph. Horrible weather, cold, rain. The news is good. Both kiss you fondly.

NICKY.

Stavka. 4 *June,* 1916.

My beloved Sunny,

I thank you tenderly for your dear letter and charming photographs. Please thank Tatiana, Marie and Ania also. I was delighted to get such a number of photographs, and I look at them with pleasure. Only I have nothing to stick them on with. Do not be afraid of Miechen and her pretentions. Alexeiev received Etter very coldly, and has kept the papers which I received from her. I enclose her letter, which you may tear up. She sent me this Pologenie of all her institutions. If you should find that this is a matter for the Verkh. Sov., then I shall send them to you. Alexeiev says that it is a question which concerns the Red Cross also, although it concerns the military authorities in a still greater degree.

You ask whether I will receive Prof. Rhein; in my opinion it is not worth doing.—I know beforehand all that he has to say to me. Alek asked me to postpone this till the end of the war, and I agreed. I cannot change my mind every two months—that is simply unthinkable !

Yesterday Colonel Kireiev (of the Escort) informed me that Vict. Er. is seriously wounded in the leg, that one of the young officers is slightly wounded, and that young Shvedov has fallen ill with typhus, so that there is not one officer left in the sotnia at present !

I cannot make out whether they were with Keller, or alone.

It is time for me to finish. God guard you, my sweet Wify ! I send you my heartfelt congratulations on Anastasia's birthday.

I kiss you tenderly.

Eternally your
NICKY.

Verkh. Sov. : Verkhovny Soviet, the Supreme Council. RHEIN : Professor G. Y. Rhein, a Privy Councillor and Honorary Surgeon to the Court. In September 1916 he was at the head of the Public Health Department. VICT. ER. : Victor Erastovitch Zborovsky, a lieutenant in the Imperial Convoy.—Sotnia : a Cossack unit, literally " hundred," equivalent to a squadron.

Telegram.

Stavka. 5 *June*, 1916.

I congratulate you on the day. Warmest thanks for dear letters and telegram. Chernovitzi was taken to-day. Our troops are pursuing the enemy. Am very happy. I kiss you tenderly.

NICKY.

Stavka. 5 *June*, 1916.

MY DEAR,

I thank you tenderly for dear letter. I have received Grabbe, and he has given me all your messages. I have absolutely no time for writing; it is such a nuisance !

Some days ago Alexeiev and I decided not to attack in the North, but to concentrate all our efforts a little more to the South.—*But I beg you not to tell anybody about it*, not even our Friend. Nobody must know about it. Even the troops stationed in the North continue to think that they will soon take part in an offensive—and this keeps up their spirit. Demonstrations of a very pronounced kind, even, will be continued to be made here for the same purpose. We are sending strong reinforcements to the South. Broussilov is calm and firm.

Yesterday, to my great surprise, I found in our little garden two bushes of white acacia in bloom—I send you a few flowers.

The weather is a little warmer and finer. Yes, I had quite forgotten to congratulate you on Anastasia's birthday.

May God guard you, my angel, and the girls! I cover your dear little face with ardent kisses.

Eternally your

NICKY.

" Not to attack in the North." The following quotation from Ludendorff is of special interest : " Russia's amazing victories over the Austro-Hungarian troops induced her to abandon her proposed offensive against the front of the Commander-in-Chief in the East, except for the move in the direction of Baranovitchi, and concentrate all her efforts against Austria-Hungary. The more the German front proved itself inviolable, the more eagerly did the Russians turn from it to hurl themselves against their weaker foe " (p. 220).

Stavka. 6 June, 1916.

MY BELOVED,

My heartfelt thanks for dear letter. The weather has cleared up to-day, but the air is more reminiscent of autumn than of the month of June. We went for a drive on the new road, and crossed the river by the beautiful new bridge near the little village of Dashkovka, 15 versts to the south of Mogilev. I took a little turn (on foot), and, of course, we were soaked by an unexpected downpour. Baby crept into one of the cars and kept dry. He always carries his little gun with him, and walks by the hour backwards and forwards on a certain path.

I began writing in the morning—now, after lunch, it has become warmer. Your Siberians, and the whole of the 6th Siberian Rifle Division, bore themselves heroically, and held all their positions against strong German attacks. They will receive reinforcements in two days' time, and, I hope, the new attack on Kovel will begin. If you look at the map you will understand *why* it is important for us to reach *that point*, and why the Germans help the Austrians to resist our forward movement with all their might.

Voeikov came back to-day from his estate, very satisfied with what he saw and heard in Moscow concerning our victory.

My dear, I love you and long for you desperately. I have seldom longed for you as much as I do now, in spite of having the Ray of Sunshine with me—probably it is after our last journey together. God guard you and the girls, my dear !

Thank A. for her good photograph.

1000 kisses from

Your old loving
NICKY.

" If you look at the map." Kovel is an important junction on the line midway between Brest-Litovsk and Rovno.

Telegram.

Stavka. 6 *June*, 1916.

I thank you warmly for your dear letters, A. for her photograph. The weather is much better, warmer; I rowed down the river. I kiss you tenderly.

NICKY.

Stavka. 7 *June*, 1916.

MY OWN SUNNY,

I thank you heartily for your dear letter and for the paste.

As we used to paste photographs into albums in former days when on the yacht, during rain, so I shall do now in bad weather.

After yesterday's lovely weather it started pouring with rain early this morning, and has not ceased till now. It is so dreary ! I told Alexeiev how interested you were in military affairs, and of those details which you asked for in your last letter, No. 511. He smiled and listened silently. Of course, these things have been, and are, taken into consideration; our pursuit will end on the river Souchava; all the narrow and broad gauge railways are being put right, and new ones are being constructed immediately behind our troops. Do not be surprised if a temporary lull now occurs in the military operations. Our troops will not move there until new reinforcements have come up and a diversion has been made near Pinsk. I beg you, keep it *to yourself;* not a single soul must know of it !

Taking all these circumstances into consideration, I come to the conclusion that I shall have to stay here for an indefinite period. I have therefore given Voeikov orders to send my train home for repairs, which it is in great need of. The Ikon of the Vlad. Mother of God returned from the front yesterday. The old priest who came with it from Moscow is delighted with the troops he saw, and with their spirit.

God bless you ! I embrace you passionately and cover your dear little face with ardent kisses, my dear little Wify.

Yours eternally

NICKY.

"I told Alexeiev how interested you were." Alexeiev's attitude towards the Tsaritsa, always irreproachably courteous, but firm and reserved, may be gathered from a statement which he made to General Denikin : "When the Empress's papers were examined [in the spring of 1917] she was found to be in possession of a map indicating in detail the dispositions of the troops along the entire front. Only two copies were prepared of this map, one for the Emperor and one for myself. I was very painfully impressed. God knows who may have made use of this map" (Denikin, p. 20). Alexeiev is said to have opposed the Tsaritsa's suggestion that Rasputin should visit the Stavka, and even to have threatened resignation if such a visit took place.

"Narrow and broad gauge railways." For strategical reasons the Russians had retained the broad gauge. But although this prevented the invader from making immediate use of the Russian railways, it also prevented the Russians themselves from making use of captured rolling-stock and from sending their own trains into the enemy's territory.

Stavka. 8 *June,* 1916.

MY TENDER DARLING,

Benckendorf is leaving to-day. He very much wants to take a letter for you, so I am sending you this postcard and a sprig of acacia. To-day is the anniversary of my arrival at Walton-on-T. in 1894. How far removed all this seems ! With tender and passionate love.

Always yours

NICKY.

" Walton-on-T."—Walton-on-Thames. The Tsar (then Tsare-vitch) arrived at Gravesend on 20th June, 1894, and left the same day by special train for Walton, where he was the guest of Prince Louis of Battenberg. He came by sea in the " Polar Star " from Kronstadt, and, to ensure his safety, a new department of the Civil Service was created by his father, Alexander III. Princess Alix or Alexandra of Hesse, then betrothed to Nicholas, came from Harrogate to stay with her sister, Princess Louise of Battenberg, at Walton. On the 24th the betrothed couple arrived at Windsor Castle as the guests of Queen Victoria. The Tsarevitch left England on 24th July.

Stavka. 9 *June,* 1916.

MY TREASURE,

Yesterday I had so much work to do that I had no time to write you a proper letter. To-day I shall be busy too, as I must receive old Koulomzin, Markov, the Minister of Finnish Affairs, and General Stakhovitch.—This will occupy all my time before dinner, and in the evening I shall have to look hastily through all my papers, as usual, and go to bed late. Last night I went to bed as late as 2 o'clock.

I have telegraphed through to Silaiev, asking him to con-tinue his course of treatment, as he has plenty of time for it.

The Germans are bringing up more and more troops to Kovel, as I had, as a matter of fact, expected; and now most bloody battles are raging there. All available troops are being sent to Broussilov, in order to give him as many reinforcements as possible. This damnable question of ammunition for the heavy artillery is beginning to make itself felt again. All Everth's and Kouropatkin's reserves had to be sent there; this, in conjunction with the transporting of troops, greatly complicates the work of our railways and of the Staff. But God is merciful, and I hope that in a few days or a week's time this critical phase will have passed!

The weather is quite incomprehensible—one day is lovely, and the next it pours with rain. The train came in late, hence your letter has only just been brought to me. I thank you tenderly, my beloved, my darling Wify.

God guard you! I kiss you tenderly.

Always all yours

NICKY.

KOULOMZIN: A. N. Koulomzin, Secretary of State and President of the Council from July 1915 to January 1917. He was President of the "Romanov Committee" and a member of the department which looked after the families of men who were absent on service. MARKOV: Lt.-General V. I. Markov, Secretary of State for the Grand Duchy of Finland. STAKHOVITCH: General A. P. Stakhovitch, formerly commander of His Majesty's Own (Life-Guard) Uhlans. He had held various military appointments, and in 1915 was appointed Director of the State Horse Breeding Department.

Telegram.

Stavka. 9 *June*, 1916.

I am very grateful for your letters and photographs. The sun seldom breaks through; it drizzles. The news is good. I kiss you tenderly.

NICKY.

Stavka. 10 *June*, 1916.

MY SWEET DARLING,

I thank you much for your letter. There was again no time for writing to you. I received the old Persian Prince, Zilli Sultan, who is returning to his country. He is the late Shah's brother, to whom we gave a reception in Peterhof.—Alexey sat next to his son and talked to him in

French all the time. God keep you, my dear Sunny! I kiss you and love you passionately and tenderly.

Eternally your

NICKY.

Telegram.

Stavka. 10 *June*, 1916.

Many thanks. To-day I received the old Persian Prince with his son. I had tea with George in the little summer-house near the road. Fine weather. The rain has ceased. I kiss you tenderly.

NICKY.

" Summer-house "—dacha : a lightly constructed summer residence. Those who were unable to maintain a dacha of their own used to hire one for the summer months. These houses ranged from mere huts or bungalows to handsome wooden buildings.

Telegram.

Stavka. 11 *June*, 1916.

Warmest thanks. Speak to S. about all these questions. The heavy rains continue. I thank Olga for the photographs. I kiss you tenderly.

NICKY.

Stavka. 11 *June*, 1916.

MY OWN DARLING WIFY,

I thank you tenderly for your dear letter, full of boring questions, most of which I have already touched upon in my conversation with St. He is an excellent, honest man, only, it seems to me, he cannot make up his mind to do what is necessary.—*The gravest* and most urgent question just now is the question of fuel and metals—iron and copper for munitions—because, with the shortage of metals, the factories cannot produce a sufficient quantity of cartridges and shells. It is the same with the railways. Trepov declares that they are working better than last year, and brings forward evidence to that effect, but complaints are being made, nevertheless, that they do not bring up all that they could! These affairs are a regular curse; from constant anxiety about them, I cannot make out where the truth lies. But it is imperative to act energetically and to take firm measures, in order to settle these questions once for all. As soon as the Duma is adjourned I shall call all the Ministers to this place for the discussion of these problems, and shall decide upon everything here. They persist in coming here nearly every day, and take up all my time; I usually go to bed after 1.30 a.m., spending all my time in a continual rush, with writing, reading and receptions!!! It is simply desperate!

It is warmer to-day, yet it rained twice. Yesterday I received two Persian princes. Baby amazed us all by conversing in French, during lunch, with the younger of the two!

God keep you!—I kiss you passionately and tenderly, my treasure, the girls as well. Give her my greetings.

Eternally yours

NICKY.

Stavka. 12 June, 1916.

MY BELOVED,

I thank you heartily for your dear letter, No. 516. Yes, it is indeed very sad that poor Joukov has died. Grabbe does not yet know what caused it, but supposes that grygea [hernia] prevented him from mounting his horse just at the moment when our cavalry began its pursuit of the Austrians. He evidently considered it humiliating to remain behind in the hospital, and shot himself, leaving a note, in which he says that he is finishing by suicide!

Alexeiev informed me that he has received a letter from one of the Commanders-in-Chief, who writes that the soldiers are in need of notepaper and postcards. Be an angel, and order as many as you can, and later on send them in separate packets in your small trains to the Commanding Officers of the armies.—The splendid 6th Siberian Division has suffered many losses, but has at the same time destroyed an enormous quantity of German troops, who have arrived from Verdun [literally, from under Verdun].—We take no prisoners in any place where the enemy is using explosive bullets ! This was announced officially the other day— the whole world must know of it ! Ask your wounded about it.

Our brave Keller has driven the Austrians out of the Boukovina, and has taken 60 officers and over 2000 men prisoners.—Lechitzky cannot hold him back. K. has just telegraphed to Grabbe that he is giving up the 1st Koub. sotnia with regret—it will now be replaced by the 4th Terskaia. *I beg you* to find out when they are being sent, and say good-bye to them !

God guard you ! I embrace you closely and kiss you tenderly, my treasure, my beloved Wify !

Eternally yours

NICKY.

Stavka. 13 *June*, 1916.

MY BELOVED SUNNY,

My heartfelt thanks for your dear letter. I congratulate you on the occasion of Marie's birthday; it is sad that we are not together.

To-day it is clear and warm at last, so that we could again lunch in the tent, after an interval of ten days.—The news is good. Grabbe is going home for a little while, and would like to see you.

I embrace you tenderly, and whisper words of love into your ear ! God guard you, my darling !

Always yours

NICKY.

Telegram.

Stavka. 13 *June*, 1916.

Hearty thanks for letters. My best wishes to dear Marie on the occasion of her birthday. I was busy the whole evening. The weather is fine at last, no rain. May God bless you ! I embrace you closely.

NICKY.

Stavka.   14 *June*, 1916.

MY SWEET, DARLING WIFY,

I thank you heartily for your dear letter.   I congratulate you on the seventeenth anniversary of our dear
Marie.   How the time flies !—I shall ask Alexeiev about the
academy building.   I am practically certain that the building will have to be cleared, as the need of officers for the
Gen. Staff is very great.   Heaps of vacancies are [being]
filled with officers who only completed the academy course
last year, and yet the number is not sufficient.   Only think—
our army has been doubled, and there have been some
losses among the officers of the Gen. Staff, hence the shortage
of them is more apparent every day.—I think it a mistake
to send so many wounded into the capital—it would be
better for them to be distributed for treatment in the
provinces.

There is again no time for writing.—Yesterday I received
Ignatiev, to-day I shall have to receive Naoumov, and
Schouvaiev to-morrow.

God guard you, my beloved treasure !

I kiss you tenderly and ardently.

Eternally your old

NICKY.

" The academy building." The Tsaritsa wished to retain this
building as a hospital for wounded, for which purpose it was then
used.   This hospital had been under the patronage of General
Soukhomlinov, but after his disgrace the patronage was transferred
to the Tsarevitch, Alexey.

Stavka.   15 *June*, 1916.

MY OWN PRECIOUS SUNNY,

I thank you tenderly for your dear letter.   I had a
very busy day yesterday : Marie's birthday church, a
lengthy report, lunch, hurried letter-writing, an excursion
on the river in the new fast motor launch, at 6 o'clock the
cinematograph, and after dinner another long report by
Naoumov.   After that I had to read through a heap of
papers, which lasted till 11.30, and then the three of us
drank tea with Dehn and Vlad. Nic.   To-day I shall receive

P

old Schouvaiev. As soon as the Gosoud. Soviet and the Duma are adjourned I shall gather all the Ministers here, approximately the 24th. After that you will perhaps manage to come here, if our military affairs do not prevent it.

I have had no time to look once into that charming book about Boy Blue !

My precious darling, I long for you too, and for your tender caresses ! It is dreary for me not to kiss anyone, except dear Baby—and even that only once in the morning and once in the evening. That is not enough for me !

The weather is simply ideal—so warm and dry. I should like to spend the whole day in the woods or on the river ! Kyrill arrived here yesterday from Poltava on his way to the Gv. Eq.—they are stationed not far from Molodechno.

God guard you ! I kiss you and the girls tenderly.

Always, darling Wify,

Your

NICKY.

Gosoud. Soviet—the Council of State.—Molodechno, a small town on what is now the eastern border of Lithuania.

Telegram.

Stavka. 15 *June,* 1916.

Hearty thanks. Ideal weather. I am sorry about the old Colonel. Both kiss you all tenderly.

NICKY.

" The old Colonel." A patient in the Tsaritsa's hospital who was dying.

Stavka. 16 *June,* 1916.

MY DARLING WIFY,

The courier has come in a little late to-day, probably because of the new movement of troops from North to South.

I send you the telegram which Alexey has received from his regiment.

Thank God, again good news from Lechitzky ! Yesterday

his army captured 221 officers and 10,200 men ! So many new hands for work on our fields and [in] our factories !

Miechen has written me a cold letter, in which she asks why I had not approved of her Pologenie ? I have sent it through Alexeiev to the Verkhov. Soviet. Perhaps you will tell them, through Iliin, to look through it and send me their opinion about it. She is simply insufferable—if I have time, I shall answer her very sharply. Coming back to my room after lunch I found your dear letter No. 520. Benckendorf has also arrived, as old Fred. intends to leave on business.

Please thank A. for Douvan's papers.

How I long for your sweet kisses ! Yes, beloved mine, you know *how* to give them ! . . .

It is very hot to-day, just now a few drops of rain have come down from a little isolated cloud. I hope to bathe in the river while Alexey runs barefoot on the bank. Did he describe to you how peasant boys played all sorts of games with him ?

It is time to finish, my precious darling.

God guard you all !

I kiss you fondly.

Eternally your

NICKY.

Lechitzky commanded the 9th Army. ILIIN : A. A. Iliin, Chairman of the Red Cross Society. DOUVAN : K. J. Douvan, the Mayor of Evpatoria.

Broussilov's offensive, in which Lechitzky played a dashing part, was entirely successful. More than 144,000 prisoners were claimed at this time, 4031 officers and 219 guns.

Telegram.

Stavka. 17 *June,* 1916.

Many thanks for letters and telegram. It rained hard here during the night, now it is clear. It is annoying about Keller. I embrace you closely.

NICKY.

Keller was wounded in the leg at Kimpoloung.

Stavka. 17 *June,* 1916.

MY BELOVED,

I thank you heartily for dear letter No. 521. What a pity that you have a gathering on your poor finger, and that you have to wear a bandage! Be careful, and look after it well.

There! poor Keller is wounded again—I heard of it this morning, before I received your telegram. I sincerely hope that it will not prove a long-drawn-out business. Brave man; this is for the third time during the war that he has paid with his health!

Next Tuesday our second offensive will begin there, and higher up, almost on the whole length of the front. If only we had sufficient ammunition for the *heavy* artillery, I should be quite easy. But now we shall be obliged to slacken the offensive to some extent in a week or two, in order to replenish our reserves, and this is being done very slowly [this is slow work] because of the shortage of fuel!

Thus, our military operations are being hindered only by the fact that the army does not receive a sufficient quantity of heavy ammunition.

One could crawl up a wall in sheer desperation!

Yesterday I bathed for the first time in the river outside the town—the water was fresh and fairly clean, the current very swift.

My tender darling, I love you and long for your caress! God guard you all! I kiss you tenderly.

Eternally your

NICKY.

Stavka. 18 *June,* 1916.

MY OWN DARLING,

I kiss you and thank you tenderly for your dear letter. I have again no time to write, as old Ivanov started talking after lunch like a wound-up machine. I am sending him to Finland for a review. He leaves to-day with Fredericks, whom I have, with your leave, given permission to kiss you on the brow. He is, it seems, very well pleased

with the commission entrusted to him, but does not know
how to carry it out.   The weather has improved; it has
become fresher, thank God, and I hope to be able to
bathe.

Everyone here is, of course, very sorry that Keller was
wounded just at the time when his cavalry corps was being
so useful.   I hope that he will soon recover.

How is your poor finger?

I miss you terribly, my dear Wify.   We have never been
parted for so long!   Let us hope that such separation is
not without purpose, and will be credited to us somewhere!

Now I must finish.

God guard you and the dear girls!   I kiss you tenderly
and passionately.

Eternally your faithful

NICKY.

Telegram.

Stavka.   18 *June*, 1916.

MY DARLING SUNNY,

I thank you heartily for your dear letter No. 523.
I know how difficult it is to write in this heat.   After a
heavy downpour the air has cooled considerably since this
morning, which is very pleasant.   The weather is grey and
cheerless, so Alexey and I will go at 4 o'clock to the cinematograph, which is being arranged for the soldiers on
Sundays.   He is, of course, delighted!

Shakh. has asked me to receive him, and I shall do so on
Thursday.   I telegraphed to old Sasha K., and have received
a very charming reply.

The troops are fighting wonderfully: many of the battalions, and even the [smaller] separate units, display so
much heroism in battle that it is difficult to remember every
instance.—Our Odessa Rifles are fighting like lions, but,
alas! only a fourth part of them has survived!—Your
Crimeans are getting ready to pursue the Austrians deep
into their rear.   Your Siberians have been taken back into
reserve for a rest, which they have well deserved, as well as
for reinforcements.   With God's help, our offensive will be

renewed in two days' time, with the assistance of large fresh forces.

I must finish now, dear.   God guard you all !   I kiss you and press you to my longing heart.

Eternally, my precious,

Your

NICKY.

Shakh. : Shakhovskoy.   SASHA K. : Alexandra Alexeievna Kozen, née Princess Kourakina, wife of General A. F. Kozen.   She was a lady-in-waiting.

Stavka.   20 *June*, 1916.

MY OWN DARLING,

I thank you heartily for your dear letter No. 524. I am glad that your finger is not worrying you any longer.

The weather changed suddenly yesterday : it became very windy, cold, and began raining hard.   To-day it has cleared up again—these continual fluctuations are astonishing.   We have been to a very entertaining performance (cinematograph) for soldiers, and laughed a great deal.

I am sending George to Arkhangelsk, in order that he may see how work is getting on there, and also that he may wish God-speed to our brigade which is going by a circuitous route to Salonica.   They are starting in a few days' time. To-morrow I hope to see our 1st Koub. sotnia, which is going to Tsarskoe—what a joy that will be !—When they return home, the 4th Terskaia will go to the front.   Yesterday evening our troops began an offensive in the direction of Baranovitchi, and we have taken the first line of trenches.

The English and French have also begun with some success.

Now, my treasure, it is time to finish.   God guard you all !   Thank the girls and Ania for their letters.   Tell her that I shall write soon.—I kiss you tenderly, my beloved Wify.

Eternally your old

NICKY.

Stavka. 21 *June,* 1916.

My BELOVED,

I am very grateful to you for your dear letter
No. 525, and for the congratulations on the occasion of the
regimental holiday of my Cuirassiers. I am very glad to
have Petrovsky with me; he settled down at once to his
life here—he is such a charming and cheerful boy. I also
like Mitia Dehn—he is so calm and reasonable, and a real
gentleman.

I shall speak to Vld. Nic. about the mud compresses for
Baby—it seems to me that it should not be difficult to
arrange for them here.

I am anxious to know what Miechen spoke to you about :
—of her own affairs, and of the paper sent to me; or of
something else?

Gen. Williams has been telling me of a stupid conversation
Boris had with an English officer at the Rifle's Mess at
Tsarskoe. B. seems to have declared that he was convinced
of the inevitability of war with England at the end of this
war, and that Baghdad had not been taken by us, because
they had not allowed it [*i.e.,* because England had not
allowed it]. All this is a lie. B. asserted that he had heard
this at the Stavka, but would not say from whom !
Buchanan and Sir Grey have come to know of this chatter—
it is all very disagreeable !

The news, on the whole, is good.

May God bless you and the dear girls, my dear little girl
of former years !

I kiss you tenderly and ardently and remain

Eternally your

NICKY.

Vld. Nic. : Dr. Derevenko.
The " stupid conversation," between the Grand Duke Boris and
the English Intelligence Officer, Thornhill, is circumstantially
described, with the sequel, by Sir Alfred Knox (p. 429). The
matter was reported to the British Foreign Office, and caused great
indignation in diplomatic and military circles, though it must have
been clear that it had no significance whatever. Sir Alfred Knox
and Thornhill visited the Grand Duke and forced him to withdraw
his allegations.

Telegram.

Stavka. 21 *June,* 1916.

Hearty thanks. I am sorry for Lady Sybil Grey. Lovely weather. The news is good. I kiss you fondly.

NICKY.

LADY SYBIL GREY, wounded on Red Cross service in Russia.

Stavka. 22 *June,* 1916.

MY DEAR ANGEL,

I thank you sincerely for your dear letter No. 526. I cannot understand how two of your Alexan. got wounded near Novoselitzy, when I know that they are stationed along the Dvina, a little to the north of Dvinsk ! Perhaps they were temporarily attached to another regiment—both those officers !

The offensive at Baranovitchi is developing slowly—for the same old reason—that many of our commanding generals are silly idiots, who, even after two years of warfare, have not been able to learn the first and simplest A.B.C. of the military art. I cannot tell you how angry I am with them, but I shall get my own way, and learn the truth !

I can say nothing about the Guards, as so far it has not been quite decided where they are to be sent. I am inclined to think somewhere to the South-west—but that is only a guess of mine. I shall inform you in good time.

I received Grigorovitch yesterday. To-day I shall receive Gen. Baranov, in connection with Kourlov's affairs in the Baltic provinces.

The Ministers are arriving here on Tuesday, after which I shall be more free. May God bless you and the girls ! I kiss you tenderly, my love, my dear Sunny.

Always yours

NICKY.

BARANOV : General P. P. Baranov, Commander of Her Majesty's Own (Life Guard) Uhlans, and Major Domo to the Grand Duke Michael Nicolaievitch. KOURLOV : General P. G. Kourlov, retired, at one time Assistant Minister of the Interior. He was allowed to re-enter the service during the war, and was made Chief of the

Baltic Provinces on the Civil Administration. He gave up this
post in July 1915.

Telegram.

Stavka. 22 *June*, 1916.

Sincerest thanks. I have only just inspected our 1st
Koubanskaia Sotnia; everything that they did was most
interesting. Lovely weather. I kiss all tenderly.

NICKY.

Stavka. 23 *June*, 1916.

MY DEAR SUNNY,
    I thank you most warmly for your dear letter No. 527.
    I thought that your poor little finger had got better, but
you say that it still worries you!
    Yesterday evening between 6 and 7 I went with Baby to
the station and inspected our dear Cossacks of the 1st
Kouban Sotnia. Nearly every one of the privates has
received a decoration.
    Of course they distinguished themselves. Both Keller
and the commander of the 2nd Kizliaro-Grebensky, to whom
they were attached, praised them highly. I have heard a
lot of interesting things from many of them. I invited
Rashpil and Skvortzov to dinner; among the other guests
they looked quite black. They will probably arrive at Ts.
Selo on the 25th. It would be very nice if you could receive
them before or after the Te Deum in the Feodorovsky
Sobor.
    The news from Broussilov is good—I hope that, after
receiving reinforcements, our troops will be able to attack
the enemy and press him further back. Our losses from
the very beginning—from the 22 of May—are staggering:
285,000 men! But, against this, the success is prodigious!
    I have spoken to V.N. about the mud compresses. He
said that everything could be easily arranged.
    May God bless you, my only beloved!
    I kiss and embrace you and the girls tenderly.

Eternally your

NICKY.

RASHPIL and SKVORTZOV: junior officers of the Imperial (Cossack) Convoy.

Feodorovsky Sobor, the Feodorovsky Cathedral or Cathedral of St. Feodor, the favourite church of the Tsaritsa, to which further reference is made in the correspondence.

Stavka. 24 *June,* 1916.

MY BELOVED SUNNY,

I thank you tenderly for your dear letter No. 528.

St. has written to me about these questions, and yesterday I received Shakh., and talked to him for a long time. A thunderstorm broke out during our conversation; it became quite dark, and the lightning struck something not far from the town. All the electric wires began to glow suddenly, as with fire—it was rather weird! The storm died down after dinner and the night was still, only with a terrible downpour of rain. To-day the weather is grey and uncertain —fortunately it is a little fresher.

Olga's Martinov has appeared; he looks well and hopes to continue on active service—a real molodetz!

What is this nonsense which is being talked about Sergey? He is at present just in the right place! How can one put a Grand Duke at the head of the question of supplies?

The news is good; the difficult sector of the front—near Galousia, Novoselki, Kolki—is at present occupied by our troops, who are driving the enemy out of it, pursuing him through marshy and wooded country. Owing to this, our front will be considerably shorter, whereas up to now it has been largely curved. Shcherbachev's troops scored an important success on the flank adjoining Lechitzky. Now I can say that the general picture is much more promising than it was 12 days ago.

I count eagerly the days before our meeting—perhaps at the beginning of July; if only you will not suffer from the heat living in the train!

May God bless you, my beloved!

I kiss you and the girls tenderly, and remain

Eternally your

NICKY.

St.: Sturmer. Shakh.: Shakhovskoy. MARTINOV: a junior officer reporting to the Stavka for duty. "Molodetz," a fine fellow, a bravo.

Shcherbachev commanded the 7th Army.

Stavka. 25 June, 1916.

MY BELOVED SUNNY,

Very many thanks for your long and interesting letter. Being already acquainted with the questions you deal with in your letter, I am delighted with the clearness and ease with which you set them down on paper and express your opinion, which I consider correct. I shall receive old St. on Monday, and shall reassure him on that score, spurring him on at the same time in other matters.

It goes without saying that Rodzianko has talked a lot of nonsense, but in comparison with last year his tone has changed and has become less self-confident !

Of all the foolish things which he has said, the most foolish was the suggestion of replacing St. by Grigorovitch (for the duration of the war), and also of replacing Trepov and Shakhov. For the post of the first he proposed the engineer Voskresensky (I do not know him), and for the post of the second—his tovarishch Protopopov. I have an idea that our Friend mentioned him on some occasion? I smiled, and thanked him for his advice.

The remainder of the questions dealt with the Duma and the Committee working for the provisioning of the army, of which he is a member. He had a very sad and submissive look—Alexeiev received the same impression.

Petia has just arrived; he wishes to have a talk with me; so far he has only remarked that his father already knows everything from him personally.

This flower is out of our garden, a small token of your hubby's love and longing for you. May God bless you, my precious darling, and the girls !

I kiss you all tenderly.

Eternally your

NICKY.

" I shall reassure him on that score "—the rumoured appointment of the Grand Duke Sergey to the head of Supplies and thus to a virtual military dictatorship.

RODZIANKO : M. V. Rodzianko, President of the Duma, one of the most important and most undeniably capable politicians of the time. He was extremely unpopular with the Imperial circle. His political views inclined to constitutional Liberalism and he was a member of the Octobrist party.

PROTOPOPOV : A. D. Protopopov. It is not easy to form a just idea of the character of this extraordinary man, who was generally, and no doubt rightly, described as insane. He became a very sinister figure during the last months of the Romanov dynasty. When a young man he was an officer in the Guards. He owned large estates in the province of Simbirsk, and was Marshal of the Nobility in that district. He was interested in various industrial concerns, and entered politics under the auspices of the Octobrist party. As a member of the Duma he played an active part on committees of all sorts. Socially he was fluent, plausible and charming. During the war he visited the Allies in company with other members of the Duma, and became involved with a German diplomat at Stockholm on the way back. He was said to be suffering from a disease which produces well-known mental symptoms. Turning on his former associates, he became a violent reactionary, and the most bombastic defender of the monarchist régime. " Behind his expansive fanfarronades and his turbulent activity," wrote Paléologue (Vol. III., p. 110), " there is nothing but cerebral erethism. He is a monomaniac who will presently be put under lock and key." Rasputin had met him at the house of Badmaiev, a Mongol charlatan, where Protopopov was being treated for his disease. It was certainly through Rasputin's influence and friendship that he was appointed to the Ministry of the Interior in October 1916. He was a friend of Madame Vyroubova's, and discussed political affairs with her. Why such a man was recommended by Rodzianko is a mystery. " Tovarishch "—comrade or associate.

Petia—Prince Peter of Oldenburg—evidently wished to discuss his divorce.

Telegram.

Stavka. 25 *June,* 1916.

Warmest thanks. Lovely weather. I hope the leave-taking with the Cossacks has passed off all right. Both embrace you tenderly.

NICKY.

Stavka. 26 June, 1916.

MY SWEET ANGEL,

Hearty thanks for your dear letter. I do not see the necessity for your or the girls' presence at the opening of the exhibition of military trophies. I do not understand why they make so much noise on this occasion. There is no time for writing; I only wish to say that I love you deeply and passionately. God guard you, my beloved ! I kiss you ardently.

Your

NICKY.

Stavka. 27 June, 1916.

MY DARLING,

I thank you tenderly for dear letter. Of course you can bring A. with you, though it would be more restful if we could spend those few days by ourselves !

I have returned Keller's telegram to you; I have told Alexeiev to inform him that his corps will be kept for him until his return !

How intolerable that Gherm. has again appeared on the horizon !

I shall speak to St. to-day. The conference of Ministers takes place to-morrow some time during the day. I intend to be very ungracious to them, and to let them feel how I value St., and that he is their President.

I fail to understand why the opening of the exhibition of military trophies has suddenly grown to be such a solemn ceremony, and still think your presence entirely unnecessary, or even the girls' presence.

It seems to me that Misha's Georgievsky Komitet does all this for its own glorification. I have received a telegram from their Vice-President—Sen. Dobrovolsky (a friend of Misha's)—informing me of the day of the opening.

How splendid it would be if you came here between the 3 and 11 of July ! That is Olga's namesday. To-morrow Baby's mud treatment begins. Mr. Gilliard hopes to get a month's leave—the poor man is really tired out.

May God bless you and the girls ! I kiss you tenderly, my sweet Sunny.

Eternally your

NICKY.

GHERM : Ghermogen, the Bishop of Saratov. He had been driven into retirement at the Nicolo-Ougreshky Monastery on account of his hostility to Rasputin. Now, while Rasputin was absent, he was released from his retirement through the influence of Bishop Volgi of Vladimir, and was receiving newspaper reporters.

Georgievsky Komitet—the Committee of St. George, a patriotic organisation

Telegram.

Stavka. 27 June, 1916.

Hearty thanks. Beautiful weather. I have only just received Sturmer. The news is good. I kiss you tenderly.

NICKY.

Stavka. 28 June, 1916.

MY DEAR SUNNY,

Many thanks for your dear letter.

A time of frightful bustle began for me yesterday, which is, in fact, continuing to-day.—I have received St.; we have discussed everything. Then Grigorovitch with Roussin stayed till 11 in the evening.

The rest have arrived to-day. The sitting begins at 6 o'clock in the evening and will last till dinner-time. Then several people are waiting to be received—I shall have to postpone it till to-morrow. Alas ! I have no more time ! May God bless you, my angel, my dear girl !

I kiss you and love you infinitely.

Eternally yours

NICKY.

ROUSSIN : Admiral Roussin, Chief of the Naval General Staff.

Telegram.

Stavka. 28 June, 1916.

Many thanks for letter. I have only just returned from the conference. All is well. . . .

Telegram.

Stavka. 29 *June,* 1916.

Deepest thanks. I had to receive three Ministers to-day, so could not write. Delightful weather. . . .

Stavka. 30 *June,* 1916.

MY PRECIOUS,

I thank you tenderly for both your dear letters. I could not write to you, as I was literally walking on my head, thanks to these Ministers, each of whom wished to be received separately. Now, at last, I have done with them !

Grabbe requests you to order Zborovsky to go to the Crimea for the improvement of his health. If it would be possible to place him in the Escort's barracks at Livadia he could take his old mother and sisters with him !

My head is still spinning round from all the matters which I thought of, or heard of, when the Ministers were here, and I find it very difficult to put my thoughts in order.

The thought of your early arrival here brightens everything up for me. Baby constantly asks me about the day of your arrival, and whether you will be here on his birthday ? He stands the mud treatment very well, and is as cheerful as ever. Vl. Nic. advised me to take iodine, which I am doing, without feeling any unpleasant results so far.

The weather is fine, not hot ; the nights are fortunately cool ; I bathe every day.

Igor is going to Ostashevo for a month. Petrovsky's turn has come too ; Daragan and Ghenritzi (a dragoon) are coming in their places.

May God bless you and the girls ! I kiss you and them tenderly. Give A. my greetings, and thank her for the radishes.

Eternally, my dear Sunny, your

NICKY.

PETROVSKY : Colonel N. A. Petrovsky of the Life-Guard Cuirassiers, A.D.C. to the Tsar. DARAGAN : Colonel G. M. Daragan of the Empress's Own Life-Guards, A.D.C. GHENRITZI : Captain A. V. Ghenritzi of the Life-Guard Dragoons, A.D.C.—The radishes were grown by patients in Mme. Vyroubova's hospital.

Telegram.

Stavka. 30 June, 1916.

I thank you for letter and Olga for the photographs. I saw an interesting French picture at the cinematograph to-day. Delightful weather, colder. There is no necessity to be present. I have ordered the parade to be postponed on this account. Both kiss you tenderly.

NICKY.

" No necessity to be present—" at the opening of the exhibition of war trophies.

Stavka. 1 July, 1916.

MY BELOVED,

I thank you heartily for dear letter No. 535.

How nice that you were present at the moleben [Te Deum] and took leave of our Cossacks ! To-day my ouriadnik Mouravitzky left me, and in his place arrived a new one with four crosses. He is called Svetlichny. The first was an excellent fellow—Baby loved him; he used to play all sorts of amusing tricks in the water, together with Nagorny, while bathing, and used to talk to Igor in Little-Russian.

I send you a lot of photographs which were taken by Derevenko. He asks you to take all the ones you like best. Yesterday's performance at the cinematograph was interesting—we were shown Verdun.

I permitted the families of the military to be present, so that all the side boxes were full of ladies and children, the chairs were occupied by the husbands, and the whole upper part, as usual, by soldiers. The air was not as good as [it is] without the ladies. I wonder why. I must finish. Daragan has arrived for 10 days. God guard you, my precious, sweet Sunny !

I kiss you and the girls tenderly.

Eternally yours
NICKY.

Ouriadnik—orderly, a military servant. NAGORNY : a sailor who was always in personal attendance on the Tsarevitch, and who accompanied the family to Siberia. He was killed by the Bolsheviks at Ekaterinburg.

Telegram.

Stavka. 1 *July*, 1916.

Warmest thanks. I am sure that the leave-taking has passed off well. I shall see them here. At last I am free. . . .

Stavka. 2 *July*, 1916.

My PRECIOUS WIFY,

My warmest thanks for dear letter No. 536. I am writing, as usual, after lunch, having come in from the garden with wet sleeves and boots, as Alexey has sprayed us at the fountain. It is his favourite game with Solovoy, the French General Janin, Petrovsky, Gen. Williams and the Japanese. Great animation prevails while it lasts, and peals of laughter ring out ; sometimes other guests take part in it as well. I keep an eye on order, and see that things do not go too far. I hope you will see this game when you arrive. It is so hot now that it does not take a minute to get dry. Solovoy is a cheerful and kindly lad, and Baby likes him very much. George has arrived ; thanks for the greeting sent by him. He was very interested in Arkhangelsk, and tells all the details very well.

Old St. has already asked me to receive him ; I shall do so to-morrow, on Sunday. He will probably bring with him the scheme of the chief question which was worked out during our last sitting.

There is a temporary lull now at the front, which will come to an end about the 7th. The Guards will take part too, because the time has come for breaking through the enemy's lines and taking Kovel. You will be here by then, and I shall be still happier !

God guard you and the girls ! I kiss you passionately.

Eternally yours, my love,

NICKY.

Q

" The time has come for breaking through the enemy's lines."
Of this day (16th July, new style) Ludendorff wrote : " On 16th
July the Russians, in enormous force, poured out from the Riga
bridge-head . . . and gained ground at once. We went through a
terrible time until the crisis here was overcome. . . . These battles
were not yet over at the end of July, when there were some indications that the attacks at Baranovitchi and along the whole course
of the Stockod would be resumed. We awaited these with a sinking
heart . . . our nerves were strung to the highest pitch " (pp. 226-7).

Telegram.

Stavka. 2 July, 1916.

Many thanks. Of course young Besobrazov may be
granted an extension of sick leave for another two months.
We have a thunderstorm here too, but not a big one. Both
kiss you tenderly.

NICKY.

Stavka. 3 July, 1916.

MY OWN BELOVED SUNNY,
Many thanks for dear letter.
V. Dolg. has arrived, and Aunt Olga has passed through
to Kiev on the same train. I did not manage to see her,
as I was busy with the Staff.
There is again no time ! Good news is coming from the
Caucasus. Oh, how happy I am, and Baby too, to be
seeing you soon !
God guard you, my darling Wify !
I kiss you tenderly and passionately.
Eternally your old
NICKY.

V. Dolg. : Prince Dolgorouky. Aunt OLGA : the Dowager Queen
of Greece.

Stavka. 4 July, 1916.

MY OWN TENDERLY BELOVED WIFY,
My warmest thanks for your dear long letter. Nicolai
Mikh. has arrived to-day to discuss several questions in

connection with the Imper. Historical Society, as well as with regard to his last journey on the northern rivers. Needless to say, I shall receive any brave officer whom you may send to me. Let them ask through the Staff. I constantly receive officers, colonels and generals who are returning from the front, and invite them to lunch and dinner. Many of those who have been dismissed from their appointments come with complaints, and their cases are examined here. Mogilev is like an enormous hotel, where crowds of people pass through, and where one always sees the most diverse types of men.

The weather is simply wonderful—would that I could stay all day long in the water. While Alexey is splashing about near the bank I bathe not far away from him with Kira, Petrovsky, my Cossacks and sailors.

The 4th Sotnia has arrived this morning; I have said good-bye to them, though, as a matter of fact, they are not leaving till to-morrow morning. So many good friends !

May God guard you on your journey ! This is my last letter.

I kiss you and the girls fondly, and am awaiting you eagerly.

Yours eternally, Sunny mine,

NICKY.

Telegram.

Stavka. 5 *July*, 1916.

Hearty thanks for dear letters and cornflowers. It is very hot. Both are expecting your arrival with excitement. We kiss all fondly.

NICKY.

Telegram.

Stavka. 12 *July*, 1916.

I am touched, grateful for the letter. He is feeling well—temp. 36.6. It feels very sad and empty. Happy journey. Both embrace you closely.

NICKY.

Stavka. 13 *July,* 1916.

MY OWN BELOVED,

My heartfelt thanks for both your dear letters, for the little morning note from the train, which I did not read till day-time, and for the parting letter, which Baby handed to me during St.'s report. He is quite well, thank God! slept very soundly next to his old father, and is, as usual, full of life and energy.

It is I who ought to thank you, dear, for your coming here with the girls, and for bringing me life and sun in spite of the rainy weather. I am afraid that you will be tired after all the running up and down, hither and thither. Of course I did not succeed in telling you half of what I had intended, because, when I meet you, after having been parted for long, I somehow become stupidly shy, and only sit and gaze at you, which is by itself a great joy to me.

I am so glad that we shall meet before A.'s birthday! When we were coming back from the station Baby began to think aloud, and suddenly uttered, " Alone again," very tersely and clearly.

A small party of us are now going up the river to his favourite bank. The weather is calm and cloudy, very mild. God protect you, my beloved Sunny, and the girls! I kiss you fondly.

Your old, tenderly devoted and adoring hubby

NICKY.

Stavka. 14 *July,* 1916.

MY OWN DARLING,

Nicky's train was over 3 hours late; something had happened to the engine. I shall receive him before dinner. The weather is fine, warm. I intend to send Baby for a row on the river, and shall myself go for a drive in the car; shall walk the latter part of the way over both the big bridges, take a boat at the white summer-house [dacha], which you saw, and meet Baby there.

I hope to take you there when you come next, as it will be a new walk.

We have scored some big successes on the Caucasian

front. To-morrow our second offensive begins along the
whole of Broussilov's front. The Guards are moving forward to Kovel ! May God help our brave troops ! I cannot
help getting nervous before a decisive moment, but after
it has begun a deep calm comes over me, and terrible
impatience to hear the news as soon as possible.

Eristov is a very interesting man, and all that he says is
clever and accurate. His ideas with regard to the war are
also very sound. Walks and tea-drinking are very convenient for this sort of conversation.

Dear, ask Tatiana to send me a blue box of my notepaper
of this size.

It is time to finish !

God guard you and the girls !

I kiss you tenderly, my own Sunny, the girls and A.

Eternally your

NICKY.

NICKY : Prince Nicholas of Greece, son of King George I of
Greece, generally referred to by the family as " Greek Nicky."
" Our second offensive "—the brilliant advance of the 11th Army
under Sakharov. ERISTOV : Prince G. N. Eristov, a colonel in the
Life-Guards and A.D.C. to the Tsar.

Stavka. 15 July, 1916.

MY BELOVED,

I thank you tenderly for dear letter. It is a great
joy to me to see and read what is written by your dear hand.

Yesterday I had a very lengthy and interesting conversation with Nicky. He has left this morning for Kiev to see
Mamma, then he will again return to Pavlovsk and, of
course, visit you.

I found him looking nervous and older, so I gave him an
opportunity for speaking out and for explaining Tino's
message. I must confess that the Allied diplomats have,
as usual, made many blunders : by supporting this Venizelos
we ourselves might suffer. Tino thinks that this policy of
the Allies will imperil the dynasty, and will prove [to be] a
foolish playing with fire.

All that Nicky told me is based on official documents, the copies of which he has brought with him. He intends to let only a very few people know of this, therefore I have decided to tell you before his arrival.

The old man leaves to-day. It is time to finish this letter. God guard you, my only and my all, my girl, Sunny! I kiss you ardently.

Your old
NICKY.

TINO : King Constantine of Greece.

Telegram.

Stavka. 15 *July,* 1916.

Many thanks to you and Olga. Good news. A lovely day with a slight wind. Both kiss you tenderly.

NICKY.

Stavka. 16 *July,* 1916.

MY BELOVED SUNNY,

Warmest thanks for dear letter. I have again no time for writing, as old Koulomzin has come with the report. The Guards attacked yesterday, and have moved forward considerably; thanks be to God!

They and Sakharov's army have captured over 400 officers, 20,000 men and 55 guns.—May God protect you and the girls! I kiss you tenderly, my darling Wify.

Eternally yours
NICKY.

SAKHAROV : General V. V. Sakharov, commanding the 11th Army, had been one of the most efficient staff officers in the Japanese War. On the previous day he had entered Brody—Boehm-Ermolli's headquarters—and in twelve days he took 40,000 prisoners and many guns.

Telegram.

Stavka. 16 *July,* 1916.

Hearty thanks to you and Tatiana. The news continues to be good. Delightful weather. I think of you, kiss you tenderly.

NICKY.

Stavka. 17 *July,* 1916.

MY BELOVED SUNNY,

Thank you tenderly for dear letter.

Thank God, our brave troops, in spite of heavy losses, are breaking through the lines of the enemy and moving forward ! The number of prisoners taken and of heavy guns is increasing every day. The guns which we have taken are almost exclusively German, and a third of the prisoners are also German.—They cannot withstand our onslaught in the open field. The Guards are also attacking and performing miracles. I am very happy about Paul.

It is a good thing that you receive St.—he likes your suggestions.

We take the little cadet Makarov with us on our river trips—he is a good boy, and plays quietly with Baby.—Our vaccination has taken, so that, alas ! we shall not be able to bathe for a few days.

I must finish. God guard you, my angel ! I kiss you and the girls tenderly.

Eternally yours

NICKY.

Stavka. 18 *July,* 1916.

MY TREASURE,

I have again no time to write a long letter.

Vielepolsky has arrived, and I had a long time with him. He would very much like to see you and explain this stupid affair in a few words. You know everything, and so it would not take long.

Feodorov has arrived and V.N. is leaving to-day. It is clear but windy. *I love you so deeply !* May God keep you, my dear Sunny, and the girls ! I kiss you tenderly.

Eternally your

NICKY.

Telegram.

Stavka. 18 *July*, 1916.

I am deeply grateful to you and Anastasia. Your Siberians are attacking Brody and are performing miracles. A lovely dry day. Both kiss you tenderly.

NICKY.

Stavka. 19 *July*, 1916.

MY DARLING WIFY,

I thank you heartily for your dear letter and for N.P.'s telegrams, which I return herewith. I did not know that they had already taken part in such serious battles. God protect them! If only they will not throw themselves forward on a mad, thoughtless impulse! That is my constant fear!

The lists of killed and wounded officers are sent to Petrograd to the Glavn. Stab; here we receive only the lists of colonels and regimental commanders.

Just at present there is a lull there again; fresh reinforcements are being sent. The offensive will probably be renewed about the 23rd. The regiments have to be replenished constantly, and that takes a long time.

Yes, to-day it is exactly two years since this terrible war was declared. God alone knows for how much longer it will last!

Yesterday I received our Vielepolsky and Count Olsoufiev, a member of the Council of State, who has been to England, France and Italy.

He has lost his head completely over the daughters of silly Misha. How funny! He saw Olga and Tatiana at Iza's and told them the same thing.

Now, my angel, I must finish.

God protect you and the girls!

I kiss you tenderly and passionately.

Your old hubby

NICKY.

The first passage refers to the Gvardeisky Equipage.—Glavn. Stab: Glavny Stab—Headquarters. IZA: the Baroness Buxhoev-

den, a favourite lady-in-waiting who accompanied the Imperial
Family to Tobolsk, together with Countess Ghendrikov and Mlle.
Schneider, and was the only one of the party who managed to
escape with her life.

Telegram.

Stavka.   19 *July*, 1916.

I thank you and Olga heartily.   It is colder, rained twice.
I have read the copies of both telegrams with interest.
Both kiss you fondly.

NICKY.

Stavka.   20 *July*, 1916.

MY OWN DARLING WIFY,
    I thank you heartily for your dear letter.
I send you this little note, which I received in Olga's
letter—please tell me what I am to answer to her first
question.   You see, I am writing with my new pen, which
you sent me by Chemodourov.   Teteriatin is going to-day,
after a five weeks' stay here.   To-day is the anniversary of
the moleben and the levee at the Winter Palace ! !   Do you
remember the crowd on the landing place when we were
leaving?—How far removed all this seems, and how much
has been lived through since then !
    Yesterday I saw a man whom I liked very much—Proto-
popov, Vice-President of the State Duma.—He travelled
abroad with other members of the Duma, and told me
much of interest.   He was formerly an officer in the Konno-
Grenadiersky Regiment, and Maximovitch knows him well.
    It appears that the Roumanians are at last prepared to
take part in the military operations !   The Turks have
been ordered to send part of their troops from Constantinople
to Galicia, to the assistance of the Austro-Germans.
    This is curious; but so far they have not appeared.
    Well, beloved Sunny, it is time to finish.   God guard you
and the girls !
    I kiss you tenderly and passionately.

Your old hubby

NICKY

"Her first question." The Grand Duchess Olga had written about the dismissal of a lady-in-waiting.

Stavka. 21 July, 1916.

MY PRECIOUS,

I thank you tenderly for dear letter. I have only just seen Voeikov, who has brought me your greetings. Yes, he is pleased at having got rid of the " Kouvaka " business.

I also had advised him not to be self-confident, especially on such grave questions as the end of the war ! I like old Maximovitch very much—such a decent, honest man; it is pleasant to have dealings with him.

Please insist on the " old man " not appearing here before the 6th of August.—He was to go for a cure to the Romanov. Inst. at Sevastopol, and yet Voeikov says that he intends to return here in a short time ! I think this very foolish. As you are the only person to whom he listens, I beg you to write to him that he must rest for 3 weeks on the Siverskaia.

.   .   .   .

Eristov and Kozlianonov have gone—the first to Kiev, and thence to his regiment.—I have given him a letter to deliver to Mamma. Mordvinov and Raievsky have arrived. The latter has become stout and is much more lively— probably due to the war.

It is raining. I must finish.

May God guard you, my darling Sunny, and the girls ! I kiss you. ardently.

Eternally your old

NICKY.

" Kouvaka "—the name of a mineral-water factory in the province of Penza which belonged to Voeikov. "old man "—Count Fredericks.

Telegram.

Stavka. 22 July, 1916.

We both send Marie our best wishes, and thank you and Anastasia. Bad, rainy weather. We kiss you tenderly.

NICKY.

Stavka. 22 July, 1916.

MY OWN DARLING,

Tender thanks for sweet long letter.

I am glad that you think of adding a wing to your hospital, so as to have room for soldiers also. That is good and just. I really do not know what to advise Yedigarov. If he wants to continue in military service (which is the duty of everyone in war-time) it would be better for him to enter the Caucasian Division, but not your Crimeans, because they have already over 100 officers. Or perhaps one of the three Trans-Amur Cavalry regiments—they are magnificent regiments.

I am very sorry for him, but I cannot meddle with the private affairs of the Nijegorodzy.

I forgot to congratulate you on the occasion of our Marie's namesday.

The weather is disgusting—cold, and it pours with rain every half-hour, but we shall nevertheless go for a drive in our cars, as it is bad for one to remain indoors all the time.— In addition, we have a cinematograph performance this evening.

Grigorovitch has arrived—I received him yesterday; he is going to Arkhangelsk. Baby and I await your arrival with impatience—your charming presence is worth the running backward and forward, or "bustle," as you call it.

Now I must finish, my angel.

God guard you and the girls !

I kiss you tenderly and passionately.

Your old

NICKY.

Telegram.

Stavka. 23 July, 1916.

We thank you and Olga heartily. The elbow of the left arm bends with difficulty, but there is no pain. He is in excellent spirits. It is showery, warmer. Both kiss everybody.

NICKY.

Stavka. 23 *July,* 1916.

MY BELOVED SUNNY,

I am heartily grateful for your dear letter.—The weather is still queer and disagreeable! The sun comes through every quarter of an hour, and then it rains in buckets. This morning, while we were still in bed, Alexey showed me that his elbow would not bend; then he took his temperature, and calmly announced that he had better stay in bed all day.—He had 36.5. As the weather is so damp I thought it would really be better for him to stay in ·bed. At present he is playing "Nain Jaune" with Voeik. and P.V. in our bedroom.

One of our Pages died suddenly just before breakfast, as he was shaving!—I am so sorry for him! He served a few years ago in the Semenovsky Regiment in the mixed company at Gatchina. And after lunch I heard that the inspector of the local river communications, who frequently accompanied us on our walks, got under a car in the street and broke his leg.

Yesterday we saw an interesting performance at the cinematograph and were very pleased.—Baby is playing, making a great deal of noise; he is cheerful, and has no pains at all.

Of course his indisposition is due to this vile damp weather! My beloved, with what impatience I look forward to your coming! Baby, naturally, does so too. God protect you and the girls!

I kiss you all tenderly.

Eternally, Sunny mine, your

NICKY.

Stavka. 24 *July,* 1916.

MY PRECIOUS,

I thank you heartily for your dear letters. I can imagine how busy you are, and how all these receptions and drives try you. Poor Sunny! Perhaps you will get a little rest here, if I do not bother you with requests to go out here and there.

Sandro is here for two days. He tells me much about

Mamma, Ksenia, who has gone there for a fortnight, and about Olga. Baby is quite well, thank God! He slept well, and is now getting up—2.30 o'clock.—Feodorov does not allow him to go out yet, so that he should not move about too much. But two of his little friends will come to him, and they will play quietly indoors.

The weather has improved, the sun is shining brightly. Darling, this will be my last letter, as you are coming now. May God guard you on the way!

In thoughts and prayers I am always with you!

Eternally, my beloved Wify, your old

NICKY.

Telegram.

Stavka. 24 July, 1916.

Hearty thanks for letter and telegrams. I shall be firm, and insist on compliance with my will. The elbow is better; got up from bed, but did not go out of doors. It is warmer, heavy rain only once. Both kiss you tenderly.

NICKY.

" I shall be firm "—with Prince Alek of Oldenburg, in regard to a scheme of Professor Rhein's which the former was opposing. " R." in the next telegram refers to Rhein.

Telegram.

Stavka. 25 July, 1916.

Hearty thanks. I received Alek this morning. We discussed many questions, but did not say a word about R. The elbow is well. We had a trip on the river. It is raining again. We kiss you tenderly.

NICKY.

Telegram.

Stavka. 3 August, 1916.

Once more—a happy journey. Thanks for dear letter. We both feel lonely. Good-night. We embrace you.

NICKY.

Stavka. 3 *August,* 1916.

MY BELOVED ANGEL,

I hate parting from you, and seeing the train carrying away you and the girls ! When you are with me there is *such peace in my soul;* I want to drive away all anxiety and unpleasantness and silently to enjoy your presence— of course, when we are alone. I thank you most tenderly for coming and giving me this happiness and comfort ! Now I shall be strong and brave till your next visit. I thank you sincerely also for your dear letter, which has somewhat soothed the pain of parting !

Baby has gone to have dinner with his two little friends, and I have received Count Bobrinsky, who did not stay long, and made a good impression on me. We dined in the tent; it was rather cold and damp—I would have preferred to stay on the balcony. After saying prayers with Baby I managed to finish all my papers, which always gives me some satisfaction !—Then I went for a lovely walk along the main road, and came back by the long bridge in wonderful moonlight. The air was very fresh—that is very good for one before going to sleep.

Sleep well, dear Sunny !

4 August.

The weather is wonderful and very warm.

I hope you slept well and travelled comfortably ! Baby and I felt very lonely at lunch, during our journey—in a word, the whole day till night-time. God guard you, beloved Wify, my treasure ! I cover you with passionate and tender kisses. I kiss the girls fondly.

Eternally your

NICKY.

Stavka. 5 *August,* 1916.

MY BELOVED,

Our usual drab life has begun. The bright " Sunny " days have gone, and I live in the dear memories of the past ! Darling mine, how I love you, and how intimately accustomed I am to your constant presence ! Each parting is so hard to bear, and each time I long more and more for

us to be together always. But *duty* comes before everything; we must submit and try not to repine, although it
is not easy.

After yesterday's lovely weather it rained several times
during the night; to-day the weather is unsettled—impossible to say whether it will be fine or showery! But the
air is very warm, and we intend to go for a drive in the
car up to the place which we call " skerries."

I receive every day one or another of the Ministers, and
this, together with my papers, has prevented me from seeing
Botkin's brother (the sailor) and old Dudel Adlerberg.

It is time for me to finish, beloved. God guard you
all !

I kiss you ardently.

Your old
NICKY.

" Skerries "—thus printed in the Russian edition. DUDEL
ADLERBERG : General A. A. Adlerberg, on the retired list.

Stavka. 6 August, 1916.

MY PRECIOUS SUNNY,

I thank you tenderly for your first long letter. There
is again no time for writing to you at length and for answering all your questions.—Constant receptions of Ministers or
others !—It turns out that Youry Troubetzkoy has arrived;
I shall receive him before dinner.

.   .   .   .

It is very hot.

Give A. my warmest greetings and wish her a happy
journey—I have not had a free minute to write to her.
God guard you, my beloved Wify !

I send 1000 tender kisses to you and the girls.

Eternally your old
NICKY.

YOURY TROUBETZKOY : General Prince Y. I. Troubetzkoy, formerly
the commander of the Imperial Escort, in command of the 2nd
Cavalry Division during the war.—" A happy journey." Mme.

Vyroubova and Mme. Lily Dehn, accompanied by Rasputin, were starting for Tobolsk, to pray before the relics of a new saint, recently canonised through the influence of Rasputin. This journey was undertaken by the wish of the Tsaritsa, who had vowed either to visit Tobolsk herself or to send thither her chosen representatives. The party, in a special saloon, followed the same route which was taken, a year later, by the Imperial Family on their way to exile and death.

Telegram.

Stavka. 6 August, 1916.

Both thank you tenderly for dear letters. Beautiful weather. I thank you also for the congratulations on the occasion of the regimental holiday. . . .

NICKY.

Stavka. 7 August, 1916.

MY BELOVED DARLING,

I thank you warmly for your dear letter. Thank A. for the copy she has sent me.—I have again no time to write, as Alek suddenly appeared this morning; I have only just received him, after lunch. Fortunately he was calm, spoke of Rhein's affairs and others, but did not grumble. I shall receive Mamantov this evening, and Makarov not until to-morrow, Monday. I shall order him to suppress this affair with Lopoukhin.

It is very hot; I am afraid a thunderstorm is gathering.

Good-bye till our next meeting! God guard you, my dear Wify!

I kiss you and the girls tenderly.

Eternally your old

NICKY.

" The copy she has sent me." A copy of a letter from N. P. Sablin, making serious allegations against General Besobrazov, then commanding the special Guard Corps. It was by such letters and messages that the Tsar was swayed in making appointments and in ordering dismissals. LOPOUKHIN : V. A. Lopoukhin, Acting Secretary of State, Governor of Vologda and formerly of Toula. There is no reference elsewhere to the " affair."

Telegram.

Stavka. 7 August, 1916.

Hearty thanks for dear letters. To-night I shall think of you particularly, my darling. A lovely day. I kiss you tenderly. God bless you !

NICKY.

Stavka. 8 August, 1916

MY BELOVED,

Many thanks for dear, short letter. I thought of you with particular tenderness last night and this morning, when you were receiving the Sacrament in our snug little crypt chapel.—It seems as though a year had passed since we went to Communion together, in those difficult days before my departure to this place ! I remember so well, that when I stood opposite the large ikon of Our Saviour, up above in the large church, some inner voice seemed to persuade me to come to a definite decision and to write to Nic. immediately about my resolve, independently of what our Friend said to me.

I beg you to thank Him for sending me the two flowers. Mr. Gibbs has arrived, but much later than I expected. Baby seems glad to see him.

In the meantime, till the 15th, there is a lull on the fronts, although fighting is still going on in the Boukovina. A strong offensive is developing in the centre of our front in the Caucasus.

I quite agree that N.P. should be appointed commander of the " Standart," but I must find a good post for Zelen. One really cannot drive a good man from his post only to give it to a better, and leave the first with nothing !

I am sure that it is not what you intended !

It is raining to-day, but very warm.—God guard you, my sweet Wify, and the girls !

Ask Tatiana to send me *at once* one of my silver cigar cases !

I kiss you tenderly.

Eternally your old

NICKY.

R

" Crypt chapel "—the Pestcherny Chapel in the crypt of the Feodorovsky Sobor, for which the Tsaritsa had a special fondness.— " It seems as though a year had passed." A year had actually passed, so that we may suspect an error in the text—probably " year " should be " years."—GIBBS : the English tutor to Alexey.— " A lull on the fronts." According to the Russian official figures, 350,845 men and 7757 officers had been taken by Broussilov's armies. Falkenhayn admits Austrian losses of " far more than 200,000 men in three days " (p. 249).—" Standart " the Imperial yacht. ZELEN.: Captain R. D. Zelenetzky of the Equipage. He had commanded the cruiser " Oleg " and also the " Standart." He was assistant to the Grand Duke Kyrill, who commanded the naval detachments at the front. In accordance with the Tsaritsa's wish, he was succeeded in the command of the " Standart " by N. P. Sablin.

Stavka. 9 August, 1916.

MY OWN DARLING,

There is no time for writing a long letter. I thank you a thousand times for your dear letter. I am very glad that you went to Communion. So far everything is quiet, only Sakharov continues his offensive. The weather is clear and cool to-day.

Mr. Gibbs has arrived and is beginning to settle down to our life here.

God protect you, my precious darling! I kiss you tenderly.

Your old
NICKY.

Stavka. 10 August, 1916.

MY PRECIOUS WIFY,

I thank you sincerely for your sweet letter. Yesterday evening I received Kyrill, who has returned from the Guards, where he spent 6 days. He saw many commanders and officers, and they all told him the same about old Besobrazov, what you already know, so that to-day I spoke to Alexeiev on the subject and told him that I wished to dismiss B. He, of course, agreed with me that it would be better to remove him and appoint a good general. We were both considering with whom to replace him—perhaps one of the brothers Dragomirov!—I am so annoyed at having forgotten to ask Kir. about Zelenetzky! But he is coming back in a week's time, and I shall be able to do it then. N.P. will probably arrive here on the 12th.—I shall be frightfully glad to see him again.

Dmitry will be here soon on his way through; I want to keep him here for a few weeks, because George told me that the boy has got it into his head that he will be killed.

I am already counting the days till your arrival! Beloved, I must finish. God guard you! I cover your beloved little face with ardent kisses.

Eternally your old
NICKY.

P.S. It worries me how to tell Fredericks about Olga's divorce. It is very difficult to write about such things.

Besobrazov : the Tsaritsa was exceedingly anxious to have this general removed from the command of his Guard Corps. Actually, he seems to have been a somewhat foolhardy and careless leader, and in this case her advice was possibly sound.

" Olga's divorce." Olga, the Tsar's sister, was divorcing her husband, Prince Peter of Oldenburg (" Petia "), and shortly afterwards she married Colonel V. A. Koulikovsky.

Telegram.

Stavka. 10 *August*, 1916.

Hearty thanks. I congratulate you on the 2 years anniversary of hard work in your hospital. It is clear, warm. Both kiss you tenderly.

NICKY.

Stavka. 11 *August*, 1916.

MY BELOVED CHILD,

I thank you heartily for your dear letter. Of course it would be splendid if you stopped for a few hours in Smolensk—it would give such pleasure to the wounded and the populace !

Excuse the blot which I have made on the envelope, but your pen is very capricious : at times it does not write, and then suddenly shoots out a blue fountain. Here everything is quiet on the front; in the Caucasus we have captured two Turkish regiments. I am expecting N. P. to-day.

I send you this paper from Maximovitch—I think it will be best to have each of them for a fortnight! Do you agree? Please return the paper to me. The Japanese Prince, Kanin, is coming here in September, so that Tatishchev and Bezak will go to meet him at Vladivostok and bring him here, and George will be attached to him here.

I must finish now, my darling.

God guard you and the girls! I kiss you fondly.

Eternally your old hubby

NICKY.

" Each of them for a fortnight "—officers of the Gvardeisky Equipage for duty as A.D.C.

KANIN : Prince Kotohito Kan-in, cousin to the Mikado. BEZAK : Colonel A. N. Bezak (retired) of the Cavalry Guards, an Equerry, and formerly A.D.C. to the Grand Duke Nicholas Mikhailovitch.

Telegram.

Stavka. 11 *August*, 1916.

Hearty thanks. N. P. has arrived, looks very well. Lovely warm weather. Good night. I embrace you closely.

NICKY.

Stavka. 12 *August*, 1916.

MY BELOVED,

I thank you warmly for your dear letter. I was very glad to see N. P. yesterday; he looks well. It is very interesting to listen to his tales—after evening tea we sat up till 12.30 o'clock; he was describing his life and experiences there. He praises our officers and men very highly —Kyrill told me that he had heard the same enthusiastic praises of the battalion from all the generals and officers.

We had, of course, expected this, but it is none the less very pleasant to hear it spoken of so eloquently. Summon Count Nirod, and explain everything to him for the old man. —The date is not settled yet. Olga wishes it to be made public only after the 15th of August. She also requests that her affairs should be talked over with the steward of her estate —Kodzevitch—in order to avoid complications in the future.

To-day I received Colonel Tatarinov, our military attaché in Roumania. He brought this important document, signed by them. On the 15th they will at last begin to attack the Austrians on their front.

Good-bye till we meet next, my beloved, precious Sunny. —God keep you and the girls ! I kiss you all tenderly, and remain

Eternally your old

NICKY.

NIROD : Count M. E. Nirod, a member of the Council of State.
" The steward of her estate "—originally in Russian : oupraviliaushchi kontorou.

Telegram.

Stavka. 12 August, 1916.

Warmest thanks. The time is not settled, but it must be got ready very soon. This is the answer to your question. I embrace you closely.

NICKY.

" It must be got ready." The divorce of the Grand Duchess, and its public announcement.

Stavka. 13 August, 1916.

MY BELOVED SUNNY,

I thank you heartily for your dear letter. I too have nothing interesting to tell you.

Old General Pau has come back from the Caucasus—he looks well; thin, with a handsome grey beard. He leaves to-day, and hopes to have the happiness of saying good-bye to you !

For Dragomirov's post I have chosen Gen. Gourko, who commanded the 5th Army, and is acquainted with the work on a large staff,—I intend to appoint him instead of Besobrazov.

I have no time for more now, my angel. God guard you

all! I kiss you passionately and tenderly, my precious child!

Eternally your old

NICKY.

GOURKO : General Basil Gourko, a very able, and at times a very brilliant commander. He was fifty-three. As a young soldier he had seen active service in the Pamirs. In 1899–1900 he was military attaché to the Boers, and was captured by the English. He served with distinction in the Japanese War, and became military adviser to the Octobrist party. At the beginning of the war he commanded the 1st Cavalry Division, and he succeeded in retiring with small losses after the disaster of Tannenberg. He was then promoted to the command of the 6th Corps, and in 1916 to the 5th Army. His book, in spite of certain prejudices, is remarkably fair and reasonable, and in many respects a valuable document on the war.

Telegram.

Stavka. 13 *August*, 1916.

Many thanks. Warm, misty weather. I am very grateful to you for having ordered Benck. to deliver the message. Both kiss you tenderly.

NICKY.

Stavka. 14 *August*, 1916.

MY PRECIOUS DARLING,

Tender thanks for dear letter. It is so sweet of you to have told Benckendorf about Olga's affairs, because it would have been very unpleasant for me to have informed the old man of all this in writing.

I have been afraid the whole time of what Bobrinsky told you. But it is very difficult indeed to find a man capable of being at the head of the Department of Supplies. St., being now President of the Council of Ministers, has the other Ministers under him, but if one of them got the better of him the others would not then follow his lead, and even if they did follow his lead intrigues would begin, and things would not go smoothly. There is, of course, one way out —Krivoshein's idea—to make the Minister of War master of the whole situation. But I doubt whether Shouv. or even Belaiev are the right men for this. The second of these is an extremely weak man who always gives way in everything and works very slowly. He had some disagreements with S., and hence they had to part. B. has been appointed to the Council of War.

I must finish now. May God guard you, my dear Wify, my own girl!

I kiss you and the dear little daughters fondly.

Eternally your old
NICKY.

"What Bobrinsky told you." Bobrinsky (the Minister of Agriculture) had said that Sturmer had too much to do, and that it was difficult to work with him. Sturmer's insufficiency and arrogance were weakening his position on all sides.

Stavka. 15 *August,* 1916.

MY OWN DARLING,

I thank you warmly for dear letter.

To-day is the regimental holiday of my Shirvantzy. If I am not mistaken, they are to be sent to the South as reinforcements to Sakharov and Shcherbachev. Broussilov has decided to begin his offensive on the 18th with all his armies simultaneously.

You know now that Roumania has at last declared war on Austria. This will undoubtedly help our troops in the Boukovina.

Zaionchkovsky's troops crossed the Danube yesterday, as had been decided, and are now traversing the Dobroudja. —Part of our Black Sea Fleet has entered Constanza in order to help the Roumanians, in case German submarines should attack them.

The weather is very queer; it rains heavily, it is windy, and from time to time the sun appears.

It is time to finish now.

God guard you, my little darling Wify! I kiss you and the dear girls.

Eternally your
NICKY.

The military situation in the East was now regarded as so threatening by the German Supreme Command that they decided, in spite of Allied pressure on the Somme, to transfer four divisions from the Western Front. But the great Russian offensive was already losing impetus, and it was not long before the turn of the tide. Broussilov's advance was certainly one of the most notable military achievements of the war. Nearly a million of the enemy were put out of action, and the Russians captured an enormous amount of material. Whether, after the counter-attacks of Linsingen, Bothmer and Falkenhayn, the Russians could have recovered sufficiently for a second blow, is an open question. An extremely interesting passage in this correspondence (21st to 24th September) shows how the influence of Rasputin was really the decisive factor.

Telegram.

Stavka. 15 *August,* 1916.

Warmest thanks for letter and little ikon. It is colder and clearer. In thought we are together. I embrace you closely.

NICKY.

Stavka. 16 *August,* 1916.

MY OWN DARLING,

My heartfelt thanks for your sweet, long letter, which has given me great pleasure. I return these photographs to Tatiana.

At times, when I turn over in my mind the names of one person and another for appointments, and think how things will go, it seems to me that my head will burst! The greatest problem now is the question of supplies. If we succeed in finding suitable men, all will go well, and the factories will work at high pressure. Perhaps Schouv. will prove suitable; possibly Bel. will do as Minister of War! I shall talk it all over with Alexeiev.

I have sent my prikase to poor Besobrazov, as Gourko is already on his way to take up his post. This meeting will not be of the most pleasant for either of us!

I shall send for St. and inform you about Raiev.

You probably know from the newspapers that Germany has declared war on Roumania, and Italy on Germany. Now the question remains whether Bulgaria will follow their example.

It is time to finish, my own darling Sunny.   God guard you and the dear girls !

I kiss you tenderly and remain

Eternally your old

NICKY.

BEL. : General M. A. Belaiev, succeeded Schouvaiev as Minister of War.

Telegram.

Stavka.   16 August, 1916.

Hearty thanks.   The weather is clear.   We are now going to the cinematograph.   Both kiss you fondly.

NICKY.

Stavka.   17 August, 1916.

MY TREASURE,

I thank you tenderly for your dear letter.   I am sending you some of Derev.'s photographs to choose from —make a mark on those which you would like to have, and return them.

Dmitry has arrived to-day; we talked for a long time, and about many things.   He asked permission to go up to town for about five days and bring his things for a permanent stay here.   He is happy at the thought of seeing you all soon.

O. Shavelsky has returned from his visit to Shcherba-chev's army, and is full of splendid impressions.   I was glad to hear excellent accounts of Misha's doings with his 2nd Cavalry Corps.   He, I mean to say Misha, asks permission to be allowed to come to stay with me for a few days.

I received Gourko yesterday;   had a serious talk with him, and later the three of us conferred together with Alexeiev.   Thank God, he seems just the sort of man I was in need of !   He understands perfectly how to conduct himself with the Guards and so forth.   Besobrazov has not arrived yet.

The weather is good on the whole, but during the day it is always dull.

Baby's little companion is also leaving to-morrow—he will miss him greatly !

Farewell till our next meeting. God guard you, my dear child ! I kiss you and the dear little daughters tenderly, and remain

Eternally your old

NICKY.

Telegram.

Stavka. 17 *August,* 1916.

Hearty thanks. It is a pity that you have such weather. Here it is clear. We count the days before your arrival. Both kiss you fondly.

NICKY.

Stavka. 18 *August,* 1916.

MY OWN DARLING,

I thank you tenderly for sweet letter. To-day the weather is at last delightful and warm, as in summer.

Well, yesterday I received Besobrazov, had a long conversation with him, and was pleased with the manner in which he bore himself; this showed me once more what an honest and well-bred man he is ! I have given him leave for two months. He intends to go through a course of treatment at the Caucasian watering-places [spas], and asks to be given any appointment in the army. I have promised him that if his health permits and if some vacancies occur in one of the Guard Corps to appoint him there ! He was very good at the head of a Guard Corps, so why not give him a lower post, in which he can be useful, with his ability, in spite of having occupied a higher [position] ?

Gourko, with whom I discussed this the other day, told me that it was a sensible plan—to appoint generals (of course those who have not done anything wrong [not incurred any guilt]) back to their penultimate positions; as it was, for instance, with Scheidemann or Mishchenko, and others. I quite agree with him.

Dmitry is going back to-day. I wait for you with great impatience, and intend to keep you here as long as possible.

God guard you, my beloved, my darling Sunny!
I kiss you tenderly.

Your old

NICKY.

Stavka. 19 *August,* 1916.

MY OWN TREASURE,

My warmest thanks for dear letters. Yes, up to now
we have managed the whole time to lunch and dine in the
tent in fine weather and on the balcony in wet.

You ask which Gourko has been given the new appoint-
ment? It is the little General who commanded the 1st
Cavalry Division in Moscow. Groten approved of him as
Commanding Officer. Up to now he commanded the 5th
Army at Dvinsk, and now Dragomirov is being appointed
in his place.

Thank God, the news is good—on the first day of our
offensive we took 300 officers and over 15,000 Austrian and
German soldiers prisoners. The Roumanians have, it seems,
been successful also: for a start, they have occupied three
towns not far from the frontier. How terrible, what you
write about Petrovsky's wife! Poor boy!

The weather is wonderful, real summer; I hope it will
last until your arrival!

.   .   .   .   .   .

Good-bye till we meet next, dear. May God guard you
and all! I kiss you very tenderly.

Eternally your old

NICKY.

P.S. Tell Tatiana to bring with her, also, 8 boxes of
Serbian tobacco.

Kisses.

GROTEN: General P. P. Groten of the Imperial Escort. He
commanded the 1st Soumski Hussars, and then the Life-Guard
Grenadiers.

"The news is good." The Russian troops were advancing in
Volhynia, and at the same time the Roumanians were moving
forward and had occupied Hermannstadt.

Stavka. 20 *August,* 1916.

MY TENDERLY BELOVED,

My heartfelt thanks for dear letter. I, too, am in a great hurry, because I had to receive crowds of people after lunch.

I am mad with joy at the thought of seeing you soon.

I send you this little paper which Grabbe handed to me. I do not know in which battle these poor fellows were killed and wounded ! It was quite near the Roumanian frontier—at Dorna-Vatra.

Our troops had orders to attack there.

At last it has become warm !

Benckendorf has arrived and has brought me a paper from Freder. concerning Olga's divorce. It will have to be sent on to the Synod, and then everything will be in order. Now I must finish, my precious. God guard you !

This is my last letter. Your loving and impatient hubby kisses you tenderly.

NICKY.

Stavka. 4 *September,* 1916.

MY BELOVED WIFY,

Thank you tenderly for your dear letter and for those few lines which you wrote on a piece of paper and left in my pocket-book. It is I who ought to thank you for coming here for the sake of us both : it is not so very comfortable for you in the train—all sorts of noises and the whistles of the engines continue all through the night ! We are very much more comfortable in this house, so that Alexis and I ought to be grateful to you. It was very sad and distressing coming back from the station. I plunged into my papers and he went to have his dinner. He said his prayers hurriedly and is now sound asleep.

It is cold and damp outside, and I intend to go to bed early. During dinner Sergey and Kyrill were my neighbours; the latter had only just returned from the inspection of our river flotilla on the Prypiat, and he told me much of interest. The others made a lot of noise at the table, as I foresaw at lunch.

My dear child, how I long for our evening talks! Though the others were sometimes in the way (Dmitry and Igor, etc.), it was none the less great joy to see each other. This time there was luckily no bustle. I was so glad that you spent this anniversary here!

I am convinced that your stay here gives pleasure to everyone at Headquarters, especially to the lower ranks. Dmitry is so sorry that the girls have gone—their presence puts him always in a good humour. I think that Igor also regrets their departure, but I have no intention of asking him about it!

5 September.

Good-morning, my dear!

The sun is shining and warming us, but in the shade it is cold. And you, poor dears, are being carried back to the North, where autumn is in full swing and the leaves are getting yellow and are falling. Your dear letter has greatly consoled me—I have read it several times over and kissed the dear lines.

To-day is the regimental holiday of the Cavalry Guards. We have only just finished lunch, and think of going for a motor drive in the wood, as it has again clouded over.

Artillery cross-fire is going on at the front, and strong counter attacks by the 7th Army, where our troops have driven the enemy back, inflicting heavy losses. In Roumania, by the Danube, their troops held out better, but the general situation is good. The Serbs are attacking at Salonica and have hurled back the Bulgars.

My dear, I must finish. God guard you all! I kiss you all tenderly.

Your old

NICKY.

In regard to the military situation, it may be noted that heavy fighting was in progress at Merisor in Transylvania. The Russian and Roumanian forces were compelled to retire, and fell back to the Rasova-Tuzla line.

Stavka. 5 September, 1916.

MY BELOVED,

I am beginning this letter before going to sleep, as I have a strong desire to talk a little with you quietly. All my papers are sealed, and I have only just finished drinking tea with some of my suite. I am glad to hear that you arrived safely. It is a pity it is so cold. Here it is cool too. Baby and I felt cold in our rooms, and I gave orders to have the stoves lit, so as to remove the dampness. The windows are left open in the day-time—in this way the air is kept fresh. My pen writes appallingly badly; when I have finished writing and shut it up the ink splutters out in bubbles !

To-day we went for a walk on a new and pretty road, the beginning of which we have often passed before—it reminded me of the road in Spala. All along the road there are picturesque places and beautiful trees.

After tea I received Shakhovskoy and had a long talk with him. He is really a good, honest man. He told me some interesting things about N. and others in the Caucasus, where he has been lately, and has seen them all !

6 September.

Good-night, my dear; it is time to go to sleep.

The weather is bright and warm again. In the morning I was busy and had no time to write. God guard you, my beloved, and the girls ! I kiss you tenderly, and also A. and our Friend.

Eternally your

NICKY.

Stavka. 7 September, 1916.

MY DEAR,

Your letter has not arrived yet, as the train was late, owing to a slight mishap with another train. Mamantov was due to arrive by it.

Fortunately it is much warmer to-day—the weather is grey and windy. Yesterday's cinematograph was really very interesting. We talked of it the whole evening !

Grigorovitch has arrived with Roussin. In his opinion, things are not quite satisfactory with the Supreme Command of the Baltic Fleet. Kanin has become weak, owing to his illness, and has allowed them to get slack. Therefore it is necessary to replace him by someone else. The most suitable person for the post would be the young Admiral Nepenin, the Chief of the Liaison Service of the Baltic Fleet. I have agreed to sign the appointment. The new Admiral has already gone to sea to-day. He is a friend of Kolchak of the Black Sea, his senior by two years, and just as strong-willed and able. God grant that he may prove worthy of his high position!

I am constantly thinking of you, my dear, and am very glad that our Friend has arrived. May God bless you and the girls, my beloved Wify! Fond kisses.

Eternally your old
NICKY.

" Liaison Service of the Baltic Fleet "—in Russian in the original : " Nachalnik Sloujbi Balt. Flota."
Admiral Kolchak, well known later as a " White " leader.

Telegram.

Stavka. 7 *September,* 1916.

Many thanks for the dear letters and for the photographs, also for both the telegrams. There is no news. Everything is quiet these days. I kiss you all tenderly.

NICKY.

Stavka. 8 *September,* 1916.

MY BELOVED SUNNY,

Your dear, long letter with the enclosures of a few petitions has given me tremendous pleasure. I am extremely grateful to you for it.

What you told me yesterday of Grabbe and what he told Nini greatly surprised me. I remember some time in the summer Igor spoke of arranging tennis here, expressing the hope that I would come and watch the play. I answered him that he should mind his own business and not interfere with other people's. The same evening at tea I was left alone with Grabbe, and he told me how right I was to refuse to visit that place, which is frequented by Mme. Soldat[en-kov] and other ladies, as it would probably have given rise to all sorts of absurd gossip. So I do not know how to reconcile these two facts—I mean, what Grabbe told N. and then me.

My beloved, you may be quite sure that I shall *not make her acquaintance*, whoever may wish it. But you, for your part, must not allow A. to bother you with stupid tale-bearing—that will do no good, either to yourself or to others.

Indeed, the losses in the poor Guards were again very heavy; so far I know no details.

Good-bye, may God bless you, my darling Wify,
Many kisses.

Eternally your old
NICKY.

" The enclosures of a few petitions." These were from humble people, asking for personal favours.—NINI : Mme. Nini Voeikova, the wife of General Voeikov and daughter of Count Fredericks.— Mme. SOLDATENKOV ; apparently the wife of a captain in one of the squadrons of the Emperor's Own Cossacks.

Stavka. 9 *September,* 1916.

Thank you with all my heart for your dear, long letter, in which you pass on Friend's message.

It seems to me that this Protopopov is a good man, but he has much to do with Factories, etc. Rodzianko has for a long time suggested him for the post of Minister of Trade, instead of Shakhovskoy. I must consider this question, as it has taken me completely by surprise. Our Friend's opinions of people are sometimes very strange, as you know yourself—therefore one must be careful, especially with appointments to high offices. I do not personally know this Klimovitch. Would it be wise to discharge them at the same time ? That is, I mean to say, the Minister of the Interior and the Chief of Police ? This must be thought out very carefully. And whom am I to begin with? All these changes make my head go round. In my opinion, they are too frequent. In any case, they are not good for the internal situation of the country, as each new man brings with him alterations in the administration.

I am very sorry that my letter has turned out to be so dull, but I had to answer your questions.

May God bless you and the girls. . . .

Eternally your old

NICKY.

This letter is of peculiar interest, since it shows that the Tsar did not always concur in Rasputin's choice of men for the higher offices of the State. It is not easy to say whether this independence of opinion was due solely to the absence of the Tsaritsa's personal influence, or whether it was the result of contact with sensible advisers like Alexeiev. Rasputin, according to the Tsaritsa's letter of the previous day, was urging the desirability of appointing Proto-popov to the Ministry of the Interior. The appointment was actually made in the following month, but the Tsar's hesitation is noteworthy.

KLIMOVITCH : General E. C. Klimovitch was formerly the Mayor of Rostov and Kerch, and was Chief of Police in Moscow. The Tsaritsa desired his dismissal because he " hated our Friend "—a reason which was generally sufficient. The Minister of the Interior was A. N. Khvostov.

Telegram.

Stavka. 9 September, 1916.

Many thanks for your dear letters. It is clear, colder. Silaiev has arrived. Tender kisses.

NICKY.

Stavka. 10 September, 1916.

MY BELOVED,

Best thanks for your dear letter. Please thank the girls for their letters—I have no time to answer them. The photographs sent to them by Demenkov are very interesting. Sturmer and Count Nirod have arrived for to-morrow's reception of the Japanese Prince. I shall receive them both separately to-day before dinner.

S

So, as I have learnt from your telegram, the poor Princess Ghendrikova is dead.   For her sake and her children's sake that is a merciful release.

You wish me to come home for a day or two, but unfortunately that is at present quite impossible : in view of the enormous preparatory labour for the coming operations I cannot now absent myself from my Staff.   I am afraid the atmosphere of Petrograd is depressing you, which is not noticeable here.   I would, of course, have come with pleasure, in the first place to see you and secondly to have a bathe in my reservoir.   God grant that I may be able to do so in the autumn, as I did last year !

Baby has probably already written to tell you that we are conducting some excavations near the little chapel.

I must now finish.   May God bless you and the girls ! I kiss you and them tenderly, my darling Sunny.

Eternally your old

NICKY.

Telegram.

Stavka.   10 *September*, 1916.

Thank you with all my heart for your dear letters.   It shall be done.   Please tell Nastenka that I am very grieved about her mother's death.   Clear, cold weather.   Both kiss you tenderly.

NICKY.

" It shall be done "—refers to the appointment of Protopopov. —NASTENKA : Countess Ghendrikova, a lady-in-waiting, one of those who accompanied the Imperial Family to Siberia, and was there killed by the Bolsheviks.

Telegram.

Stavka.   11 *September*, 1916.

It would be better to send your seventh train to the Caucasus.   I am just off to the station to meet the Prince. A beautiful sunny day.   Love.

NICKY.

" The Prince."   Prince Kotohito Kan-in, already referred to.

Stavka. 11 *September*, 1916.

MY OWN DARLING,

Warmest thanks for your dear letter. I have only just finished having lunch with Prince Kanin. He is a pleasant man and speaks French very well. He visited us in 1900. Fortunately the weather is bright and warm. He brought charming Japanese presents for me and Baby. I have no time for more. I embrace you fondly, my own darling, and the girls.

Eternally your old

NICKY.

Stavka. 12 *September*, 1916.

Many thanks for your dear letter and your love. Yesterday's reception of the Japanese went off beautifully. We received him with great pomp, and the weather was ideal. In the course of the day George went for a drive with the Prince, and we met them at the place where we are excavating, close to the future chapel.

He has brought me and Alexis some exquisite presents from the Emperor and himself. I shall send them to Tsarskoe—please have the boxes opened and look over the things. The most beautiful of all is a cloisonné picture representing a peacock—it is terribly heavy, but of admirable workmanship.

Alexis was very glad to see the Japanese General with whom he played last year—he has now arrived with the Prince's retinue.

George looks after them as a careful tutor would look after children. Mamma is receiving them to-day at Kiev. You will see them on the 15th. I would like also to pay you a visit. . . . When will it be possible, though?

Now I must finish. May God bless you and keep you well! Warmest greetings to you, to the girls and to her.

Eternally yours, my darling,

NICKY.

Telegram.

Stavka. 12 *September,* 1916.

Hearty thanks. Yesterday's visit went off successfully. Beautiful weather. Both kiss you fondly.

NICKY.

Stavka. 13 *September,* 1916.

MY DEAREST WIFY,

My very best thanks for your dear letter. This time I must take Miechen's part; a few days ago she passed here on her way and left a letter, in which she asked permission to be allowed to stay in Livadia, in one of the houses under the Court jurisdiction, adding that it would be inconvenient for her to stay at a hotel in Yalta. I then telegraphed her my consent. What else was to be done?

I am sending you a few illustrations out of a newspaper and a letter from Mavra, with a cutting, which I have not read. It is very warm to-day, 11° in the shade, and the air is beautiful, so that we are going up the river, as usual, which we have not done for over a week. Yesterday we excavated in another place, but again found nothing. It is funny how Alexis loves digging.

There is little news from the front, because we are preparing a new offensive. Kira has received a long letter from Drenteln; he will bring me a copy, and then I shall send it along to you. The only means of saving our sailors is by sending them to the Black Sea—there they can rest, and with God's help prepare for the final expedition to Constantinople, as was intended last spring.

Now good-bye. May God bless you and the dear girls! I kiss you and them fondly, my darling,

Eternally your

NICKY.

" This time I must take Miechen's part." The Tsaritsa had written complaining of the " beastly impertinence " of Miechen—the Grand Duchess Marie Pavlovna—in applying to the Marshal of the Court for linen and servants.—MAVRA : the Grand Duchess Elizavieta Mavrikievna, wife of the Grand Duke Constantine Constantinovitch. —" Saving our sailors "—of the Equipage.

Stavka. 14 *September,* 1916.

MY DARLING,

Thank you warmly for your dear letter. It is very sad that you are not feeling very strong; take care of yourself, if not for your own sake, then at least for mine, and for the sake of the wounded. I am forwarding you Drenteln's letter to Freder. I was quite sure that, with the departure of Besobrazov, the Guards would be at a loose end—I think I have already spoken to you of it! Gourko would undoubtedly have been better at the head of the Guards than General Kaledin, though the latter is a good general and was very successful during our last offensive in May. I had no time to include the Guards in my reserves, as they were hurried off into new positions. Of course the enemy had time to fortify his lines and bring up an enormous quantity of heavy artillery and troops. God only knows how this new offensive will end!

For the last few days the weather has been splendid and warm, but to-day it is much colder.

God guard you, my darling Wify. Tender kisses to you and the girls.

Eternally your

NICKY.

KALEDIN : General Kaledin, then commanding the 8th Army, was Ataman of the Don Cossacks. He committed suicide when his men went over to the Revolution.

Stavka. 15 *September,* 1916.

MY PRECIOUS,

I am very, very grateful to you for your dear letter. It seems to me that you ought to speak to Sturmer about Daisy's telegram, as the matter concerns two Ministries—the War Ministry and that of Foreign Affairs. I am also sending you a letter which I received yesterday from Dolly, Evgeni's daughter. She brought it herself, and insisted on being allowed to see me. Owing to deceit and false tales at the station, she penetrated into Feodorov's room, where she told him a long story of some detachment of hers, of her wish to get through to the South, away from Dvinsk, and so forth.

Nilov, who now replaces Voeikov, was most indignant, and got her out of the house only by promising to deliver this letter. Dreadful! She requests the title of Duchess of Leuchtenberg—after that, you may be sure, she will demand money from the districts, to which she has no shadow of right.

A little while ago I received Silaiev; he has returned to the regiment, but does not know for how long he can remain. It is such a pity !

My dear, I am already dreaming of our meeting in the near future. Though I am inundated with work, in thought I am always with you.

Yes, only think of it, it is fifty years since Mamma came to Russia !

May God guard you ! Many fond kisses, my beloved, for you and the girls.

Eternally yours

NICKY.

DAISY: Princess Margaret of Sweden. DOLLY: Baroness Daria Grevenitz, formerly the wife of Prince Kotchubey, daughter of the Duke of Leuchtenberg.

Telegram.

Stavka. 15 September, 1916.

Hearty thanks. I am glad to know that the visit has been successful. Sandro has arrived from Kiev for a day. Clear, cold weather. Many kisses.

NICKY.

Stavka. 16 September, 1916.

MY OWN DARLING,

Thank you with all my heart for the dear letter. I am glad that the visit of the Japanese and lunch with them passed off all right, but I am very sorry that you tired yourself out. Take care of yourself and do not overtire your poor dear heart. To-day I wrote to dear Mamma and to Sandro. It appears that that idiot Rodzianko has written him a very impertinent official letter, to which Sandro intends answering very sharply. He read out to me some extracts from both of the letters—Rodzianko's and his own. His answer is very well expressed.

As far as I can judge from Kyrill's words, a slight misunderstanding occurred in connection with the " Standart." I have never given any orders to Grigorovitch, but only asked him about this post for Zelenetsky in the future and expressed to him my desire that N.P. should get our yacht after Z. I spoke of this to the Admiral also; he took it quite calmly, only asking if it could be done towards the end of the war, when the boilers will be put in and the repairs of the yacht finished. Apart from that, Z. really does everything for Kyrill in the Equipage, as he is often absent. And finally, I wish to have N.P. by me during the war, and he could not absent himself from the service if he was Captain now.

You understand, do you not?

I must finish now, my beloved Girly. May God guard you and the dear girls. Many kisses.

Eternally your old

NICKY.

Stavka. 17 *September*, 1916.

MY TENDERLY BELOVED,

. . . . . .

After a few bright days the weather has taken a sudden turn for the worse, and now it rains incessantly; it is warm and dark, but perhaps it's just as well, as in any case we could not have gone out, because of Baby's swelling on the foot, or rather instep. He cannot put on his shoes, but fortunately there is no pain. He is dressed and is spending the whole day in the room with the round windows! Of course I shall go for a turn in the garden. On board ship, or at Livadia, we should be pasting photographs into albums in such weather.

I told Alexeiev about our sailors' battalion—they will be sent back at once after this battle. Seven corps will take part in the offensive. If only God would grant them success!

How many weeks already I have worried over this If

we had more heavy artillery, there would not be the slightest doubt as to the outcome of the struggle.   Like the French and English, they paralyse all resistance solely by the terrible fire of their heavy guns.—That was the case with us at the beginning of our offensive.

May God guard you and the girls !   I kiss you tenderly, my dear Sunny, my only and all.   Kisses for the girls.

Eternally your
NICKY.

Stavka.   18 September, 1916.

MY OWN DARLING,

The Reports are finished sooner than usual, and I will take this opportunity of beginning my letter to you before lunch.   To-day there will be a lot of visitors, because it is Sunday.   Alek has also returned from his journey to Reni and Roumania.   The weather is bright and clear, quite unlike yesterday.   Baby's swollen foot is better—he is quite cheerful.   During the day we played " Nain Jaune " together. I went to Vespers, after which O. Shavelsky introduced me to an old local priest; he is 95 years old, but looks not more than 70.—I have only just finished lunch and a talk with Alek.

Best thanks for your dear letter.—No, I have not told Petia of his release yet—anyway, it will soon be made public !

Sandro thinks that Olga ought to wait, but she will not listen to him.

I shall speak to Sergey about those 40 guns at T.S.   He told me a little while ago that heavy artillery was being concentrated there.   Why act behind his back?

Who sent me the last photographs?   Am I to select a few for myself, or are they all intended for me and Alexis?   The old Ivanov came back from Finland a few days ago—he cannot stand that country !

I must finish, my darling.   God take care of you and the girls !   I kiss you all tenderly, and her also.

I embrace you closely, my treasure.

Eternally your old
NICKY.

" I have not told Petia of his release." A reference to the divorce of Prince Peter of Oldenburg.—" Olga ought to wait "—before marrying Colonel Koulikovsky.

" Those 40 guns at T.S." Artillery, mostly of English manufacture, shipped to Arkhangel, was being massed at Tsarskoe Selo, and apparently delayed there before being sent to the front. The matter concerned the Grand Duke Sergey as Inspector-General of Artillery.

Stavka. 19 *September*, 1916.

MY OWN DARLING,

Thank you very much for your charming and loving letter. Last night I looked through all your letters, and noticed that in June you suddenly jumped from No. 545 to No. 555. So that now all your letters are numbered wrong. How do you know that Goutchkov and Alex. write to each other? I never heard of it before.

Is it not a curious coincidence that the Colonel who is in charge of the heavy artillery which is now being formed up at T.S. came here on duty and had lunch with me a little while ago? I asked him questions about many things, and he told me that every battery has one sentry on guard; that on two nights thefts had occurred, owing to darkness —on one occasion the sentry himself proved to be the thief— and that some very expensive metal component parts of the heavy English guns are being constantly stolen on their way from Arkhangelsk to T.S. Sergey knew all about it already, and all necessary precautions will be taken.

Before his departure Fred. sent me a whole bundle of letters of Count Pahlen's to his wife, in which he condemns in very sharp terms the military censorship, the rear, and so forth. The old man requests me to deprive him of Court rank, to which I give my consent, though I realise that it is too severe a punishment. Mamma has also written to you about it.

I must finish, my beloved Wify. God guard you! I kiss the girls and you, my own darling.

Eternally your

NICKY.

Alex. : Alexeiev. The examination of private correspondence in the " Black Box " department of the Post Office was a matter of routine; but it is probable that the statement concerning this correspondence came from Mme. Vyroubova. Count Pahlen's letters, referred to below, were doubtless intercepted by the postal authorities in the course of their duty.

PAHLEN : Count C. C. Pahlen was a Marshal of the Court, a Senator and a Privy Councillor.

Telegram.

Stavka. 19 *September,* 1916.

Warmest thanks for letter and information. It is cold and dull as before. Hope you will soon be better. Both embrace you.

NICKY.

Stavka. 20 *September,* 1916.

MY DEAR SUNNY,

Best thanks for your letter. To-day arrived Grabbe, Maximovitch and N.P.—up to now there were only a few of us. Baby's foot is better and he walks again freely.

Together with military matters, the eternal question of supplies troubles me most of all. Alexeiev gave me to-day a letter which he received from the charming Prince Obolensky, the President of the Committee of Supplies. He confesses frankly *that they cannot alleviate the situation in any way,* that they are working in vain, that the Ministry of Agriculture pays no attention to their regulations, that the prices are soaring and the people beginning to starve. It is obvious where this situation may lead the country.

Old St. cannot overcome these difficulties. I do not see any other way out, except by transferring the matter to the military authorities, but that also has its disadvantages ! It is the most damnable problem I have ever come across ! I never was a business man, and simply do not understand anything in these questions of supplying and provisioning.

I must finish now, my own. May God preserve you and the girls ! Many kisses.

Eternally your old

NICKY.

Telegram.

Stavka. 20 September, 1916.

Sincerest thanks. We have also dull, rainy weather. I have just come back from the cinematograph. The news is not very good. Embrace you tenderly.

NICKY.

Stavka. 21 *September,* 1916.

MY BELOVED,

The train is very late to-day and your letter has not yet arrived. The weather is again bright and not very cold. Thank Tatiana for the photographs and ask her to send me some more of my note-paper (one of the blue boxes). My yesterday's sense of depression has passed off. I told Alexeiev to order Broussilov to stop our hopeless attacks, so as to withdraw the Guards and part of the other troops from the front lines, give them time to rest and make up their strength. We must launch an attack near Galitch and more to the south at Dorna-Vatra, so as to help the Roumanians and cross the Carpathians before the winter sets in. The reinforcements necessary for this will be sent up.

N.P. told me that he was pleased with your general appearance. Try to get well, my darling, before you come down here in a fortnight's time!

To-day is Paul's birthday and the namesday of Dmitry and Dm. Sherem., so at lunch we each drank a glass of champagne to please them.

The sun is shining divinely and there are still many green leaves.

I must finish, my dear. I love you so much, and am longing for you so terribly. God preserve you and the girls. I kiss you all tenderly, and her as well.

Eternally, my dear Girly,

Your old

NICKY.

268 THE LETTERS OF THE TSAR

Telegram.

Stavka. 21 September, 1916.

Best thanks for dear, long letter. I have received Count Bobrinsky. He made a good impression. A lovely sunny day. Both kiss you tenderly.

NICKY.

Stavka. 22 September, 1916.

MY BELOVED SUNNY,

I thank you with all my heart for your 2 dear letters, especially for the last long one ! I received Bobrinsky and had a long conversation with him. He has known Protop. for many years, thoroughly approves of him, and is sure that they will both work together amicably. He spoke also of the telegram which they had both sent ! I was pleased with that.

Al. never mentioned Goutchkov to me. I only know that he hates Rodzianko and laughs at his belief that he knows everything better than anybody else.

What has been driving him to despair for a long time is the enormous number of letters which he receives from officers, their families, soldiers, and so on, as well as anonymous ones, all of which request him to draw my attention to the plight of the towns and villages, caused by the high prices of food and commodities !

I am sending you a few photographs—duplicates—as I am putting my albums in order, before pasting them in.

Broussilov has asked permission to continue the attack, as Gourko will help him on the right flank, and I have permitted it.

My pen is very bad. Farewell. God guard you and the girls, my precious ! I kiss you fondly.

Eternally your old

NICKY.

"Broussilov has asked permission to continue the attack." After reading this letter on the following day the Tsaritsa telegraphed : " He [Rasputin] approved of your original plan to stop [the offensive] and begin in another place. Now you write otherwise. May God help us." The " original plan " to which she refers (to stop the main offensive and to attack near Galitch and at Dorna-Vatra) will be found in the Tsar's letter of the 21st. The telegram appears to have been delayed, and the Tsar did not receive it till the 24th.

Telegram.

Stavka. *22 September,* 1916.

Hearty thanks. It is warm, windy. Hope you feel better. Am very grateful for yesterday's long telegram. Kiss you tenderly.

NICKY.

Stavka. *23 September,* 1916.

MY BELOVED,

Tender thanks for your dear, long letter, in which you state so well your conversation with Protop. God grant that he may turn out to be the man of whom we are now in need! Only think, Shack. wanted to obtain that post! Yes, truly, you ought to be my eyes and ears there in the capital, while I have to stay here. It rests with you to keep peace and harmony among the Ministers—thereby you do a great service to me and to our country. Oh, my precious Sunny, I am so happy to think that you have found at last a worthy occupation! Now I shall naturally be calm, and at least need not worry over internal affairs.

I am returning Bressler's letter to A.—that is a hopeless case, as his brother could not clear himself of the charges against him. Perhaps it would be better if he sent me a petition.

Thanks for sending me the photographs. The weather is warm, but in the morning there was a thick mist. This time a year ago I was returning to Tsarskoe Selo for the first time, after spending a month here! And to-day it's five months, the day of your namesday, since I have left home. Oh, how tired I am of Mogilev!

At the same time, I have a lot to do—hardly time enough to paste my photographs in the album.—I must finish this letter now. May God protect you, my angel, my heart, my intellect and my soul! Tender kisses for you and the girls.

Eternally your old

NICKY.

Stavka. 24 September, 1916.

MY PRECIOUS DARLING,

The train is late again and I have not yet received your letter. Read this telegram from Miechen and tear it up. Let me thank you again, my dear, for your long letter. You will really help me a great deal by speaking to the Ministers and watching them. I have only just received your telegram, in which you inform me that our Friend is very disturbed about my plan not being carried out. When I gave this order I did not know that Gourko had decided to gather almost all the forces at his disposal and prepare an attack in conjunction with the Guards and the neighbouring troops. This combination doubles our forces in this place and gives hopes for the possibility of success. That is why, when Al. read out the explanatory telegrams from Brouss. and Gourko, with the request to be allowed to continue the attack, which was then already in full swing, I gave my consent the next morning. To-day Br. asked permission to send General Kaledin to Lechitzky and to appoint Gourko commander over all these troops, including the Guards, which, from a military point of view, is quite correct, and with which I thoroughly agree. Now I shall be calm in the assurance that G. will act energetically but with caution and intelligence. These details are for you only—I beg you, my dear! Tell him only : Papa prikazal priniat razoumniye mieri ! [Papa has ordered to take sensible measures !]

Many thanks, my dear, for your letter, which has only just been brought to me at 2.15 instead of 11.30. The weather is very warm, but damp and rainy. God guard you, my only one, my beloved Sunny . . .

Eternally your old

NICKY.

The reference is to the telegram quoted below. These passages are of great historical interest, for they exhibit Rasputin's influence on the course of military operations—with the result shown in the Tsar's letter of the 27th, three days later. In reply to the present letter, the Tsaritsa begs her husband to " stop this useless massacre," and on this day she telegraphed : " He is very disturbed that your plan was not carried out. You foresaw everything quite correctly, and B. ought to obey and fulfil your orders. Now there are again useless sacrifices. Your thoughts are inspired from above."

Stavka. 25 September, 1916.

MY OWN DARLING,

Thank you with all my heart for your dear letter. I am returning Pahlen's letter to you. Yesterday I wrote to the old Count Nirod, to see that this injustice should be put right and the Court rank returned to Pahlen by the 5th of October. I am sending you my photograph, taken in Evpatoria, as I already have it. To-day the weather is wonderful and summer-like—12° in the shade—it is so pleasant !

Two new Roumanian officers have arrived—one of them the son of old Rosetti (mother née Girs), the image of his father, only he does not cry every minute. The other is quite a boy—Alexis likes him tremendously ; he will probably make friends with him. You must come by the 4th of Oct. —it is the day of our Cossack festival,— of course the 3rd would be better still. My love, my treasure, how happy I am at the thought of seeing you in a week's time, of hearing your sweet voice and pressing you in my arms ! Excuse the bad writing, but my pen is old and wants renewing.

I have just got your telegram. I can imagine how you received the Synod. It is disagreeable to see among them only one Member : Sergey of Finland.

I must finish now. God protect you, my own darling, and the girls. Many kisses.

YOUR OLD NICKY.

" It is disagreeable to see among them——." The meaning is : " It is disagreeable to see, among them, one member—Sergey of Finland."

Stavka. 26 September, 1916.

MY OWN DARLING,

Hearty thanks for dear letter. You ask me so many questions that I must think them out before answering. On Wednesday I shall receive Prot. and speak about the Governor of Petrograd. I doubt whether it would be wise to appoint Andrian. to this post; he is an honest man, but frightfully weak, a regular simpleton : he was formerly a military judge. He would not do for the present difficult times. As for Obolensky, he could be offered the Winter Palace after poor Komarov, if you have nothing against it. —Your friend Khogandokov was appointed Hetman by Delegation of the Amur Cossack Army only a few months ago ! I really do not know what kind of a Gov[ernor] he would have made.

I am sending you Nicky's letter and Sturmer's paper on the question, which may interest you. I must finish !

May God preserve you, my dear Sunny, and the girls ! Fond kisses.

Eternally your

NICKY.

ANDRIAN. : General Andrianov, the Prefect of the Moscow police. KOMAROV : General V. A. Komarov, Chief of the Court Ministry at Petrograd.

Stavka. 27 September, 1916.

MY BELOVED SUNNY,

Fondest thanks for dear letter and photographs. I am in despair at the thought of you not being well, and at your heart being again enlarged ! You have evidently worked too hard and overtired your heart. I beg you to be careful and to look after yourself.

The weather is again warm and bright : at times it rains.

Everything is quiet at the front these days, as considerable forces are being gathered and concentrated at the extreme left flank—Dorna-Vatra—to help the Roumanians.

My dear, Broussilov has, on the receipt of my instructions, immediately given orders to stop, and only asked whether it was necessary to send back the incoming troops or allow them to continue their movement. Then he proposed Gourko instead of Kaledin. After this he sent a paper with a plan by Gourko concerning the new joint attack, which he thoroughly agrees with, and so do Alexeiev and Poustov. I have given my consent to this new plan. That is, briefly speaking, the whole story.

Last night I managed to write to Olga; please give her my letter.

At the end of every walk we eat potatoes and chestnuts. Baby enjoys these snacks in the heart of nature immensely; the others do too. I must finish, my beloved. May God preserve you and may He send you a speedy recovery! I kiss you, the girls and her. Thank her for her letter.

With sincerest greetings, my treasure,

Eternally your old

NICKY.

Broussilov's offensive was now definitely brought to an end. That the ending was not entirely due to the military position, but was largely caused by the influence of Rasputin, is now made clear. This influence was apparently suspected by many, and it is indicated by the following passage in Gourko's book : " The weariness of the troops had its effect . . . but there can be no question that the stoppage of the advance was premature, and founded on orders from Headquarters, under a pretext which could not be openly spoken about, whereas, amongst our Allies, if not in the Press, such reasons were publicly mentioned or whispered." It is true, however, that the Russian losses had been considerable.

Telegram.

Stavka. 27 September, 1916.

Best thanks. I have received the Roumanian Ambassador and officers with letters from there. It is warm, dry. In thought I am with you. Both embrace you fondly.

NICKY.

Stavka. 28 September, 1916.

MY BELOVED,

Tender thanks for sweet letter and precise instructions for my talk with Protop. Last night I was fairly busy. We were shown part of a very interesting English

T

military film. Then I received the Roumanian Ambassador, Diamandy, and Nando's Adjutant, Angelesko, who brought me a letter from both. It appears that they are living through a terrible panic in Bukarest, created by the fear of the enormous advancing German army (which is imaginary) and the general lack of confidence in their own troops, who run whenever the German artillery opens fire !

Alexeiev foresaw this, and has told me several times that it would have been more advantageous for us if the Roumanians had kept their neutrality. Now, whatever happens, we must help them, and because of that our long front gets still more extended, as their borders are open to the enemy, whom they cannot withstand. We are collecting all available corps there, but the transport of troops wastes much valuable time.

To-morrow arrive Paul, Makarov and also the Serbian deputation from the King with the military decorations. The weather continues to be warm, but cloudy and dismal. I have sent for a few of our Eastern carpets, and they have greatly improved both rooms. Farewell. God guard you, my dear Sunny ! I kiss you and the girls tenderly.

I remain
Eternally your old
NICKY.

NANDO : King Ferdinand of Roumania.

Telegram.
Stavka. 28 September, 1916.

Hearty thanks. I have received the new Minister, talked with him for two hours. Made a good impression. Hope you are not tired. It is warm, windy. Tender kisses.
NICKY.

" The new Minister " : Protopopov.

Stavka. 29 September, 1916.

MY BELOVED,

Your dear letter No. 603 has arrived only at 2 o'clock, at the same time as the telegram—probably the train was late owing to the storm. Thank you most warmly for all you have written to me. True, it is strange that Obolensky came in such a way to our Friend—Lily's brother!

Well, yesterday from 6.15 to 8.15 I had a talk with Protop. I sincerely hope that he will prove suitable and will justify our expectations; he is, it seems, inspired by the best intentions, and has an excellent knowledge of internal affairs. Your little list with the questions was before me; only I did not touch upon the question of Rub.—It was getting late, and the guests in the other room were very noisy!

What joy, that we shall see each other soon! It would be splendid if you arrived on Monday at 5 o'clock to tea!

Baby and I find that the time is long overdue for us to see again mother and wife, sisters and daughters. The weather is warm but very windy; there is probably a gale raging on the Baltic Sea. At 6 o'clock we are going to the cinematograph to see the rest of the English war pictures; those which we have seen already were remarkably interesting and entertaining!

I shall receive Paul during the day—this will most likely be his first Report! I must finish, my own. God preserve you! I kiss you tenderly, my beloved darling, you and the girls.

Eternally your old

NICKY.

"Strange that Obolensky came in such a way to our Friend—Lily's brother." The meaning is: "It is strange that Obolensky, who is Lily's brother, should have come in such a way to our Friend." In the Tsaritsa's letter of the preceding day she says: "Obolensky asked to see our Friend and sent a fine car for him." She then describes in detail the interview between Prince Obolensky and Rasputin, making it clear (perhaps unintentionally) that the Prince was seeking the aid of the peasant. The Lily referred to here is Princess Elizavieta Nicolaievna Obolenskaia, a lady-in-waiting.

RUB.: D. L. Rubinstein, a Jewish banker and speculator. He had been closely associated with Court circles, and was believed to have been in touch with German financiers during the war. Like Manus, the banker, he allied himself with Rasputin. The Tsaritsa wished him to be sent away, in order to avoid open scandals.

Telegram.

Stavka. 29 September, 1916.

Sincerest thanks. Paul has arrived; looks well. A clear evening. I saw an interesting English film. Both embrace you tenderly.

NICKY.

Stavka. 30 September, 1916.

MY PRECIOUS WIFY,

Warmest thanks for your dear letter. Belaiev has only just left me. He is being sent to Roumania in the capacity of adviser and head of the military mission, in accordance with the example of the French. Yesterday I received the Roumanian General who is going to Bukarest.— Paul has a good healthy appearance. He has found a small comfortable house here and has quite settled down. He has asked leave to be allowed to come to tea only, as he prefers lunching and dining at home. After the 5th he will visit the Guards. To-night I am receiving the Serbian officers, who have brought me—and apparently for all of you— military medals ! I have no idea what their decorations are like.

The weather is warm but very windy, with intermittent rain and sunshine. All the same, we are going for a row on the river. Since the summer I have only had three free evenings after dinner; two evenings I played dominoes, and on the third I sorted out the photographs for the album to paste them in all at the same time. I am immensely glad of our meeting in the near future !

I can add nothing more of interest. God guard you, my dear Sunny ! I kiss you and the girls tenderly, and her also. I hope the journey will not tire you.

Eternally your very loving old

NICKY.

Telegram.

Stavka. 30 September, 1916.

I consent. Good-night. My blessings.

NICKY.

" I consent." The answer to the Tsaritsa's telegram of the same date, in which she says : " Please allow the Metropolitan and Raiev to come to you on Monday with the Holy Image from the Synod. Telegraph reply."

Stavka. 1 October, 1916.

MY PRECIOUS, BELOVED SUNNY,

Thank you with all my heart for your dear letter and note concerning the Erivan Regiment. After my last conversation with Silaiev I have been busy on this matter and am seeking a successor for him.

I made inquiries through Kondz. as to who was the first candidate; the answer was as follows—first Michabeli, then the Prince Shervashidze and finally Gelovani.

In the present case this sounds like a mockery, does it not? I shall find out from Paul, who knows the Guards, who is a likely candidate for them. It is, alas! a year since I lost touch with them.

And so, God willing, in two days' time we shall see each other!

Your telegram of yesterday has worried me considerably— about the ikon of the Synod. Why such a desperate hurry? I have already fixed the reception of several persons for Monday, just on the day of your arrival, and now besides that the Metrop[olitan] and Raiev are to come!

Yesterday arrived a General and two officers with their Ambassador from the Crown Prince of Serbia with military awards for me and Baby and handsome crosses (the Cross of Mercy) for you and all the girls.

What a difference! These people, who have lost their country, are full of faith and humility, whereas the Roumanians, who have only been a little shaken, have completely lost their heads and their faith in themselves!

May God protect you on your journey, my beloved Wify! I kiss you and the girls very tenderly, and remain

Your loving and expectant old

NICKY.

KONDZ.: General P. C. Kondzerovsky, attached for duty to the Stavka. MICHABELI: Colonel E. I. Michabeli or Machabeli, of the

14th Georgian Grenadier Regiment, then in temporary command of the 16th Mingresky Grenadier Regiment. He was an ardent separatist, and was supposed to have been in touch with the directors of the German espionage during the war. GELOVANI: Colonel Prince C. L. Gelovani of the 13th Erivan Grenadier Regiment. RAIEV: N. P. Raiev, a Secretary of State and a member of the National Education Committee, the new Procurator of the Synod.

Telegram.

Stavka. 3 October, 1916.

Thanks for telegram. Baby has a deranged stomach, so will not meet you. We embrace you tenderly.

NICKY.

Stavka. 12 October, 1916.

MY BELOVED,

You are leaving us again to go back to your work and wearying cares! Thank you deeply and warmly for your visit here, for all your love and caresses! How I shall miss them! God grant that in two to two and a half weeks we shall meet again. Before that I see no possibility, alas, of leaving here. I had great hopes of being able to go together to the South and of spending a few days together in our train.—Perhaps it will happen some day.

I shall miss you particularly in the evenings, which belonged to us.

May God bless your journey and your return home! *Take care of* yourself and do not get overtired. Tenderly I kiss your dear little face, my own Sunny. . . .

Eternally your

NICKY.

Telegram.

Stavka. 12 October, 1916.

We are very sad. Thanks for dear letters. It is lonely in the house. Good-night. Embrace you tenderly.

NICKY. ALEXEY.

Stavka.   13 *October,* 1916.

My tenderly beloved, dear Sunny,

Thank you with all my heart for dear letter.

I must tell you a piece of good news : I shall try to come for 2–3 days.   I hope to leave on the 18th and spend these three days with you, my beloved.

Alas !   To-day there is no time for more, but I have told you the thing that matters most !

God keep you and the girls !   Eternally your old
                                        Nicky.

Telegram.

Stavka.   13 *October,* 1916.

Thanks for the telegram.   Hope you have arrived safely. The sun is hiding.   I am touched by their letter.   Sleep well.   Tender kisses.
                                        Nicky.

Stavka.   14 *October,* 1916.

My treasure,

All day yesterday Baby looked pale and sad; I think he was fretting.   But to-day he played as usual, quite cheerfully, in the little wood by the old Stavka.

At dinner he complained of a headache, and he was put to bed, at which he was very pleased.   His temperature rose rapidly and he felt very unwell.   He went off to sleep before 9 o'clock and slept soundly all the night. . . . This morning his temperature is quite normal, he is cheerful, but all the same we are keeping him in bed.   Vl. Nic. thinks all this is still the result of his first cold or that he has eaten something indigestible.   In any case I hope that all is done with now.

Oh, how happy I am at the thought of being able to come home for a few days and see you and the girls !   I asked Al. about it and he said that it was quite practicable;   he remembered that last year I had also gone home about the 20th.   He thinks that later on I could go to the South— Reni, etc.—to review the troops.   How pleasant to feel that one is not tied to one place !

Yesterday Paul brought his son, who gave me a book of his verses. To-day they have both gone to make an inspection of the Guards. I asked P. to speak to Brouss. and Gourko.

I must finish, my dear Sunny. May God keep you all! Many kisses.

Your
NICKY.

Telegram.

Stavka. 14 *October*, 1916.

Thanks for information. It is finer here too. Am keeping the Little One in bed. A chill on the stomach. He is very cheerful. Both embrace you.

NICKY.

Stavka. 15 *October*, 1916.

MY BELOVED,

Thank you tenderly for your first sweet letter from Ts. Selo. *I am so happy* that I can come for a few days. Thank God, Alexey has quite recovered. He has got up to-day, but as he coughs a little we have decided not to let him out in the air. The weather is lovely, the air so pure and sunny! In the morning there was a slight frost.

To-day arrived Mitia D. and Dm. Sheremetev to replace Kira and Igor.

Ministers come to see me every day; I hope they will leave me in peace for the few days that I am at home!

After your departure I sent a telegram to Tino and then learnt that things in Athens have taken a turn for the better. Please God! Besides that, Sturmer has composed an official, frankly amiable telegram to Tino—of course in cipher—in my name, which will, I hope, improve the situation and will enable him to notify the Powers that he is undertaking on his own initiative those measures which the Powers wanted to impose on him rudely and by force.

Now, my dear Sunny, I must finish. God keep you and

the girls. I hope to start on Tuesday at 12.30, shall get
to T. S. at 3.30 before tea.   I kiss you all tenderly.
Eternally your
NICKY.

Mitia D. : Captain Dehn.—" Before tea "—on the following day.

Telegram.
Stavka.   15 *October,* 1916.

Hearty thanks for letter and telegram. A bright, cold,
sunny day. The Little One is well, cheerful. We kiss you
tenderly.
NICKY.

Stavka.   16 *October,* 1916.

MY TREASURE,

Sincerest thanks for dear letter; thank Tatiana
also. This will be my last, as we are leaving Mogilev in
48 hours.

Yes, my little one, of course I very much want to go to
Communion with you, as I have not fasted since the first
week of Lent. I shall try to eat as little as possible during
these days.

Thank God, Baby has recovered and can go out again,
but he must observe a strict diet. It is amusing to hear
his complaints, that he is hungry and that he is given too
little to eat.

For the last two days the weather has been gloriously
sunny, but now it is again cold and dull—0°. The river
keeps on rising—in some places near Smolensk and Kaluga
the meadows are flooded owing to the heavy rains.

Yesterday all the Quartermasters of the army arrived
here for a conference under the chairmanship of the Chief of
the Commissariat; they had dinner with me and told me a
mass of interesting things. The whole army requires daily
2676 wagon-loads of victuals and fodder for the horses !
This alone constitutes 400 trains per day.

It is time, my beloved Sunny, to dispatch the courier.

May God preserve you and the girls. Many kisses for you, them, and A.

YOUR NICKY.

What joy, that we shall soon see each other !

Telegram.

Stavka. 16 *October*, 1916.

Best thanks. It is cold, dull. In thought I am always with you. Both are well. We kiss you tenderly.

NICKY.

Stavka. 17 *October*, 1916.

MY PRECIOUS SUNNY,

I was mistaken yesterday, thinking that I was writing to you for the last time. I am so accustomed to you coming here and my remaining that I thought I would not have enough time to write again.

In 24 hours we are starting on our way and I am quite excited at the thought of the journey and reunion with all my dear ones *in my own home.*

Protopopov spent nearly two hours with me last night. I sincerely hope that God will bless his new work of responsibility ! He has firmly decided to carry it through to the end, in spite of all difficulties. But I am afraid that the difficulties will be great, especially for the first two months !

Fabritzky appeared during dinner; I was glad to see him—enormous, healthy, sunburnt and energetic. His naval brigade is being converted into a division at Nicolaievo, where I hope to inspect them later on.

I have just received your dear letter No. 610. Tender thanks.

Mordvinov did not sneeze, reading Anastasia's letter, but laughed a lot when I told him what she had done. It is two years since he has been able to invent a punishment for her.

Now I must finish this, *my very last letter !*

God guard you and the girls.
I kiss you tenderly, my beloved Wify.

Eternally yours

NICKY.

FABRITZKY: Rear-Admiral S. S. Fabritzky, at one time commander of the battleship " Amuretz."

Telegram.

Stavka. 18 *October,* 1916.

I prefer Mass at 11 in the fortress.

NICKY.

Telegram.

Smolensk. 26 *October,* 1916.

Both have slept well, feel better. Greyish, warm weather. We miss you terribly. Thank you tenderly for your dear letter. Both embrace you closely.

NICKY.

Telegram.

Stavka. 26 *October,* 1916.

Arrived safely. It is sad and lonely without you and the girls, especially here on the platform. Close embrace.

NICKY.

Mogilev. 26 *October,* 1916.

MY PRECIOUS, BELOVED DARLING,
With all my old loving heart do I thank you for your sweet letter, which you left on my table as you were saying good-bye. We both felt so sad when the train moved off and you stood at the door. Presently we had a glimpse of your car, which was carrying you all back home. Then Baby went to his coupé to play, and I received old Trepov, who stayed with me until our halt at Tosno !
After saying prayers with Alexey I played a game of dominoes with Dmitry, Grabbe and N. P. We all went to bed early and slept well.
We got up late—Baby even after 10 o'clock. At Smolensk we stopped, took a little walk, and I received Rausch. All

day long I read a very interesting English book which has
only just come out : " The Man who dined with the Kaiser."
When I have finished it I will send it to you.

Al. played his favourite " Nain Jaune." Before our
arrival here his nose started bleeding, so that we had to
send for Isanianz, who cauterised it.   Now all is well.

We were met by the usual people and after a few words
of greeting I let them go.   I walked up and down the platform, thinking of you and the girls.   I was struck by the
stillness which reigned around—I was expecting all the time
to hear the wild shrieks of Anastasia or Marie, plaguing
Mordvinov.   Instead of that, Alexey's cat ran away and
hid under a big pile of boards.   We put on our greatcoats
and went to look for her.   Nagorny found her at once
with the aid of an electric torch, but it took a long while
to make the wretch come out.   She would not listen to Al.
At last he caught her by the hind legs and dragged her
through a narrow chink.

At present it is quite still in the train.   Alexey has gone
to bed, and many of the retinue have, of course, gone to
the cinematograph !   I feel very lonely, but am glad that
I can write to you; I imagine that I am talking to you
quietly.

Last night I received the following telegram from dear
Mamma : " Is it true that we shall meet soon?   Would
very much like to know when and for how long, because
M. P. will come 29.   Shall I have time to *put her off* ? "   I
laughed while reading this, and immediately telegraphed
the necessary details.

When you get this letter we shall already be in Kiev.   I
am vexed that for a few days you will have no letters from
me, because I shall hardly have time to write.   In any case,
this can count for two.

Ah, my treasure, my love, how I long for you !   It was
such *real* happiness—those six days at home !

Embraces for the girls and A.

Eternally, my Sunny,

Your very own old

NICKY.

Rausch : Baron E. A. Rausch von Traubenberg, Assistant Commandant of the troops in the Minsk Military District.—" The Man who dined with the Kaiser." " My Secret Service, by the Man who dined with the Kaiser," published in March 1916.— Alexey's cat : Zoubrovka, a kitten from Mogilev, the favourite pet of the Tsarevitch.—" The following telegram from Mamma." This telegram was transcribed in Russian in the original letter, with the exception of the words " put her off," which are in English.

Telegram.

Stavka. 27 October, 1916.

Warmest thanks for dear letter. I have only just finished lunch and am going back to the train. We are leaving at six o'clock. It is cloudy, warm. The dining saloon looks gay and bright. Embrace you closely.

NICKY.

Telegram.

Kiev. 28 October, 1916.

Arrived safely. A touching reception. Mother met us. Foggy, calm weather. The three of us lunched snugly together. Hearty greetings from all of us.

NICKY.

Kiev Station. 28 October, 1916.

MY BELOVED DARLING,

We arrived this morning at 10.30 and, only think ! were met by Mamma, Paul and Sandro. Besides them there were three Generals, the District Governor and the Mayor. As Baby and I had to call in at the Sofiisky Sobor, Mamma drove straight home to the Palace and we arrived a little later.

The troops and all the schools—military and others—were drawn up along the streets. Order was exemplary, but unfortunately the weather was none too pleasant : it was foggy and dark, but not cold. I went through our old rooms with mixed feelings. The past and the death of the unhappy Stolypin came back to me so vividly.

We sat in my room till lunch time, looking through Mamma's interesting albums; she likes this room, as it is bright in the mornings. Then we three lunched together, and for the first time Baby ate with appetite.

It has been announced that the courier ought to leave at once. May God keep you, my beloved, and the girls! I kiss you tenderly.

Eternally your

NICKY.

Telegram.

Kiev. 29 October, 1916.

Best thanks for dear letter. It is dull, but warmer. Have visited four military colleges this morning. Our suite lunched at Mamma's. The three of us drove through the town. Saw Olga; she is better. Am leaving, very pleased with everything seen. Embrace you closely.

NICKY.

Mogilev. 30 October, 1916.

MY BELOVED,

We have only just arrived here, amidst terrible rain and wind. I am writing in the train, so as not to lose time, and to send off the courier punctually.

I have brought away with me the best impressions of Kiev. Mamma was very kind and charming. In the evenings, during our games of " puzzle," we had long talks. We saw Olga twice; she got up yesterday and looks well, but thin—such a calm, good expression on her face. She has written requesting permission to be married on Saturday the 5th November. Of course she asked Mamma about it too, and I took her side, saying that in my opinion it was best to finish with this affair. If it must happen, let it happen now! She wants to take leave for a fortnight and then return to her work. Mamma intends staying on in Kiev for a while, as she is very fond of it.

To-morrow I shall describe to you the details of our stay there, but now I must finish. God keep you, my beloved! Best thanks for your two letters. I kiss you all.

Eternally your

NICKY.

Stavka. 30 *October*, 1916.

MY DEAR TREASURE,

My warmest thanks for your sweet letter, which I found on the table on my return home. It was a great consolation to me to get both your letters, as I felt depressed coming back. Kiev seems like some wonderful dream; everything passed off so well there, and everybody was so cordial!

Now I shall tell you all in order. In my last hurried letter from Kiev, written in the train, I got to where the three of us were having lunch. At 2.30, the students from one of the schools for ensigns, who had completed their course and were promoted to the rank of officer, were drawn up in the courtyard. Mamma looked on out of a window and approved of everything; she was particularly pleased with Baby for keeping behind me! After that we drove to Olga's hospital and spent about an hour with her. She lay on a wicker couch, something like garden furniture. I saw several of her nurses, whom I had met before, and two doctors.

The wounded came down to see us off. Tat. Andr. was tremendously pleased to be able to speak to Alexey. From Olga we went to have tea with dear Mamma, and then I went to the train. He had his dinner while I read and wrote. At 8 o'clock I dined with Mamma and spent a very cosy evening. The next day, the 29th, from 9.30 till 12 o'clock I visited four military colleges; three of these colleges were quite new and I began with them. First of all the Nicolaiev Military College and the Nicolaiev Artillery College—both beyond the town boundary, not far from each other. Beautiful big new buildings, here and there not quite finished. Then I had to cross the whole town to get to the Alexeiev Engineering College, also a huge and well-planned building, with a magnificent view down the Dnieper. On the way to the Palace I looked in at the old Military College, now named in memory of Kostia. Luckily I arrived back in time for lunch at 12.30. Mamma invited all my suite and her own, as well as Ignatiev (the Governor) with his wife (daughter of Julius Uroussov). Baby spent the whole morning in the garden; his cheeks were rosy and he amazed everyone at the table by his appetite. He talked very nicely with Zina Mengden and behaved very well.

In the afternoon Mamma took us for a charming trip on the other side of the river. The view of the town from there was lovely, but, alas! sunless. We returned over another bridge and, passing by Olga's hospital, got out, and were glad to find that she had got up. But she was still feeling a little weak. Later we had tea at Mamma's with Paul and M. P. She presented Mamma with a very pretty ikon from the whole family with everyone's signatures on the back—only our signatures and the children's, of course, are not on it. She was very cold to me, and did not say a word about Livadia! Mamma thought that very strange. Paul was in high spirits. He had only recently seen the whole of the Guards and was full of enthusiasm. Having had dinner with Mamma, I left Kiev in pouring rain.

31 October.

I have received your dear letter and thank you with all my heart for your kind advice. I have always thought that the question of supplies ought to be decided at once, only I had to wait for this paper. Now it is done: may God help us! I feel it is right.

The weather is warm. Yesterday it rained heavily. It is time to finish. God guard you, my angel, and the girls!

I kiss you tenderly.

Eternally your
NICKY.

"Schools for ensigns"—skola praporshchikov.

Kostia, referred to previously: the Grand Duke Constantine Constantinovitch. He died in 1915.

"He had recently seen the Guards, and was full of enthusiasm." How false this impression must have been is made evident by an entry in Sir Alfred Knox's diary, dated 28th October, 1916 (p. 488): "I hear whispers that the Russian infantry has lost heart and that anti-war propaganda is rife in the ranks. It is little wonder that they are downhearted after being driven to the slaughter over the same ground seven times in about a month, and every time taking trenches where their guns could not keep them."

ZINA MENGDEN : a lady-in-waiting to the Dowager Empress.
M.P. : " Miechen "—the Grand Duchess Maria Pavlovna—*v. ante.*
" Now it is done." The control of Supplies had been placed in
the hands of the Minister of the Interior—Protopopov.

Telegram.

Stavka. 31 *October*, 1916.

Sincere thanks. All is done. I have telegraphed to the
old man. Do not overtire yourself. It is warm, sometimes
the sun comes through. Embrace you closely.

NICKY.

Stavka. 1 *November*, 1916.

MY PRECIOUS,

I have read and re-read your dear letter many times
—especially that part in which you tell of your conversation
with St. and Protop. There is nothing to forgive you for, on
the contrary, I must be deeply grateful to you for so far
advancing this serious matter by your help.

Now I understand the meaning of Gr.'s telegram which I
received in Kiev and sent on to you yesterday. But I
could not write the necessary words, not having the Minister's paper before my eyes. Now it is done, and I am calm,
though I am fully conscious of the great difficulties which
are awaiting us for the first two months. Yes, let us be
firm and wait !

Since I was last here the military situation of Roumania
has improved, and our army is concentrating more satisfactorily than I expected, in view of the difficulties of
transport. On our way from Kiev we met four military
trains going from Riga to the South; we heard singing and
saw masses of gay young faces at the windows.

Yesterday we drove to the monument, I went for a walk
and later on we ate some baked potatoes. It was quite
warm.

Dmitry has departed, as he has to have his cheek operated
on (from the inside); he hopes to see you. Igor is due to
arrive here soon—what a pleasure ! The fat Belgian,
Williams and Janin have come from the Boukovina—they

U

were delighted with all they have seen; were presented to Mamma.

May God keep you, my only and all! I kiss you and the girls tenderly.

Eternally your old

NICKY.

"Now it is done." A further reference to the transfer of Supplies to Protopopov. See the preceding letter and telegram.

Telegram.

Stavka. 1 *November,* 1916.

Sincerest thanks for dear letter. We have been to the cinematograph. Was very busy later. Saw Veselkin. Embrace you closely.

NICKY.

Stavka. 2 *November,* 1916.

MY PRECIOUS,

I am deeply grateful to you for your dear letter, and am sending my best wishes to our Olga for her birthday. Yes, 21 years have passed—nearly a whole generation. I remember living then in that old green dressing-room!

There was a downpour of rain yesterday; during the night it snowed heavily and now there are 3° of frost. The landscape is absolutely wintry. The cars find it difficult to drive through the streets. Our Fourth Sotnia was presented this morning. The officers and men have a healthy, energetic look and sunburnt faces. They are going in small detachments to Tsarskoe S. to fetch their things, new equipment and boots.

Nicolai Nic. has come for one day; we had a long talk together last night, of which I will tell you in my next letter. —I am too busy to-day.

God preserve you, my dearly beloved Sunny, and the children. Sincerest greetings to all.

Eternally your old

NICKY.

Stavka. 3 *November*, 1916.

MY BELOVED TREASURE,

Thank you most sincerely for your dear letter.

The Little One is suffering from a strained vein in the upper part of his right leg, a small swelling, but no great pains—during the night he kept on waking and groaned in his sleep.

Feodorov has ordered him to lie quietly in bed. He is very cheerful and surrounded by his three tutors, so that there is a dreadful noise in the next room.

Vl. Nic. will be able to tell you the details of the leg trouble, as it began when he was still here.

Obolensky appeared here yesterday, happy and beaming at having got rid of his post. He will get an appointment in the 3rd Caucasian Corps, which he chose himself.

Gen. Alexeiev is unwell and laid up—he has a high temperature. Feodorov says that his kidneys are out of order; he is calling in Sirotinin. This complication is of great importance to me. I was hoping to go somewhere or other on the front in the near future, but now I shall have to stay here for the present.

Poustovoitenko is very well informed of everything and makes a very good assistant. So far I am not thinking of taking anybody from outside.

Perhaps in a week's time you will be able to come here? I am sending you Nicolai's letters, which he did not send to me but brought with him—they will give you an idea of what we spoke about.

God guard you, my own Sunny, and the girls! Tender kisses.

YOUR OLD NICKY.

" Happy . . . at having got rid of his post "—as President of the Committee of Supplies.

Alexeiev's illness, at this stage, was extremely unfortunate. A week after this letter was written he was sent to the Crimea for a rest, and was succeeded temporarily by General Gourko. Although Gourko was an able and conscientious man, the change of the Chief of Staff at such a moment could only be regarded as a dangerous necessity. Alexeiev returned to his post shortly before the Tsar's abdication.

SIROTININ : Dr. V. N. Sirotinin, Court Physician.

Telegram.

Stavka. 3 *November,* 1916.

Hearty congratulations on Olga's birthday. We are sorry that we cannot be with you. It is cold and dull. Both kiss you tenderly.

NICKY.

Stavka. 4 *November,* 1916.

MY DARLING SUNNY,

Warmest thanks for dear letter.

Baby's leg hurts from time to time and he cannot get off to sleep the first part of the night. When I come to bed he tries not to groan any more and goes to sleep quicker.

Feodorov says that the swelling is going down satisfactorily, and as his temperature is only slightly above the normal, I hope that in a few days he will be able to get up.

To-day I have little time for writing, because I have received the old Prince Vassilchicov, Trotzky and Dashkov, who have returned from Moscow. They have spent exactly a month there, visiting and inspecting hospitals, and saw 76,000 wounded, of whom 16,000 have received decorations. They found everything in perfect order.

In a few days' time I shall send George to the South-west front to thank the troops and distribute awards to the heroes.

Alexeiev is feeling a little better to-day. Feod. is insisting on his staying in bed at least a week longer, because, besides illness, he is tired out with work, not having had enough sleep all this time. He is looking better.

Kyrill has come for two days; he has gone now to Abo.

May God guard you, my treasure, my beloved Wify, and the girls! I kiss you fondly.

Your old

NICKY.

VASSILCHICOV: General Prince S. I. Vassilchicov, formerly commander of the Life-Guard Hussars, then, in succession, of the 12th and 1st Cavalry Divisions and of the Guard Corps. DASHKOV: General D. Y. Dashkov of the Cavalry Guards, a member of the suite.

Telegram.

Stavka. 4 November, 1916.

Best thanks. Am sorry that I sent you those two letters, not having read them myself. Greyish, mild weather. Tender kisses from both.

NICKY.

Stavka. 5 November, 1916.

MY PRECIOUS DARLING,

Most grateful to you for your dear letter. I am so sorry that I have upset you and made you angry by sending you the two letters of N., but as I am in a constant hurry I had not read them, because he had spoken exhaustively of the matter for a long time.

But he never once mentioned you, discussing only the stories about spies, factories, workmen, disorders, Ministers and the general internal situation! Had he said anything about you, you do not really doubt that your dear hubby would have taken your part? I must add that he did not at all want to give me his letters—I simply took them from him, and he gave them up rather unwillingly. Of course I am not defending him, but am only explaining things as they were.

Baby's leg is a little better. He slept very well, and it hurt only for about a quarter of an hour in the evening.

Yesterday I received the famous General Manikovsky, the chief of the Ordnance Department. He told me much concerning the workmen, the terrible propaganda among them and the enormous amount of money distributed among them for strikes—and that on the other side no resistance is offered, the police do nothing and nobody seems to care what may happen. The Ministers are, as usual, weak—and here is the result!

It is time for me to finish, my darling. God bless you and the girls! Fond kisses.

Eternally your old

NICKY.

" The two letters of N." These letters, written by the Grand Duke Nicholas and intended only for the Tsar's perusal, contained allusions which were extremely painful to the Tsaritsa. They provoked, from her, a hysterical outburst. She was "utterly disgusted." His conduct, she said, was loathsome and treacherous. He himself was "the incarnation of evil," hated by all who were loyal and trustworthy.

Telegram.

Stavka. 5 November, 1916.

Thank you deeply for dear letter. The leg is much better. It is cold, clear, 7° of frost. Have received a charming reply from Georgie B. Close embrace.

NICKY.

Georgie B.—Prince George of Battenberg. See note to telegram of 7 April, 1916.

Stavka. 6 November, 1916.

MY PRECIOUS,

I thank you most sincerely for your loving letter. To-day is the holiday of the Hussars and also of the Gvardeisky Equipage, so that we had several Hussars and Naval officers here. I had long conversations after lunch, so I have now absolutely no time to write more fully.

The weather is bright—at last, after three weeks of darkness, the sun has shown himself. Baby is feeling much better, though last night he had severe pains for an hour.

Please return Georgie's telegram to me. I must finish. God keep you, my beloved Sunny, and the girls!

I love you with all my soul.

Eternally your old

NICKY.

Stavka. 7 November, 1916.

MY BELOVED SUNNY,

Thank you tenderly for dear letter.

N. has arrived with Petiusha to-day, bringing with him only the respectable people of his suite. The fat Orlov and Yanushk. remained behind! He has not changed, and looks well in his cherkeska. Yesterday I received Sirotinin, and he reported to me what, in his opinion, ought to be done with Alexeiev. He requires *a rest* in the Crimea for 6–8 weeks. They hope that this will be long enough for him to get well and gather strength. This morning I told Alexeiev about it, and he, of course, submits to their decision.

He strongly recommends Gourko as his successor. I had also thought of him, and have therefore agreed to his choice. Not long ago I saw Gourko; everyone speaks well of him, and at this time of year he can easily leave his army for a few months.

How stupid of Pogul. to get divorced!

Baby's little leg is quite well. I hope that to-morrow he will get up. Yesterday he tried to walk a few steps and he had no pain. He slept all the night without waking up.

God keep you, my darling, and the girls! In thought I am always with you.

Eternally your very loving old

NICKY.

" N. has arrived with Petiusha to-day." This visit is referred to by Sir J. Hanbury-Williams (p. 130), who makes it clear that the Tsar did not share the Tsaritsa's hatred of the Grand Duke. The Tsar, he says, was very pleased, and " spoke so cordially about him [the Grand Duke] that it is hard to believe all these stories about jealousy, etc."

Stavka. 8 November, 1916

MY BELOVED, PRECIOUS WIFY,

Thank you very much for your dear letter.

All these days I have been thinking of old St. He, as you say rightly, acts as a red flag, not only to the Duma, but to the whole country, alas!

I hear of this from all sides; nobody believes in him and everyone is angry because we stand up for him. It is much worse than it was with Goremykin last year. I reproach him for his excessive prudence and his incapacity for taking upon himself the responsibility of making them all work as they should do. Trepov and Grigorovitch would have done better in his place. He is coming here to-morrow (St.), and I will give him leave for the present. As to the future, we shall see; we will talk it over when you come here. I am afraid that with him things will not go smoothly, whereas in time of war that is more important than at any other! I do not understand how it is, but nobody has confidence in him!

It will be splendid if you come here on the 13th. What a funny letter Baby has written to you! He is quite well and, God willing, gets up to-morrow.

N. and P. are lunching and dining with me; so far all conversations have passed off well. They are leaving to-night.

God guard you, my precious, and the girls. Thank her for the ikon.

Eternally your very loving

NICKY.

Telegram.

Stavka. 8 *November*, 1916.

Sincerest thanks. The weather is warmer. The Little One is quite well. Both send our love.

NICKY.

Stavka. 9 *November*, 1916.

MY BELOVED DARLING,

Thank you with all my heart for your letter and for your desire to help me in my difficulties.

I am receiving St. in an hour, and shall insist on his taking leave. Alas! I am afraid that he will have to go altogether—nobody has confidence in him. I remember even Buchanan telling me at our last meeting that the English Consuls, in their reports, predict serious disturbances if he remains. And every day I hear more and more about it. This must be taken into consideration.

Baby is up and quite well, though he is a little thinner, and pale. There are masses of things I want to discuss with you, but I have no time for writing.

I am so happy that I shall see you soon!

May God guard you, my only and my all, and the girls! Warmly I kiss you, fondly I love you.

Your old

NICKY.

Telegram.

Stavka.   9 November, 1916.

Many thanks. I have spoken to the old man. He is returning to-morrow. He will inform you of my decision. Both kiss you tenderly.

NICKY.

Telegram.

Stavka.   10 November, 1916.

Have done it.   Good-night.

NICKY.

"Have done it." Yielding to the irresistible force of opinion, and seeing, at last, something of the real state of affairs, the Tsar dismissed Sturmer, both from the Ministry of Foreign Affairs and from the Presidency of the Council.   The Tsaritsa was not averse to his dismissal as Foreign Minister, but was anxious that he should be retained as President of the Council.   Here, as in most of her views, she was reflecting the opinion of Rasputin.   See her letters of the 9th, 10th and 11th November.

Telegram.

Stavka.   10 November, 1916.

As you have nobody to accompany you, I am sending Voeikov to-day.   Fond kisses from both.

NICKY.

Stavka.   10 November, 1916.

MY PRECIOUS SUNNY,

Many thanks for your dear letter. When you receive this you will probably know already from St. about the changes which it is imperative to bring about at once.

I am sorry for Prot.—he is a good, honest man, but he jumps from one idea to another and cannot make up his mind on anything. I noticed that from the beginning. They say that a few years ago he was not quite normal after a certain illness (when he sought the advice of Bad-maiev). It is risky to leave the Ministry of Internal Affairs in the hands of such a man in these times !

Old Bobrinsky will have to be replaced too. If we find a clever and energetic man for his post, then I hope the

298 THE LETTERS OF THE TSAR

question of Supplies will be put right without alterations in the present system.

While these changes are in progress, the Duma will be prorogued for about eight days, otherwise they would say that it was being done under pressure from them. In any case, Trepov will try to do what he can. In all probability he will return on Sunday, bringing with him the list of persons whom we had discussed with him and St.

Only, I beg you, do not drag our Friend into this. The responsibility is with me, and therefore I wish to be free in my choice. The poor old man was calm and touching.

God protect you, my beloved darling. . . . Fond kisses for all.

Eternally your
NICKY.

The Tsar had informed Sturmer of his intention to dismiss Proto-popov also—a wise decision, but due rather to the force of circum-stances than to his own initiative. When the Tsaritsa heard of this, she resolved to save the Minister of the Interior at all costs. Palé-ologue is wrong in saying that she decided to leave at once for the Stavka. Her visit had been arranged some days previously. It will be seen from the penultimate paragraph of this letter that the Tsar was anxious to conceal his decision from Rasputin.

Telegram.

Stavka. 11 *November,* 1916.

Cordial thanks for dear letter. I shall wait for the appointment until our meeting. Gourko has arrived; began working together yesterday. Have not written to you to-day—had no time. Kisses.

NICKY.

" The appointment "—of a new Minister of Foreign Affairs.

Telegram.

Bolgoe. 12 *November,* 1916.

Hearty thanks for letter. It is bright, thawing. Wish you a pleasant journey. . . .

In the train. 4 *December*, 1916.

MY TENDERLY BELOVED, DARLING SUNNY,

I have not read your letter, as I love to do that in bed before going to sleep. But I thank you in advance for all the love and kindness which are poured out in them. I shall post this in Tosno and hope that it will reach you to-night.

Yes, those days spent together were difficult, but *only* thanks to you have I spent them more or less calmly. You were so strong and steadfast—I admire you more than I can say. Forgive me if I was moody or unrestrained—sometimes one's temper must come out!

Of course it would be great happiness to be always together in these difficult times. But now I firmly believe that the most painful is behind us and that it will not be as hard as it was before. And henceforth I intend to become sharp and bitter.

God grant that our separation may not last long. In my thoughts I am always *with you*—never doubt that.

With all my loving heart do I embrace you and the girls. Keep well and firm, my dear little birdy, my own and my all. Sleep sweetly and calmly.

Eternally your old hubby

NICKY.

Give her my kind regards.

" Those days together were difficult." The Tsaritsa had fought successfully for Protopopov, and he was retained in office.

" I intend to become sharp and bitter." The word here translated as bitter is " yadoviti "—literally " poisonous."

Telegram.

Stavka. 5 *December*, 1916.

Have arrived safely. A lovely clear day; 2° of frost. Thank you once more for dear letter. Hope you are feeling well. Both kiss you tenderly.

NICKY.

Telegram.

Stavka. 6 *December,* 1916.

Hearty thanks for good wishes and presents. The Little One handed them to me in the name of you all last night. Clear, windy weather. In thought and prayer I am with you. Embrace you closely.

NICKY.

6 *December,* 1916.

MY DEAR,

My very best thanks for your sweet kind letter, also for yesterday's presents and for those which came to-day with your letter !

I drank in each tender word written by you. In the morning we went, as usual, to church, and coming back I inspected all the officers and men lining our route. It is their holiday to-day and I congratulated them.

Then I received the members of the Staff, after which I listened to the usual report, a short one on this occasion, as I spoke to Gourko last night.

We have just finished lunch. The weather is lovely here, heaps of snow and such light dry air. The journey went off very well. In the train we slept till goodness knows what hour. I went for a walk with A. at each station.

I have read with delight " The Wall of Partition," and feel soothed by it.

A mass of telegrams, as usual.

Olga will be pleased and surprised at being appointed Colonel-in-Chief of the 2nd Koubansk. Plastounski Battalion. I remembered that two of them had no Colonels-in-Chief; I thought it right to give her the second, and to Boris, who inspected them all there, the 5th battalion.

Well, good-bye, my darling. May God bless you and the girls !

With loving kisses from your old

NICKY.

" Yesterday's presents." The 6th December was the Tsar's namesday.—" The Wall of Partition," a novel by Florence Barclay. —Olga, the Tsar's daughter.

Telegram.

Stavka. 6 December, 1916.

I thank you and the children with all my soul for letters and games. God bless you ! Sleep well.

NICKY.

7 *December,* 1916.

MY DEAR SUNNY,

I am infinitely grateful to you for your sweet letter. I will tell Fredericks about the telegrams received by you from Astrachan. That man frequently telegraphs to me. I remember, at the time when Stolypin was still alive, he used to send me similar well-wishing telegrams. He was one of those who did not approve of the speeches of Schouvaiev and Grigorovitch in the Duma.

Yesterday I was inundated with telegrams, as they were not forbidden : an enormous number arrived ! I have not yet finished answering them.

The cinematograph was extremely interesting last night. We know at last who is the " mysterious hand."

Her cousin and fiancé, would you believe it ? This caused tremendous excitement in the theatre.

On the 17th all the Commanders-in-Chief are coming here for a military conference, as it is time to prepare our plans for the coming spring. I hope that the day after that I shall be able to start for home !

You can be quite sure, my beloved, that I shall know how to answer Trepov when he appears.

In the evening I run through several chapters of your English book : that refreshes the brain greatly.

May God bless you, my own, and the girls !

I kiss you all tenderly and remain

Your ever loving hubby

NICKY.

" The telegrams received by you from Astrachan." This is a mistake : the telegrams in question came from Arkhangel. In the German edition of the Tsaritsa's letters they are described as coming from " the Monastery Patmi." This is sheer nonsense, and should read " the Monarchist Party," as transcribed in the Russian.

Telegram.

Stavka. 8 *December,* 1916.

Many thanks for dear letters and photographs. General Williams' son has died of illness. He is going to town for a week. Clear, cold day. Tender kisses.

NICKY.

8 *December,* 1916.

MY DEAREST,

Thank you very much indeed for your sweet letter. I shall receive Trepov on Monday the 12th Dec. Do not worry yourself, my dear. Now I am calm and *firm,* and know what to answer. He is coming here to settle also some serious railway questions with Gourko.

I have handed over the telegrams to Fredericks. He asked, before printing them, to find out about the man who sent them. I think, too, that that would be more correct. The reply will go through Kalinin, so that you can find out beforehand from him and decide there.

Luckily I have not many papers, but during the last days I had to receive " Dudel " (Adlerberg), Solovov and Ozerov. The book you sent me is very elegantly produced. I am glad to have " Hadji Murat." Yes, I can imagine Olga's wild joy. Grabbe and all our Cossacks were also very moved. Grabbe showed me Olga's answer—it is very good !

Every evening I enjoy a chapter of " The Wall of Part[i-tion]," and shall soon have finished it.

We have now a proper good winter with lots of snow. I must finish. God bless you and the girls !

I kiss you fondly, my Sunny, and love you infinitely. Cordial greetings to them and to A. Thank her for her letter and present.

Always your old

NICKY.

Kalinin : Rasputin's name for Protopopov; the intentional and humorous continuance of a mistake made at their first meeting. OZEROV : General S. S. Ozerov of the Imperial suite, formerly the commander of the Preobrajensky Regiment.—" Hadji Murat," a short posthumous work by Tolstoy. Hadji Murat (or Murad) was the lieutenant of Shamil, the leader of the Mohammedan element in

the Caucasus.—"Olga's wild joy"—over her appointment as
Colonel-in-Chief. See letter of the 6th.

Telegram.

Stavka. 9 December, 1916.

Warmest thanks. I have ordered the old Count to entrust
the matter concerning the telegrams to Kalinin. It is clear,
7 degrees. Both embrace you tenderly.

NICKY.

Stavka. 9 December, 1916.

MY BELOVED SUNNY,

Thank you most sincerely for your tender letter. I
am very glad to hear of your decision to visit Novgorod, the
most ancient city of Russia. You will feel quite different
after your return. I have always noticed that, after a tour
of the country. The Governor of Novgorod is an excellent
man, and I like him very much. His name is Islavin.
Please give him my kind regards.

I have changed the day for Trepov's reception, having
fixed it for to-morrow—Saturday.

I intend to be sharp, firm and ungracious. Thank you
for the photographs—I am afraid I have already got them.
Fredericks has received letters simultaneously from Wrangel
and Larka Vorontzov. Both complain bitterly of Misha's
wife, who does not allow them to speak to him, even if it
is only about his health. Judging from what they write,
the doctors who attend him insist on serious treatment and
a rest in a warm climate. If he remained a little longer in
the Crimea it would do him a great deal of good; but he,
or perhaps she, wishes to return to Gatchina, of which the
doctors do not approve, and nobody can penetrate to Misha
to explain it to him. I am therefore thinking of telegraphing
to tell him that he should remain there for another month.

My dear heart, I must finish. May God bless you and
your journey!

I kiss you warmly and tenderly.

Your old hubby

NICKY.

WRANGEL : Colonel Baron P. M. Wrangel, A.D.C. to the Tsar. Well known later as a leader of the "White" counter-revolutionaries. He was in the Cavalry Guards.

Telegram.

Stavka. 10 *December,* 1916.

Many thanks for letter. Read it with interest. Alexey understands that you could not write. Best wishes and blessings for your journey.

NICKY.

10 *December,* 1916.

MY BELOVED ANGEL,

Many thanks for dear letter. Yesterday, driving through Alexey's favourite wood by the old Stavka, we went in, and stayed for a minute to pray before the ikon of the Mother of God. I am glad to have done it, as it was your special wish.

I thank you also for giving me details of the conversation between Kal. and A.

I hope that your excursion will be successful and that you will like Novgorod. I went there once in the summer of 1904, just before Baby's birth.

Things do not look too bright in Roumania—chiefly owing to the fact that our troops cannot get through to them because of the congestion of refugees on the railways. In the Dobrudja our troops had to retire to the very Danube, as there were too few of them to defend a long and thin front.

By about the 15th of Dec. the concentration of our forces will, I hope, be more or less accomplished, and perhaps towards Christmas we shall begin our offensive. As you see, the position there is not a very happy one.

Now I must finish, my treasure. May God bless you and the girls ! Give my kind regards to A. and tell her how sorry I am that she suffers so much with her leg.

I kiss you warmly and tenderly, my Sunny.

Your old

NICKY.

" Kal. and A." Protopopov and Mme. Vyroubova.

Stavka.   11 *December*, 1916.

MY BELOVED DARLING,

Owing to it being Sunday, I have no time to write a letter—church, reports and a big lunch! To-morrow I shall write fully about my conversation with Trepov. I hope the visit to Novgorod will not tire you! It is thawing to-day, which is very disagreeable. May God bless you, my little Birdy! I kiss you and them tenderly.

YOUR NICKY.

Telegram.
Stavka.   11 *December*, 1916.

Sincerest thanks for letters and telegram. I am so glad that you were pleased with Novgorod. Hope you are not tired. It is warm, snow. Embrace you closely.

NICKY.

Stavka.   12 *December*, 1916.

MY DEAR HEART,

Again I have no time to write a long letter. I have just received a very interesting civil engineer, who has returned from Germany after spending two years there. He was with Dr. Kressen. He told me many things, and it was he who kept me such a time. His name is Weinberg, the grandson of a Jew.

I am very glad that you were satisfied with what you saw in Novgorod.

God bless you, my Sunny! With many kisses from
Your old
NICKY.

Stavka.   13 *December*, 1916.

MY BELOVED SUNNY,

Endless thanks for your long interesting letter with the many details of your trip to Novgorod. You saw more there than I did in 1904. Of course it would be splendid if we could go together in the spring! Thanks too for the ikon—I am very glad to have this particular one.

X

Kyrill came to-day with N. P. They both had lunch and raved about the battalion and Odessa.

Well now, about Trepov. He was quiet and submissive and did not touch upon the name of Protopopov. Probably my face was ungracious and hard, as he wriggled in his chair. He spoke of the American note, of the Duma, of the near future and, of course, of the railways. He unfolded his plan concerning the Duma—to prorogue it on the 17th of December and reassemble it on the 19th of January, so as to show them and the whole country that, in spite of all they have said, the Government wish to work together. If in January they begin blundering and making trouble he is prepared to hurl thunders at them (he told me his speech in brief) and close the Duma finally. That might happen on the second or third day of their New Year's session! After that, he asked me what I thought. I did not deny the logic of his plan, as well as another advantage which came into my mind—namely, that if it all fell out as he thinks, we would get rid of the Duma two or three weeks earlier than I had anticipated (in the middle of Jan. instead of the middle of Feb.).

And so I approved of his plan, but took from him a solemn promise that he would stick to it and carry it out.—I went to pray before the ikon of the Mother of God before this conversation, and felt comforted after it.

I was delighted yesterday at Paul's arrival. He came to tea and to-day he will make his report. I have just seen Vlad. Nic.—Serg. Petr. is leaving for Moscow. Yesterday I gave an audience to Toll—the commander of my Pavlograd Hussars. He looks contented, but more stupid than ever.

I must finish. God bless you, my dear, my heart and my soul! Kisses for you, the girls, and A.

Your old

NICKY.

"The American Note." President Wilson's note, addressed to all the belligerent Governments, asking them to make known their respective views on the conditions under which the war might be terminated.—"Vlad. Nic." Dr. Derevenko. "Serg. Petr." Dr. Feodorov.

Telegram.
Stavka. 13 *December*, 1916.

Hearty thanks. Wrote to you to-day in detail. Am happy to get your ikons. The weather is mild. Both embrace you tenderly.

NICKY.

Telegram.
Stavka. 14 *December*, 1916.

Many thanks for dear letters and two telegrams. I have ordered him at once to thank those kind people in our name. It is clear, 3 degrees of frost. Do not overtire yourself. Tender kisses from both.

NICKY.

14 *December*, 1916.

MY DEAR,

Tender thanks for the severe written scolding. I read it with a smile, because you speak to me as though I was a child.

It is unpleasant to speak to a man one does not like and does not trust, such as Trepov. But first of all it is necessary to find a substitute for him, and then kick him out—after he has done the dirty work. I mean to make him resign after he has closed the Duma. Let all the responsibility and all the difficulties fall upon his shoulders, and upon the shoulders of his successor.

I am sending you two lists of candidates which he left with me, and a letter, sent by him yesterday, in which he again returns to the question of appointing Makarov as President of the Council of State.

Rouchlov is a very good, spiritually strong and respectable man, who loathes Kokovtsev and the others. You know that the President of the Council of State is newly appointed every year, as well as all the members.

Things are not well in Roumania. We have sent and keep on sending troops, but they are obliged to make long marches (three weeks) because of the shocking condition of the railways. Now it has at last been decided to put them under our control.

The 17th of December has been fixed as the day for the meeting of the Generals as, up to then, Gourko has several conferences.

I must finish now. God bless you, my darling, my Sunny! With fond kisses to you and the girls, I remain

Your " poor little weak-willed " hubby

NICKY.

KOKOVTSEV : Count Kokovtsev, a former President of the Council of Ministers, had warned the Tsar against Rasputin as far back as 1912, soon after Rasputin's appearance at the Court. It goes without saying that he fell into immediate disfavour.

Telegram.

Stavka.   14 December, 1916.

Have carried it out immediately. I sent the paper yesterday. Good-night.

NICKY.

" Have carried it out." In the Tsaritsa's telegram of the same date she says : " I have sent you copies of two telegrams sent to me. Please pay special attention and weigh the exact meaning of the words. Order Fredericks to thank ' warmly' from ' us.' They must be supported." This is a further reference to the messages from the " Monarchist Party " of Arkhangel. See the Tsar's letter of the 7th.

15 December, 1916.

MY BELOVED,

Sincere thanks for your sweet letter. It is so full of questions that I do not know how to answer them all.

The most important one, concerning Voeikov, I shall decide when I come home. I consider it absolutely necessary to establish peace and quiet among the entire population of the country. This, combining with the changes in the Gos. Sov. [Council of State], will do an infinity of good in the sense of refreshing the whole atmosphere.

I have only just received the Roumanian Minister, who brought me thanks from Nando in answer to my greetings to him, in which I tried to encourage him. Diamandy is a good honest man, who looks at the situation from the right point of view. I am glad that you liked my Prikase. It was

written by Gourko—perhaps a little drawn out, but I found
it difficult to abridge, as the meaning might have suffered
from that. On Saturday I shall be busy with my Generals
and hope to depart on Sunday after dinner. What joy!

To-morrow our Bagration-Muchransky is coming back
from Stockholm and Copenhagen. Yesterday I received
the other Bagration, who spoke with great admiration of
you and of his magnificent division.

To-day the weather is fine, 3 degrees of frost, and it has
cheered me up. . . .

Ever you " poor little weak-willed " hubby

NICKY.

" Concerning Voeikov." Voeikov had brought the Tsar certain
monitory " representations " from the nobility of Moscow.

" I am glad that you liked my Prikase." This was an Order of
the Day addressed to the troops, containing the words : " The hour
of peace has not yet come. . . . God will bless your arms : He will
cover them with eternal glory and will give us a peace worthy of your
glorious deeds, oh, my glorious troops !—such a peace that future
generations will bless your holy memory ! " Paléologue was
impressed by this " noble and courageous language," but he did
not know that it was Gourko's and not the Tsar's.

BAGRATION-MUCHRANSKY : General Prince D. P. Bagration. He
commanded a brigade of the Caucasian Cavalry Division. " The
other Bagration "—General A. I. Bagration.

16 *December*, 1916.

MY DEAR,

Tender thanks for you sweet letter. No, I am not
angry with you for the other, written by you, I perfectly
understand your desire to help me !

But I cannot change the day for the reassembly of the
Duma (1st January), because the day is already fixed in the
Proclamation, which will appear in the newspapers to-morrow.

We have eaten the staritza's apple and have both found
it excellent. I have read the description of your visit to
Novgorod in the " Roussk. Inv.," the only newspaper which
I read, and was very pleased with it.

I hope to get the chance of leaving on Sunday, if our conference does not last too long. Many questions must be
discussed.

We had many foreigners to lunch to-day: two Roumanians, three Englishmen and one Frenchman. Of course, all military. It is amazing how many foreign officers come to Russia every fortnight!

You had better not receive Dubrovin just now.

The other day I ordered Voeikov to telegraph to Kalinin that I wished him to get well. Yes, I also think that it will be well to confirm his appointment as Minister. Only a little while ago I was looking through his papers and found among them one of his letters—such a delightful and peaceful one. Now I must finish. May God bless you, my dearest Wify, and the girls!

Tender greetings and kisses sends to you
Your " poor weak-willed little hubby "

NICKY.

" The staritza's apple." The apple was given to the Tsaritsa by Marie Mikhailovna, a celebrated " staritza " or holy woman of Nijni, with the request that the Tsar should eat it, and the assurance that the war would soon be over. She was said to be over 100 years old, wore irons and never washed. Her crazy utterances and false predictions were received with reverence by the Tsaritsa.

Roussk. Inv.—the *Roussky Invalid* (Russian Pensioner), the semi-official organ of the War Office.—DUBROVIN : Dr. Dubrovin, an ultra-Conservative, founder of the reactionary " Union of Russian People."

Telegram.

Stavka. 16 December, 1916.

Hearty thanks for dear letter. The fatigue which you feel is the result of your journey. To-morrow at 5 o'clock the conference with the Generals begins. It is colder, but clear. Tender kisses.

NICKY.

Stavka. 17 December, 1916

MY BELOVED ANGEL,

Gourko's report was finished sooner than usual, so I came home and settled down to write.

Everth came yesterday and I saw him during dinner. He looks fresher and younger than he did in April. The others are arriving to-day. Belaiev has arrived from

Roumania. He will remain until the end of our sittings [conference], then will return to report the results to Nando and Sacharov, after which he desires to take an active part in the war and command a division.

I have just received your sweet, long letter, for which my best thanks. When I return, we will study these lists together and decide upon all these questions. I have said nothing to old Fredericks about Balashev or about Prince Golitzin, as I do not know who he is or what he has said. You see, I do not read newspapers here.

How can you think that Generals would discuss political questions at a military conference? I should like any one of them to touch upon such a subject in my presence!

I am so happy to be coming home again, perhaps to stay a little into the New Year. . . .

And so this is my last letter. I hope that you will feel better and stronger; do not do too much. God bless you, my own, my beloved Sunny! I kiss you and our dear girls tenderly.

Ever your old hubby
NICKY.

To-morrow morning I shall think of you.

BALASHEV : P. N. Balashev, the leading member of the Nationalist party. GOLITZIN : Prince A. D. Golitzin, a Secretary of State. He was one of the directors of the Russo-British Bank, and was at one time Marshal of the Nobility in the Government of Kharkov.

Telegram.

Stavka. 17 December, 1916.

Sincerest thanks. It is dreadful that there is no train for Voeikov till to-morrow. Could not Kalinin help? Tender kisses.

NICKY.

Telegram.

Stavka. 18 December, 1916.

Hearty thanks. Am leaving at 4.30. Was very busy last two days. Here also the sun is wonderfully bright; 14° of frost. The conference is sitting for the last time. Am with you in thought. Tender greetings.

NICKY.

Telegram.

Orsha Station. 18 Dec., 1916.

I have only just read your letter. Am horrified and shaken. In prayers and thoughts I am with you. Am arriving to-morrow at 5 o'clock. Heavy frost. The conference closed at 4 o'clock. I bless you and kiss you.

NICKY.

" Am horrified and shaken." The Tsaritsa's letter had told him of the disappearance of Rasputin and of the rumour of murder.

Telegram.

Bolgoe. 22 February, 1917.

Am travelling well. In thought with all of you. Feel lonely and sad. Am very grateful for letters. Embrace all. Good-night.

NICKY.

The Tsar was now on his way to the Stavka for the last time. A fortnight after the dispatch of this telegram he was no longer an Emperor, and was placed under arrest. During his stay at Tsarskoe Selo he had learnt the details of the murder of Rasputin. It is doubtful if he realised the significance of that murder, or if he had the slightest idea of what was taking place in the capital and throughout Russia. Actually, the first signs of the Revolution had already shown themselves, the army was on the brink of mutiny, and the better part of the population was sick of war, enervated, hungry and desperate. Yet, in his next letter, the Tsar is thinking seriously of " taking up dominoes in his spare time." It is this strange blindness, this concern with trifles, which gives the correspondence such a peculiar tragic quality.

Telegram.

Stavka. 23 February, 1917.

Arrived safely. It is clear, cold, windy. Am seldom coughing. Feel again firm, but very lonely. Thank you and Baby for telegrams. In thought am always with you. Am terribly sad. Kiss you all tenderly.

NICKY.

Telegram.

Stavka. 23 February, 1917.

What a nuisance ! I was so hoping that they would escape measles. Sincerest greetings to all. Sleep well.

NICKY.

Stavka. 23 *February,* 1917.

MY BELOVED SUNNY,

Sincerest thanks for your dear letter, which you left in my coupé. I read it with avidity before going off to sleep. It was a great comfort to me in my loneliness, after spending two months together. If I could not hear your sweet voice, at least I could console myself with these lines of your tender love. I did not go out once till we came here. I am feeling much better to-day—there is no hoarseness and the cough is not so bad.—The day was sunny and cold and I was met by the usual public [people], with Alexeiev at the head. He is really looking very well, and on his face there is a calm expression, such as I have not seen for a long time. We had a good talk together for about half an hour. After that I put my room in order and got your telegram telling me of Olga and Baby having measles. I could not believe my eyes—this news was so unexpected. Especially after his own telegram, in which he says that he is feeling well. In any case, it is very tiresome and disturbing for you, my darling. Perhaps you will cease to receive so many people? You have a legitimate excuse—fear of transmitting the infection to their families.

In the 1st and 2nd Cadet Corps the number of boys ill with measles is increasing steadily. At dinner I saw all the foreign generals—they were very sorry to hear this sad news.

Here in the house it is so still; no noise, no excited shouts! I imagine him sleeping—all his little things, photographs and knick-knacks, in exemplary order in his bedroom and in the room with the round window!

Ne nado! On the other hand, what luck that he did not come here with me now, only to get ill and lie here in our little bedroom! God grant that the measles may pass without complications; it would be so much better if all the children fell ill with it at the same time!

I greatly miss my half-hourly game of patience every evening. I shall take up dominoes again in my spare time. —The stillness round here depresses me, of course, when I am not working.—Old Ivanov was amiable and charming at dinner. My other neighbour was Sir H. Williams, who is delighted at having met so many of his compatriots here lately.

You write about my being firm—a master; that is quite right. Be assured that I do not forget; but it is not necessary to snap at people right and left every minute. A quiet, caustic remark or answer is often quite sufficient to show a person his place.

Well, my dear, it is getting late. Good-night. May God bless your sleep. . .

24 February.

It is a very cloudy, windy day, and snowing heavily— no sign of spring. Just received your telegrams about the children's health. I hope they will all get it together this time.

I am sending you and Alexey Orders from the King and Queen of the Belgians in memory of the war. You had better thank her yourself. He will be so pleased with a new little cross! May God keep you, my joy! I kiss you and the children. In thought and in prayer I am with you all.

Your little hubby

NICKY.

Telegram.

Stavka. 24 February, 1917.

Many thanks for both telegrams. Please do not overtire yourself running from one invalid to another. The train is late owing to a storm. My cough is better. Tenderest kisses for all.

NICKY.

Stavka. 24 February, 1917.

MY DARLING, SWEET SUNNY,

Thank you with all my heart for your dear letter. And so we have now three children and Ania ill with measles! Try to make Marie and Anastasia get them too; it is simpler so; better for all of them, and also for you! And all this has happened since I left home, only two days ago!

Sergey Petrovitch is anxious to know how the illness is developing. He thinks that for the children, and especially for Alexey, a change of climate is absolutely necessary after their recovery—soon after Easter. To my question where, in his opinion, it would be best to go, he advised the Crimea. He told me that he has a son (I never knew of this) who caught the measles, and for a whole year the boy coughed incessantly, till he was sent to the South, where he recovered quickly and completely. While he was telling me of this, there were tears in his eyes. It is really splendid advice, and what a rest it would be for you! Moreover, the rooms in Tsarskoe must be disinfected, and most likely you will not want to go to Peterhof—where can we live then?

We shall think this out in peace on my return home, which I hope will be soon!

My brain is resting here—no Ministers, no troublesome questions demanding thought. I consider that this is good for me, but only for my brain. My heart is suffering from separation. I hate this separation, especially at such a time! I shall not be away long—direct things as best I can here, and then my duty will be fulfilled.

25 February.

I have just received your morning telegram. Thank God that there are no complications! For the first days the temperature is always high, and falls gradually towards the end. Poor Ania! I can imagine how she feels and how much worse she is than the children.

It is now 2.30. Before going for a walk I shall go to the monastery and pray to the Holy Virgin for you and the children. The last snowstorms, which ended yesterday, have put the armies in a critical position all along our South-western railway lines. If the movement of trains is not restored at once, real famine will break out among the troops in 3–4 days. It is terrible. Good-bye, my love, my dear little Wify. May God bless you and the children!

Ever your most loving little husband

NICKY.

Telegram.

Stavka. 25 February, 1917.

Tender thanks for dear letter. To Marie also. My thoughts never leave you. Cold, windy, greyish weather. I send you and the invalids my heartiest greetings.

NICKY.

Telegram.

Stavka. 26 February, 1916.

Thank you most sincerely for dear letter—Anastasia also —and for the news. Am glad they are not feeling bad. Heartiest greetings to all.

NICKY.

Stavka. 26 February, 1917.

MY BELOVED,

The trains are all mixed up again. Your letter came after 5 o'clock yesterday, but No. 647 arrived just before lunch. Many kisses for it. Please do not overtire yourself, running about among the sick ones.

See as much as you can of Lily Dehn—she is a good sensible friend.

Yesterday I visited the ikon of the Holy Virgin and prayed fervently for you, my love, for the dear children, for our country, and also for Ania. Tell her that I have seen her brooch, pinned to the ikon, and touched it with my nose when kissing the image.

Last evening I went to church. An old woman—the Prelate's wife—thanked me for the money which we have given. This morning, during the service, I felt an excruciating pain in the chest, which lasted for a quarter of an hour. I could hardly stand the service out, and my forehead was covered with drops of perspiration. I cannot understand what it could have been, because I had no palpitation of the heart; but later it disappeared, vanishing suddenly when I knelt before the image of the Holy Virgin.

If this occurs again I shall tell Feodorov. I hope Chabalov will be able to stop these street disorders. Protopopov must give him clear and definite instructions. If only old Golytzin does not lose his head !

Tell Alexey that Kulic and Glina are well and remember him. May God bless you, my treasure, and the children, and her !

Eternally your

NICKY.

" The Prelate's wife." The wife of Archbishop Constantine of Mogilev and Mstislav. CHABALOV : General S. S. Chabalov, the Military Governor of the Oural Provinces.—Kulic and Glina : pets.

Telegram.

Stavka.   26 February, 1917.

Thank you heartily for telegrams. Am leaving the day after to-morrow. Have finished here with all important questions. Sleep well. May God bless you all !

NICKY.

It was on this day that the Tsar received Rodzianko's historic telegram, in which the news of the outbreak of the Revolution and of the peril of the dynasty was conveyed in no uncertain words. He was told that there was anarchy in the capital, that the Government was paralysed, and that any delay would be fatal.

Stavka.   27 February, 1917.

MY TREASURE,

Tender thanks for your sweet letter. This will be my last one. How happy I am at the thought that we shall see each other in two days' time ! I have a great many things to do, and therefore my letter will be short.

After yesterday's news from the town I saw many frightened faces here. Fortunately, Alexeiev is calm, but he thinks it necessary to appoint a very energetic man, so as to compel the Ministers to work out the solution of the problems—supplies, railways, coal, etc. That is, of course, quite right. I have heard that the disorders among the troops are caused by the company of convalescents. I wonder what Paul is doing ? He ought to keep them in hand.

God bless you, my dear Sunny ! Many kisses for you and the children. Give her my greetings.

Eternally your

NICKY.

"This will be my last one." True : this was actually the last letter written by the Tsar to his wife.

"After yesterday's news." Probably a reference to Rodzianko's telegram; but it was now generally known that the Revolution had gained the upper hand, and that it was too late to think of concessions.—"The company of convalescents"—rota viyzdoravlivaiushchikh : men sent to the capital for light duty.

Telegram.

Stavka. 27 February, 1917.

Best thanks for letter. Am starting to-morrow at 2.30. The Cavalry Guards have received orders to leave Nov. for town immediately. God grant that the disorders among the troops will soon be stopped. Sincere greetings to all.

NICKY.

Nov. : Nijni-Novgorod.

Telegram.

Viazma. 28 February, 1917.

Left this morning at 5 o'clock. In thought I am always with you. Wonderful weather. I hope that you are feeling well and are calm. Many troops have been sent from the front. Heartiest greetings.

NICKY.

Telegram.

Lichoslavl. 28 February, 1917.

Thanks for news. Am glad that all is well with you. Hope to be home to-morrow morning. Embrace you and the children. God guard you !

NICKY.

The Imperial train was stopped at Vishera, on instructions to the railway staff sent from Petrograd, and was diverted to Pskov. Here the Tsar telegraphed to Rodzianko intimating his readiness to make concessions, and received the grim reply : "It is too late." On the evening of 1st March the Tsar sent for General Rouszky (whose headquarters were in Pskov) and handed him a Ukase which made the Cabinet responsible for the Duma. Throughout the night the Commanders-in-Chief were in telegraphic communication with each other, with Alexeiev (lately returned to the Stavka) and with Rodzianko, and it was agreed that the only possible course was to demand the abdication of the Tsar (Denikin, p. 50; Gourko, p. 274). On the following day General Rouszky informed the Tsar of this decision. He listened with no visible emotion, and at 3 o'clock he sent Rouszky a signed act of abdication. This act had been prepared at the Stavka and forwarded to Pskov (Denikin, p. 50). He abdicated in favour of his son, but shortly afterwards consulted Professor Feodorov (Gilliard, p. 165) : " Sergey Petrovitch, tell me frankly, is Alexey's malady incurable ? " " Sir, our science teaches us that we have here an incurable disease. Those who are afflicted with it may none the less reach an advanced age. But Alexis Nicolaievitch is at the mercy of an accident." On hearing this, he changed the abdication in favour of his brother Michael ("Misha"). The same evening, the delegates from the Duma—Schoulgin and the hated Goutchkov—arrived at Pskov and were at once taken to the Imperial train. There, and still with an embarrassing lack of emotion, the Tsar handed them the act. Schoulgin, who was an ardent monarchist, appears to have been the only member of the group who was deeply moved. A coat of varnish was placed over the Tsar's signature, and the delegates returned to Petrograd with the document.

Telegram.

Pskov. 2 March, 1917.

Arrived here at dinner-time. Hope that everybody's health is better and that we shall soon see each other. Close embrace.

NICKY.

This telegram was sent shortly before the deed of abdication. It is a strange example of resignation, indifference, concealment or restraint.

Telegram.

Stavka. 4 March, 1917.

Thanks, my dear. Have at last received your telegram to-night. Despair is passing away. May God bless you all ! Tender love.

NICKY.

Telegram.

Stavka. 4 March, 1917.

Hearty thanks for telegram. Mother has arrived for two days; it is so cosy and nice; we are dining together in her train. Another snowstorm. In thought and prayer I am with you.

NICKY.

The Dowager Empress hastened from Kiev on hearing what had happened at Pskov, in order that she might be with her son in the hour of his trial. The ex-Tsar, in the Imperial train, had now returned to Mogilev.

Telegram.

Stavka. 5 March, 1917.

Hearty thanks. Mother kisses you and the children. She thinks much of Sunny. It is very cold. In the town it is apparently quieter. I hope that the invalids are feeling better. I kiss you tenderly.

NICKY.

Telegram.

Stavka. 5 March, 1917.

Thanks for news. The old man knows nothing of his family. Could you not find out? In thought I am always with you and the children. God bless you! Sleep well. I kiss you tenderly.

NICKY.

" The old man " is presumably Count Fredericks.

Telegram.

Stavka. 7 March, 1917.

Hearty thanks for details. The old man and his son-in-law have at last left for the country. Here it is quite quiet. Am spending most of my time with Mother, who, with me, kisses you all very tenderly.

NICKY.

" The old man and his son-in-law," presumably Count Fredericks and Voeikov.

On the following day the ex-Tsar was arrested at Mogilev and he was brought to Tsarskoe Selo on the 9th.

The tragic fate of the Romanov family is now well known. On the 14th August, 1917, they started for Tobolsk in Siberia, where they arrived on the 19th. After a lengthy, but not unhappy, imprisonment in this place, the Tsar and Tsaritsa were taken to Ekaterinburg on the 25th April, 1918. Here they were joined later by their children. All were killed in the basement of Ipatiev's house on the night of 16–17th July, 1918.

INDEX

(Containing all principal references to persons and places.)

ADDENDA